How to Learn How to Think: What the Liberal Arts Are Good For, Anyway

Michael D.C. Drout
Professor of English
Wheaton College, Massachusetts

Signum Press

ISBN: 978-1-959360-05-6 (paperback)
ISBN: 978-1-959360-03-2 (ebook)

Cover: Janio Garcia, “A Young Man is Presented to the Seven Liberal Arts” after *Giovane Introdotto tra le Arti Liberali* by Sandro Botticell

1. Grammar: Elizabeth Elstob, scholar. "The Saxon Muse," she wrote the first grammar of Old English.
2. Rhetoric: Iris Murdoch, novelist, philosopher. “The purpose of literature is to prove that other people really exist.”
3. Logic: G.E.M. Anscombe. The greatest woman philosopher, she was Wittgenstein's student and translator. Some of her work explicates difference between beliefs and desires.
4. Arithmetic: Emmy Noether. The greatest woman mathematician. She made major contributions to abstract algebra. Her first and second theorems explain why symmetries indicate the existence of conservation laws in physics.
5. Geometry: Sofia Kovalevsky. The first woman to earn a doctorate in Mathematics. The first woman to become a full Professor of Mathematics. Known for defining the rotations of an irregular solid.
6. Astronomy: Chien-sheng Wu. Particle Physicist who proved that “God is left-handed" by demonstrating that "parity" is not conserved in the Weak Interaction, she was also a major contributor to figuring out how stars produce energy.
7. Music: Clara Schuman. A piano prodigy and great composer, she changed the style of piano performances throughout Europe to place greater emphasis on musicality.

More of the artist’s work can be seen at: https://janiogarcia.myportfolio.com/

To my students and colleagues at Wheaton College, Massachusetts, 1997–2023:

"That they may have life and may have it abundantly."

Table of Contents

Acknowledgments

This book has had a strange and remarkably tortuous history. It began as a set of audio lectures, *How to Think: The Liberal Arts and Their Enduring Value*, published by Recorded Books in 2013. My sincere thanks go to John Alexander for encouraging me to develop that course and for all of his support and friendship over the years. I am also grateful to Dean Kimberly C. Shankman for inviting me to speak on the topic at Benedictine College in Atchison, Kansas, where I realized (during dialogue with faculty and students) that my arguments were not as complete and convincing as I had thought them to be. There seemed little chance of fixing this, however, as the audio format does not lend itself to revision.

Then China Youth Press offered to translate *How to Think* into Chinese. Due to time pressure, my original intention was simply to convert the recorded lectures into continuous prose. But there was too much distance between the audio transcription (despite Jack Segal's meticulous work) and a written argument. I was forced, therefore, to write a new book from my notes rather than simply polishing a transcription. I am grateful to my honors students at that time—Anqi Lu, Wenzhuo Shi, Audrey Dubois, Jillian Valerio, and Rowan Lowell—who were very understanding about their professor's deadlines.

Even long after I had sent the text to the translator, I found myself manufacturing excuses for returning to my argument about the Liberal Arts, at first merely tweaking the wording (in case the translator needed clarification), then adding examples or elaborations (in case I ever needed additional supporting evidence). It was not until surprisingly late in the process that I finally understood I was writing a new book; though when I finally did, it was with an enormous sense of relief: no longer constrained by the format of audio lectures or the limitations of length for the translation, I produced the argument I had always intended to write. This was not, unfortunately, the book that anyone wanted to publish (though various publishers took their sweet time in telling me so). I had finally resigned myself to self-publication when my friends at Signum Press encouraged me to submit the manuscript. I subsequently did more work on a book that had been enthusiastically accepted than I had ever done on ones I had been told to "revise and resubmit." At the prompting of my editor, I added new chapters, examples, and stories and sharpened the argument throughout. The result is once again a book entirely different than all of its antecedents, but one that, finally, makes the argument I wanted to make all along. I am extremely grateful to Corey Olsen, Amy Troolin, Sørina Higgins, Kira Tregoning, and Giovanna Chinellato for all of their help and support.

Some of the ideas I present here were originally developed in special interdisciplinary courses at Wheaton co-taught with professors Tom Armstrong, Kathy Morgan, Rolf Nelson, Silvia Schreiner, Jason Goodman, and, most of all, my good friend William Goldbloom Bloch. I would like to thank these colleagues as well as the students of these OTSOG ("On the Shoulders of Giants") classes. Thanks also to professors Michael J. Kahn, Mark LeBlanc, John Kricher, Beverly Lyon Clark†, Sam Coale, Shawn Christian, Sue Standing, and Betsey Dexter Dyer for exciting discussions over the course of twenty-five years. For help with *The Dream of the Red Chamber* material, I am indebted to my students Zhiting Lu, Wenzhuo Shi, and Peizhen Wu, and my colleague Jianyu Huo, all of whom were remarkably patient with me.

I am also grateful to the Silk family, whose ongoing support for my work has been an unfailing beacon through shadowy seas. I completed the writing and revisions of this book in the aftermath of a family tragedy that we would not have survived without the kindness and generosity of the Wheaton community (with special thanks to former Provost Touba Ghadessi) and the overwhelming love and friendship of Paula Smith-MacDonald, Deyonne Bryant, and Bill Goldbloom Bloch. In ten lifetimes I could never repay my debt of gratitude to them, or to my former Wheaton students from the classes of 1997-2023, who filled our darkest days with their life and light. First you showed me *how* to be a teacher; then you showed me *why* I am a teacher. I will never forget it.

Finally, I thank most of all my family: Raquel, Rhys, and Mitchell† (and Lancelot and Percival): you put up with a lot, but I do notice.

M.D.C.D.
June 2023
Dedham and Norton, Massachusetts

Introduction

Discovering the Value of the Liberal Arts

"The fervor of the converted" is sometimes used to describe the enthusiasm of an adult who takes up a new religion with more zeal than people who were born into the faith. Fervor, however, is not a convincing argument by itself. Indeed, too much fervor is often a sign not to trust a speaker or writer, who may be using emotion to hide weaknesses in logic. Fervor is only a useful guide when it is paired with logical reasoning so that the reader can understand not only *that* the writer feels so strongly about the subject, but also *why*. Only then can the intensity of the speaker's emotions potentially serve as additional evidence of the importance of the argument.

My having "the fervor of the converted" for the Liberal Arts[1] comes in part from my particular educational journey. I did not begin my studies in these disciplines. My undergraduate degree was at Carnegie Mellon University in Pittsburgh, a school known for science and engineering. Although I myself was studying Professional and Creative Writing, I was surrounded by future scientists and engineers who had little patience with "fuzzy" subjects, and my education was informed by their view of how unforgiving the natural and technological worlds are to errors or faulty assumptions. It was excellent training in rigorous thinking, but there were also gaps and weak spots: things that engineers and scientists did not do particularly well and problems they tended to avoid. I'll talk about some of those as we go on.

[1] Note that when I discuss "The Liberal Arts," I am focused on the history and development of these disciplines in Western culture, primarily that of Europe, North Africa, and North America in the past 2,500 years. It would be incredibly useful to synthesize the argument of this book with a similar analysis of the analogous disciplines in highly sophisticated Eastern educational traditions, including those of China, Japan, and India, but such work is beyond my capabilities. Perhaps scholars of those traditions may be inspired to create such a synthesis, which would be a major contribution to the study of human culture.

Different weaknesses characterized the next stage of my education, in Journalism, at Stanford University. Sadly, I was only a month or so into my studies when I discovered that I was not a good fit for the profession of journalism as it was practiced in 1990. Assigned to do a story on elephant seals at Año Nuevo State Park, I drove to the coast, climbed under a fence, and snuck into the restricted area to see the seals (so close that I was able to grab a piece of molted fur—and could have been bitten or crushed by a 1,300-pound animal). Then I checked out five books on elephant seals from the library and power-read them over two days to prep for an hour-long phone interview with a professor who specialized in marine mammals. I was very pleased with the resulting story, and my journalism professor did say it was "fine." However, along with the story, we had to turn in a "diary" of what we had done during our investigation—and after reading this, my professor explained that I had done the research all wrong. "The story should have taken two hours, not two days," he said. "Call the expert; get the explanation from him. Your job is to *report* research, not to *do* research." As far as journalism as a profession is concerned, this was probably good advice, but as far as I was concerned, it meant that I was never going to be a good journalist. So I left journalism for academia, first studying Old English and oral traditional literature with Prof. John Miles Foley at the University of Missouri and then completing my doctoral work in medieval English at Loyola University Chicago under the supervision of Prof. Allen J. Frantzen. Thus, out of my eleven years of higher education, four were spent at an engineering school; one at an elite, so-called "Ivy-plus" institution; two at a large state university; and four at an urban, Roman Catholic school primarily devoted to training future doctors, nurses, and social workers. In all that time, I never once set foot on a campus of that unique American institution: the small Liberal Arts college.

Perhaps that is why I was blindsided by how strongly I felt about Wheaton College in Massachusetts.[2] Within half an hour of arriving for my

[2] A significant complication throughout my career as a professor has been that there are two Wheaton Colleges, both of which are small Liberal Arts schools. I am at the Wheaton in Norton, Massachusetts, which began its history in 1834 as a female seminary and then a women's college (it is now secular and has been co-educational since 1988). The other Wheaton College, located in Wheaton, Illinois, was founded in 1860 and is a Christian

job interview, I knew that *this* was the intellectual environment I had been searching for all along—without realizing that I was searching at all. At Wheaton, everyone cared about literature and art and philosophy and science and all their interconnections. I kept expecting that at some point the mask would fall away, and I would discover that it was all an act, but that never happened. The faculty and the students really were seekers of a unified understanding of the world, the people in it, the things they have done and still do, and, most of all, how it is all related. They believed in an ideal—even if they rarely articulated it as such—of synthesis. I found where I belonged, and so I cemented myself like a barnacle to this small, beautiful college in southeastern Massachusetts and have taught and learned here for twenty-six years.

That I found my place only after a very long educational journey, and that this discovery was so unexpected, probably explains some of my fervor. Unlike people who started out on Liberal Arts campuses and who therefore always knew what they were like, I am still regularly surprised and thrilled that the communities of students and teachers that I had been seeking for so long really do exist. I evangelize for the Liberal Arts at every opportunity because I want to share good news.

My circuitous educational journey may have been an inefficient path to my eventual goal, and I would certainly not recommend it to students who already know they want to study the Liberal Arts, but my experience does perhaps make it easier for me than it might be for others to compare directly several very different approaches to education based on my own journey, those of the students I have taught over the past quarter century, and my own children's passage through the education system. I conclude that (while every type of education is valuable) study of the

---

school. My Wheaton is named after the Wheaton family of southeastern Massachusetts. The other Wheaton is named after the town of Wheaton (which is named after some members of the Wheaton family from Massachusetts who had migrated to Illinois). A major source of confusion has been that the Illinois Wheaton is home to the Marion E. Wade Center for the study of fantasy literature. For a few years in the early 2000s, the Illinois Wheaton would occasionally forward to me letters that had been sent to them on the assumption that, since Michael Drout studied J.R.R. Tolkien, he was a professor at the Illinois Wheaton.

Liberal Arts is uniquely effective at producing success in both work and life.[3] To resort to cliché: the Liberal Arts gives you the biggest bang for the buck.[4]

It should not be a surprise that this conclusion is not universally shared by all people of good will. Every intellectual discipline makes an argument for the value of its own approach (or else that discipline would not exist), and people are, quite reasonably, partisans of their own disciplines (or they would have studied something they valued more). Because we have not world enough and time, there is a never-ending competition for resources, for prestige, and for attention, and so the relative value of each discipline is certain to be a contentious topic. Despite what those of us who get paid to teach Liberal Arts might wish, arguments in favor of other approaches—and thus, against the Liberal Arts—cannot be dismissed out of hand as coming from philistines, fools, or "Yahoos."[5]

The case *for* the Liberal Arts, therefore, needs to be spelled out rather than tacitly assumed, and so in what follows I will try to live up to the best tradition of the Liberal Arts by determining what we are actually talking about, how it got that way, how we use it today, and why it has the form it has. Over the course of this book, therefore, we will assemble, piece by piece, an understanding of how the Liberal Arts arose, evolved, and now

[3] From experience and observation (rather than from survey data), I have independently come to many of the same conclusions as Richard A. Detweiler, and at approximately the same time (his book was published in 2021). If you want quantitative social science data to back up my qualitative, experiential conclusions, I recommend his *The Evidence the Liberal Arts Needs: Lives of Consequence, Inquiry, and Accomplishment* (Cambridge, MA: MIT Press, 2021).

[4] This is a similar point to that made by Randall Stross, who argues that the Liberal Arts features of a Stanford education contribute most to students' successes, and therefore the Liberal Arts need to be at the center of all education. His examples cover both time and space, tracing the influence of the disciplines through history and across the globe. *A Practical Education: Why Liberal Arts Majors Make Great Employees* (Stanford: Stanford University Press, 2017).

[5] "Yahoo" is a word coined by 18th-century satirist Jonathan Swift, who used it in his novel *Gulliver's Travels* as the name of an imaginary race of brutish and crude creatures (clearly meant to represent humans), who had to serve as beasts of burden for a race of intelligent horses he called Houyhnhnms. See? I learned that in my Liberal Arts education.

function in the world. We will thus spend the rest of this book answering in detail the question: "What are the Liberal Arts good for, anyway?" But I will give you the short version right now: the Liberal Arts teach people *how to think* and therefore how to solve even the most complex problems, the kinds of problems that are enormously important but are not always easily handled with discipline-specific methods. The thorniest, knottiest, most difficult problems that we regularly face are not always part of tasks that our employers have asked us to accomplish—they are often problems of how to live our own lives, how to make good choices in the face of confusing or conflicting knowledge, and how to explain to others why we think they should pursue a particular course of action.[6] Becoming good at solving those kinds of problems, then, leads not only to success and achievement, but also to happiness, satisfaction, and genuine contributions to society.

An essential part of learning how to think is developing the ability to distinguish between *assertions*, in which someone says, to one degree or another, "Trust me: what I am saying is true," and *arguments*, in which a person presents evidence and step-by-step reasoning to explain why you should believe something (beyond blind trust). My claim about the value of the Liberal Arts is right now mostly an assertion. I do want you to trust me—and describing my personal experience is a form of argument for why you might want to trust me on this topic—but that is not enough. Therefore, as we go on I will present evidence and explain, step-by-step, the reasoning behind my conclusion that you should study the Liberal Arts.

Before going any further, I want to emphasize that this book is not —despite appearances to the contrary at this point—going to try to convince you that you need to go to a Liberal Arts college. Nor will I be specifically "defending" Liberal Arts colleges or Liberal Arts programs in other kinds of colleges or universities against the arguments that the money

---

[6] This understanding of the value of the Liberal Arts is different from but not completely incompatible with that of Alexander A. Hanan, who argues that studying the Liberal Arts is ideal preparation for becoming a good person ('good' being defined in explicitly moral and religious terms) because such an educated person has a mind prepared to engage with important philosophical, ethical, and religious questions. *Reimaging Liberal Education: Affiliation and Inquiry in Democratic Schooling* (London: Bloomsbury, 2015).

spent on them could better be used on other things (short version of my answer: it depends on what those other things are). I'm also not directly trying to make the case that employers should hire Liberal Arts graduates or that the study of the Liberal Arts can restore our Republic and improve politics. My focus, reader, is personal, not institutional: it is on *you*. I want to convince you that *you* should study the Liberal Arts—at whatever stage of your life or education you are in, and in whatever way works for you—because if you do, you will find success and happiness, and this will happen because the study of the Liberal Arts enables achievement and unlocks joy. You can take college classes online or use some of the numerous free educational resources that have been created over the past two decades; you can buy audio or video courses or borrow them from a local library; you can ask your children, grandchildren, or nieces and nephews to make copies of their college syllabi; you can chase down the references in the footnotes in this book and read those works for yourself. Regardless of the path you take, if you study the Liberal Arts, you will better understand how the world works and your place in it. You will know why we do things the way we do them and what other ways we have done things in the past (and therefore better evaluate the things we do in the present or could do in the future). You will eventually end up running your department or office or organization—whether you want to or not—because you'll be better at solving complex problems than you would be if you had not studied the Liberal Arts.

This argument certainly has *implications* for all the other arguments about the Liberal Arts I just mentioned. After all, if people are better off for having studied the Liberal Arts, then it might make sense to support institutions that teach them. If the study of the Liberal Arts helps people solve complex problems more effectively, it seems obvious that employers would want to hire Liberal Arts grads. If each person who studies the Liberal Arts becomes a more sophisticated thinker and thus makes better social and political decisions, then an increase in the study of the Liberal Arts would presumably be a boon to politics and society. But although the main argument of the book will touch upon all these other arguments, it does not rely upon any of them. Even if they all were to be found faulty (unlikely), my argument about the value of the Liberal Arts for you could (will!) still be convincing.

That is why my primary goal for the rest of this book will be to convince you that it is in your best interest to study the Liberal Arts. And make no mistake, I *am* trying to convince you; I'm not just neutrally informing. But I want to convince you not by clever rhetorical tricks (though, because I have studied the Liberal Arts, I know some), or by asserting authority (I do have some, but not enough), or by the battering ram effect of repeated assertion (again, because I have studied the Liberal Arts, I'm capable of making the same argument over and over in different words, but that seems like a waste of time for both of us). Indeed, those approaches *should* be self-defeating, since once you followed my advice and began to study rhetoric (one of the core Liberal Arts),[7] you would start to see through my tricks and so might no longer be convinced. No, I want to convince you through an extended argument in which I explain every step and justify every piece of evidence: there will be no trying to hide weaknesses with hand-waving or flamboyant language or by saying "of course" as a way of hustling you past an insufficiently justified conclusion.

Extended arguments are most effective when they have a clear and obvious structure for organizing the material—then the role of each piece of evidence is obvious from the very beginning. Here is the plan: In Chapter 1, we will investigate the background of the Liberal Arts so that we can understand where they came from, how we ended up with them in the form they have today, and what types of disciplines fit into the category of "Liberal Arts." This historical discussion will continue into Chapter 2, but with a twist: there, we are going to investigate how the disciplines we now call the sciences split away from the Liberal Arts. I will try to explain why this happened, and we will see what this separation means for the disciplines that still remain part of the Liberal Arts.

In Chapter 3, we will discuss why the Liberal Arts evolved as disciplines intended to be used by certain kinds of people: those who were *free* and those who were in positions to lead others. Indeed, the word

[7] My audio course *A Way With Words: Writing, Rhetoric, and the Art of Persuasion* from Recorded Books (2008) is an in-depth exploration of rhetoric and how to use it.

"liberal" comes from *liber*, the Latin word for "free," which meant not only "not a slave" but also a "person who rules over others."[8] The people who educated their children in the Liberal Arts expected that these disciplines would help those children rule. They were not incorrect.

Chapter 4 goes beyond ruling: we will investigate the possibility that the study of the Liberal Arts can help make you a good person and how we might define what "good" means in this context. We will discuss the ways that the study of the Liberal Arts might lead you closer to truth and make you more empathetic and how, by studying them, you could acquire greater self-discipline. We will also investigate the possibility that the practice of doubting received dogma, which studying the Liberal Arts can produce, might be a good thing. In the end we determine that, although it seems likely the study of the Liberal Arts can make you a more moral person and one who produces a positive net benefit for your society, we cannot be sure (a conclusion completely consistent with the intellectual discipline engendered by studying the Liberal Arts).

The arguments of the next two chapters are more secure. In Chapter 5, we will discuss the biggest and most important intellectual and practical contribution of the Liberal Arts to society: their use in solving complex, messy, ill-defined problems—exactly those that are the most troubling and whose solutions seem furthest out of reach. Chapter 6 focuses on the other massive benefit of the Liberal Arts: how they preserve and transmit culture, allowing us to build upon past developments and thus to accomplish much more than we otherwise could ever hope to achieve. A dwarf can see much farther standing on the shoulders of giants, but the work of those giants must be preserved and transmitted to new generations in order for it to be made use of in this way.

At this point, much of the argument of the book will be in place. But abstract, theoretical discussions go only so far towards explaining or convincing; seeing how those abstractions work in practice is essential. In the details dwell both the devil and God (if we can believe the adages), so in Chapters 7 and 8, we will develop two case studies that demonstrate how

[8] Cicero, *Pro Sestio. In Vatinium*, trans. R. Gardner, Loeb Classical Library 309 (Cambridge, MA: Harvard University Press, 1958), 139.

the disciplines of the Liberal Arts can help us understand particularly complex artifacts from two immensely different cultures: the Old English poem *Beowulf* and the classic Chinese novel *The Dream of the Red Chamber*. These choices of topic are obviously arbitrary, in that other works of culture could easily be substituted. *Beowulf* scholarship is the subdiscipline of the Liberal Arts in which I have the most personal knowledge, as I have been studying it intensively for the past thirty years. In contrast, I only read *The Dream of the Red Chamber* for the first time in 2016, and I have had to educate myself about this masterpiece, the culture in which it was created, and the tradition of scholarship that has arisen around it. But as that education (only made possible by my previous study of the Liberal Arts) is so fresh in my mind, it can be a useful demonstration of techniques for navigating through the work of hundreds of scholars in multiple disciplines across two centuries in order to understand both a literary work that is complicated, confusing, unclear, and beautiful, and its scholarly tradition (which I find to be a human achievement that is almost as beautiful and awe-inspiring as the literary work itself). Chapter 8, then, is an illustration of how the methods of the Liberal Arts can be used to produce knowledge and reveal beauty within apparent chaos. The details of this learning process illustrate both the generalizability of Liberal Arts skills and the steps an outsider must take to begin to understand a new discipline—and a great work of art. It also shows that, with the help of the Liberal Arts, even a crusty old dog can learn a new trick or two.

Having looked at two very mature and sophisticated subfields of the Liberal Arts in Chapters 7 and 8, in Chapter 9, we turn to something brand new: Lexomics, an evolving set of methods that bring together computer-assisted textual analyses and more traditional literary techniques. It may be that, in the development of Lexomics, we are seeing a small subfield of the Liberal Arts starting to evolve into a science, or it might be the case that we are merely observing how new methods open up new areas of investigation, enabling us to address very old questions whose answers previously seemed hopelessly out of reach. Either way, our investigation of Lexomics demonstrates that far from needing to be opposed to each other, the Liberal Arts and the sciences are only effective at engaging the most complex and messy problems (again, those problems that we most desperately need to solve) when they work hand-in-hand.

Critique and self-criticism are an essential part of every Liberal Arts discipline, so it should not be a surprise that the final two chapters discuss the problems with and weaknesses in the Liberal Arts—at least the ways that they are instantiated in our culture at this particular time. In Chapter 10, I offer a critique of the contemporary Liberal Arts and the ways in which they are taught, and then, in Chapter 11, I introduce the criticisms of others and show how they might be addressed. This final chapter, then, is (somewhat of) a defense of the Liberal Arts in their current form and a celebration of a powerful and wonderful tradition, one that goes back thousands of years, includes much of the best of human culture, and—I am confident—will be precious as long as humankind endures.

Chapter 1
The Origins of the Liberal Arts

The phrase "the Liberal Arts" is a shortening of the older and more descriptive name "the Seven Liberal Arts," which for centuries described the core disciplines that educated people studied. But although our current terminology is more general (just "the Liberal Arts" rather than the number seven), the content is in some ways much more restricted, since three of the original seven subdisciplines split away to become sciences, leaving behind those disciplines that are now often called "the Humanities." In this chapter, we will trace the historical evolution of the category "the Liberal Arts" and the specific disciplines it includes.

Although the foundation of the Liberal Arts was certainly in ancient Greece, the disciplines were not grouped together and labeled "Liberal Arts" until the time of the Roman Empire. In the year 47, Julius Caesar appointed a scholar named Marcus Terentius Varro (116–27 BC) as the head of the public library of Rome.[9] Varro was a prolific writer. The most influential of his works was the *Disciplinarum Libri Novem* (*Nine Books of the Disciplines*), which was a sort of proto-encyclopedia. Although Varro divided up and classified the topics, he did not invent them. People had been learning all of this content already since ancient Greece—aristocratic Romans hired Greek scholars as tutors. Varro's great contribution was to provide *organization*. He figured out how to group all the different topics that educated people had been learning into sensible categories, devising nine fundamental disciplines: grammar,[10] rhetoric, logic, arithmetic, geometry, astronomy, musical theory, medicine, and

[9] This Varro, sadly, is not the same person as the gladiator Varro—famous from *Spartacus*. If there ever was a great Gladiator-Librarian (and I so wish there was), he had a different name.

[10] Because I am an English Professor, I cannot help noting that grammar comes first. Just sayin'.

architecture. Subsequent scholars, writers, and educators thought his was a good way of organizing knowledge—partly because of how personally powerful and influential Varro was, partly because he was organizing the library of Rome itself, and partly due to the quality of his reasoning and writing. The culture stuck with this system of classifying the disciplines for the next five hundred years.

Varro, however, did not come up with the term "Liberal Arts" (or if he did, no record survives). The first to use the phrase in writing was instead the philosopher Seneca the Younger (5 BC–65 AD), who was an advisor to Nero before that emperor commanded him to kill himself for, supposedly, conspiring in an assassination plot. In a letter addressed to Lucilius, Seneca seems to be assuming that everyone knows what the Liberal Arts are, suggesting that the category was well established in people's minds even if it was not defined by Varro. We cannot be certain exactly what Seneca saw as the core group of disciplines, but there is a good hint that they were not exactly the same as Varro's group, since Seneca says he respects no field that leads to making money (that would seem to rule out architecture and medicine). Seneca says that certain disciplines, which he calls *Liberalia studia*, are called "liberal" because they are "the studies worthy of a free-born gentleman," and indeed, the word *liber* means "free" (it is the root of the English word "liberty").[11]

To Seneca and the Roman aristocracy, the Liberal Arts were the subjects that should properly be studied by free-born citizens. These subjects were themselves all inter-connected with Roman ideas about political power, freedom, and leadership. It is important to note that, for the Romans, "freedom" did not only mean "not being a slave," but also having the qualities necessary to rule over other people. At the very least, the free Roman ruled over the members of his family, but usually he also

[11] Seneca, *Ad Lucilius Epistulae Morales*, ed. and trans. Richard P. Gummer (New York: G. P. Putnam's Sons, 1920), 348–76. To the possible criticism that the Liberal Arts *further* empowered people who built and enforced a system of social stratification and despotism, I respond that *any* tool increases the power of the people who use it. The tool is not to blame for the use to which it is put, and the tools of the Liberal Arts empower the champions of freedom as much or more as they do those who benefit from and therefore support oppression.

ruled over slaves, workers, and even other free Romans lower in the civic hierarchy. He also was expected to rule over himself.[12]

Many of Varro's disciplines would be essential to ruling. You needed grammar, rhetoric, and logic to take part in any kind of politics, because you needed to be able to communicate with people, to make speeches, and to convince others that you were right. In order to be right, you had to reason logically. You probably needed to be able to write things down, and you needed arithmetic in order to run a household or supply an army. You needed geometry for calculating the sizes of pieces of land, for determining distance and travel time, and for building.[13] You needed music and astronomy to keep track of time and the seasons and to unlock the secrets of the universe.[14] A free person needed to know the Liberal Arts in order to govern and control himself and others, to enable the interactions among the free-born population that allowed people to run the city and the empire.[15] But over the long centuries, things changed. Rome became less powerful, and new social phenomena (most significantly the religion of Christianity) affected the intellectual life of the city and what was left of the empire. Sometime between the sack of Rome by Alaric in 410 and the Vandal conquest of North Africa in 425, a scholar named Martianus Capella (360–428 AD) wrote *De Nuptiis Philologiae et Mercurii* (*About*

---

[12] I use the masculine pronoun here because the focus of the disciplines was on the education of young men who would go on to rule their own households and the civic life of Rome. However, many aristocratic young women were also educated in the Liberal Arts.

[13] Although Roman aristocrats hired professional architects and builders, they still had to know enough geometry to be sure that they were not being exploited and that their houses would not immediately fall down.

[14] To the Romans, there was no difference between the subject of astronomy and what we now call astrology, the foretelling of the future via the stars—they were both part of the same discipline.

[15] To the assertion that continued reappearances of imperialism and slavery in this historical discussion implies that the Liberal Arts are in some way tainted by their development in ancient Rome, I respond by pointing out that slavery and imperialism in their most anti-human and murderous forms were just as prevalent in Egypt, Mesopotamia, Persia, and all other advanced ancient civilizations that existed at the same time but which lacked the codified Liberal Arts.

the Marriage of Philology and Mercury) a book that was often called *De Septem Disciplinis* (*About The Seven Disciplines*), so we know that by the fifth century, the number of Liberal Arts disciplines had contracted from nine to seven.

The Marriage of Philology and Mercury is what is called an extended allegory: you are reading one story on the surface, but you are supposed to recognize that the author is really talking about something else, often something abstract. In this case, we have a description of the marriage of Mercury, who represents the pursuit of intelligence, and Philology, who represents learning through letters, the kind of learning that is written down in books rather than being the result of lived experience. In Martianus' extended allegory, the handmaidens of Lady Philology are Grammar, Logic, Rhetoric, Arithmetic, Geometry, Astronomy, and Music. They come along with the bride to the wedding and bless the union of Intelligence (Mercury) with Learning (Philology). Note that we have lost Medicine and Architecture from Varro's nine disciplines: these handmaidens still get to go to the wedding, but they have to sit off to the side at the feast and keep silent when the other "divine" or "cosmic" disciplines speak, because Architecture and Medicine are, Martianus says, about merely worldly things (such trifles such as healing the sick and keeping us protected from the elements).[16]

For various reasons—including dumb luck, but also the development of a "Late Antique" post-Roman Christian intellectual tradition—the organizing principles for the next thousand years of education come from Martianus Capella's allegorical treatise on the seven Liberal Arts. There were some changes after the rise of what is called Scholasticism in the twelfth century, but even then Martianus remained important, and his text was influential well into the Renaissance. Remarkably, Martianus was this influential despite his awkward Late Antique Latin, which is filled with odd metaphors, unusual words, strange syntax, and strained translations of Greek. For these reasons, the text of *Philology and Mercury* was hopelessly corrupted within a century of its

[16] When I teased my father, a physician, about Medicine sitting off to the side being silent, he smiled and said, "Right up until the minute somebody got sick." Touché.

composition and therefore had to be fixed by later scholars. Nevertheless, the book structured education in Europe for centuries.

Martianus is also important as the conduit through which the classical disciplines—knowledge, methods, and ways of thinking from Greece and Rome—get through to the Middle Ages (broadly, the years 500 to 1500). These centuries are called "Middle" because they occur *between* the Classical period and the rebirth of Greek and Latin culture in the Renaissance. Although we generally think of medieval culture as being distinctly different from that of the periods before and after the Middle Ages (and it is), there is also a lot of continuity across the centuries, in part because Latin remained the universal language of Europe. The seven Liberal Arts are at the heart of that continuity, though in the Middle Ages, these became divided into two subgroups: the *Trivium* ("three roads") and the *Quadrivium* ("four roads"). Our contemporary word "trivia" comes from the Trivium because these three disciplines were considered easier than the Quadrivium, so trivia was something less difficult that you would learn early in your education before you got to the more challenging material. The Trivium is composed of grammar, logic (also called dialectic), and rhetoric. In Martianus' allegory, the handmaiden Grammar is an old woman holding a knife, because she is expected to slice away the grammatical errors made by children.[17] Rhetoric is a woman dressed in full armor and carrying a sword because she can harm others with her words (her armor and her clothing are covered with writing: all of the figures of speech).

The Quadrivium is arithmetic, geometry, music, and astronomy. We might see the Trivium as being about words and the Quadrivium about numbers: arithmetic is number by itself; geometry is number in space; music is number in time; and astronomy is number in space and time, which is why it is the last. The Trivium plus the Quadrivium make up a

[17] Old Lady Grammar with her knife to me represents what far too many people—based on unpleasant educational experiences—think of the discipline of English. The image probably is a fair representation of how grammar was taught right up until the 1980s. But, given enormous progress in linguistics, grammar does not need to be a miserable experience; it can be both fascinating and fun. My audio course *A Way with Words III: Grammar for Grown-ups* from Recorded Books (2008) tries to demonstrate this approach.

marvelously rich curriculum, one that worked pretty well for hundreds of years and in many ways is still in place. There must be reasons beyond mere inertia for this stability.

One explanation is the logical progression of the disciplines, particularly in the Trivium. Grammar, logic, and rhetoric are absolutely foundational to any kind of education in a literate society, and they were particularly important in the European Middle Ages, where being literate meant being able to read a non-native language: Latin. For hundreds of years, every educated person in Europe needed to learn a new language before he or she could start learning anything else. You were not considered a *literatus* or a *grammaticus* if you could not read Latin.[18] This requirement set a high barrier to learning, but there were also some significant benefits to universal Latinity. For a millennium or more, every educated person in Europe could communicate with every other educated person using a single language. Ideas could therefore circulate relatively freely across the continent, and you only needed to know one language to read all of the important books that existed (until Greek books were brought back to Europe in the twelfth century). That is why grammar was the foundational discipline of the Trivium: you needed Latin grammar in order to do anything else.

But mastering grammar alone was not enough. Without understanding logic, you would have no way of knowing if what you were reading was true. You needed to understand how we know what we know, what kinds of things we *can* know (and what is unknowable), and how to follow an argument step by step, evaluating the evidence and the way it hangs together. You also needed to be able to recognize faulty reasoning so that you would avoid the traps of errors that others had made. Without logic, you could not be sure that anything you thought you knew was actually the truth.

---

[18] However, we are starting to discover that there was more literacy in the vernacular languages than had been previously suspected. See, among others, Rosamond McKitterick, *The Uses of Literacy in Early Mediaeval Europe* (Cambridge: Cambridge University Press, 1992).

Finally, there was rhetoric, the art of convincing people, which was essential for two major reasons. As Aristotle noted, logic was essential for reasoning, but as soon other humans were involved (and it is surprisingly difficult to avoid interacting with other humans), pure logic was no longer the only factor contributing to decision-making.[19] Those other humans could use many techniques to try to convince you that their ideas were right—whether they were or not. You needed to know what these tricks were so that you could be resistant to their effects. Rhetoric, like grammar and logic, was thus an essential foundation for additional learning, but you also needed rhetoric in order to *do* anything with your learning. In order to accomplish things in the social world you needed to be able to convince others that you were right. You therefore needed access to these same rhetorical weapons as your potential opponents and allies. Grammar and logic were essential for the study of rhetoric, which was necessary for personal success in a Greek, Roman, or medieval social context. People were educated with the expectation that they would exercise political power, and, with the possible exception of the earliest stages of the Germanic migrations when physical, violent power was at a premium and those with the most power were not literate, people could not exercise political power without rhetoric. It was an essential tool for those who would rule.

The immediate practical application of the four disciplines of the Quadrivium in the early Middle Ages is slightly less obvious. Arithmetic was indeed essential for anyone who wanted to run an organization of any complexity since it is necessary for all levels of finance down to maintaining household accounts (the idea that medieval communities used barter rather

[19] Aristotle is one of those great thinkers whose works seem deceptively simple, sometimes to the point of creating the impression that the philosopher is saying things that everyone already knows. That is the impression I got, anyway, when I first read some of Aristotle's works in the early years of my undergraduate studies. Only when I returned to them much later in life did I recognize how profound—and powerful—they are. This is in contrast to Plato, whose works almost immediately give the sense that they need to be pondered over because what seems on the surface simple has very important implications. The effort of re-examining both philosophers at multiple stages of one's intellectual life is always rewarded.

than money is a myth).[20] Geometry was less important in the day-to-day lives of most educated people than were grammar, logic, rhetoric, and arithmetic, although there certainly were applications. Music is a little trickier to understand because what was studied in the Liberal Arts curriculum was not how to *make* music, but how to understand proportion and harmony in mathematical terms.[21] Scholars saw geometry as number being applied to space and music as number applied to time. Astronomy, once you got beyond the calculation of hours, days, seasons, and phases of the moon—which is more difficult than it seems—was also less practical in application. The astrological parts of astronomy were, in the Middle Ages, really the domain of specialists. Aristocratic Romans cared about the proportion and harmony studied in music, and they were interested in many features of astronomy, but as we move further away in time and place from the Roman Empire, the final three disciplines in the Quadrivium began to seem esoteric—the proper study of specialized scholars, perhaps, but not necessarily an essential part of the education of the ruling class. Furthermore, knowledge continued to expand throughout the Middle Ages—the idea that it was a thousand years of stagnation is also a myth—and this new knowledge did not fit perfectly into the Seven

---

[20] Although the hypothesis that barter-economies preceded the invention of money is found in Adam Smith and in his followers (and, for that matter, in his predecessors), not a single such economy has ever been documented by historians or anthropologists. There is, in fact, a large and amusing literature tracing the journey of the hypothesized barter-economy as it first moved further back in time in Europe and then jumped across the sea to North America, then South America, then Asia–essentially whatever place was at "the ends of the earth" or was the most "primitive" in the mind of the economist writing the story. The barter-economy now exists in an entirely theoretical phase of human culture that was sufficiently sophisticated to have a barter-economy but not sophisticated enough to leave any records of it. See Peter Spufford, *Money and its Use in Medieval Europe* (Cambridge: Cambridge University Press, 1999).

[21] A good portion of this discipline is what we would now consider "music theory," but there is a great deal more mathematics and even physics, along with a non-trivial amount of theological speculation, in the Quadrivium discipline of music than in contemporary music theory. See the remarkably effective synthesis in Chiara Bertoglio, *Musical Scores and the Eternal Present: Theology, Time, and Tolkien* (Eugene, OR: Pickwick Publications, 2021).

Liberal Arts divisions. Study of the traditional Liberal Arts was no longer teaching all the things that people were eager to learn.

It is probably not a surprise that the knowledge that began to displace the disciplines of the Quadrivium was tied closely to the pre-eminent intellectual institution of the European Middle Ages: the Roman Catholic Church. Religion, as an area of study, had never been central to the traditional curriculum. The Roman religion had been in flux long before the fall of the Western empire, and the Liberal Arts were not seen as having a specific religious purpose. Even though Martianus Capella entitled his work *About the Marriage of Philology and Mercury*, Mercury being a Roman god is just not very important in the text.[22] In fact, the lack of explicit religious commitment was a big reason why the Liberal Arts endured so long; they were adaptable to new religions without much change.

The Roman Catholic Church was the single most important cultural institution in Europe in the Middle Ages, creating not only a set of social organizations but also a system of Christian thought. This system was not in conflict with the Liberal Arts curriculum. The Trivium was absolutely necessary for the system to work at all because of the necessity of universal Latin literacy. But by the time we reach the twelfth century, there was a gap between what educated people needed to know and what they were taught in the Quadrivium disciplines. This gap was widened by the intellectual revolutions of the twelfth century, when Latin-speaking Europe began to recover Greek learning through interaction with Islamic scholars.

The great intellectual project of that time period was the integration of Greek, Roman, and Christian philosophy. At first the influence of this project was mostly felt in the upper echelons of intellectual life. But surprisingly quickly, the work of those intellectuals we call the Scholastics began to influence education throughout Europe. The Scholastics kept the framework of the Liberal Arts, but they placed a much greater emphasis on what they, following Aristotle, called dialectic (logic)

---

[22] This is one reason why scholars are unsure about Martianus' religious beliefs. He may even have been a Christian using tropes of Roman culture for effect.

and dispute (rhetoric). The practical result, in their expanded version of rhetoric, was an idea that would be codified centuries later by the German scholar Friedrich Hegel (1770–1831) as "thesis, antithesis, synthesis."[23] One person made a claim, another put forth the opposing thesis, and then they disputed until, after fighting back and forth, they came to a synthesis that was the truth.

Sometimes, however, disputation was not sufficient for the discovery of truth: for example, when people were trying to determine the nature of God—a very important problem for medieval Christian scholars. You could not measure God or detect Him using physical methods, so if you wanted to reason about God, you had to get your data from other sources and reason in a different way. One technique developed in the Middle Ages was argument by analogy, in which you reason that because one thing is like another thing, the knowledge you have about the first thing can tell you about the second. For example, if you decide that God is like the sun, then, although you cannot gather data about God directly, information you gather about the sun can help you reason about God, and you can conclude that since the sun's light allows us to see physical objects, God must produce something analogous to light that allows us to perceive spiritual things.[24] This kind of argument by analogy could be extended nearly indefinitely, and many of the theological disputes of the later Middle

---

[23] Invariably someone will mention that some other philosopher (usually J. G. Fichte, but there are others) came up with "thesis, antithesis, synthesis" before Hegel, but all subsequent development of these ideas cites Hegel as the originator; even he did not use the precise terminology.

[24] The most extreme form of argument by analogy is satirized in the famous "Burn the Witch!" scene in *Monty Python and the Holy Grail,* in which the dim-witted characters try to determine if a woman is a witch by analogically reasoning that, since witches can be burned, they must be made out of wood, and an essential quality of wood is that it floats. Ducks also float and therefore can be assumed to share that essential quality with wood, so if a woman weighs the same as a duck, then she must be made of wood and is therefore a witch and so should be burned. It is perhaps not a coincidence that Terry Jones from the Monty Python comedy group was also a scholar of medieval literature who wrote a very provocative book on the Knight in Chaucer's *Canterbury Tales—Chaucer's Knight: The Portrait of a Medieval Mercenary* (Baton Rouge, LA: Louisiana State University Press, 1980).

Ages—including the famous dispute over how many angels can dance on the head of a pin[25]—were based on very long chains of analogical reasoning.[26]

Any school curriculum is, at its core, a set of decisions about how much of a student's time is to be spent on each subject.[27] If the time spent on logic and rhetoric increased, as did the time spent on theological matters, something had to give. That something was music and astronomy, and to a lesser degree geometry. At the same time, the universities were becoming more and more specialized, starting to gather so much knowledge that scholars also had to become specialized in ways that did not match the old disciplines. This specialization then led to further subdivisions within the disciplines. In the very long view, the newly developing sciences stole most of the good stuff from the Quadrivium and built new disciplines from it (that process will be the focus of the next chapter).

At the end of the Middle Ages, the Protestant Reformation, the Roman Catholic Counter-Reformation, and the Wars of Religion all

---

[25] The answer depends on whether or not angels, as supernatural beings, would have any physical size at all or if they were purely immaterial (all the participants in the debate assumed that angels existed). It is not certain that the problem in this precise form was ever actually debated, though the question of whether or not two angels could be at the "same" place was discussed by Thomas Aquinas in this *Summa Theologiae*, First Part, Article 52, Question 3.

[26] To be fair to many generations of philosophers in the Middle Ages, both the power and the perils of analogical reasoning were recognized. See, for example, Thomas Gallus, "The Celestial Hierarchy," in *Medieval Literary Theory and Criticism c.1100-c.1375*, ed. and trans. A. J. Minnis and A. B. Scott (Oxford: Clarendon Press, 1988), 173-92.

[27] In my quarter-century of experience, I have found that there are only three types of curricula—fully sequential (the most intellectually effective, but everyone hates it), "Chinese menu" (pick one from column A and one from column B; this solves political problems and makes faculty happy), and free form (string together courses, and *post facto* justify them; this makes students happy). Although I was one of the writers of a college curriculum that lasted a remarkable two decades (possibly more from inertia, but I like to think it also had some intrinsic brilliance), I nevertheless believe that no form is inherently better than any other, and that whether or not a given curriculum is effective at a given time is entirely dependent upon whether or not the faculty believe in it: when they do, it works, but as soon as they stop, it fails, regardless of its actual structure.

contributed to this dynamic process, bringing about a substantial revision in the curriculum. The Protestant Reformation challenged many of the intellectual systems that had developed in the medieval church, and the Counter-Reformation responded to these critiques and worked to put the Roman Catholic Church's intellectual house in order. The Wars of Religion raised the stakes very high indeed.

Perhaps the deepest and most fundamental change in the Liberal Arts, particularly in the Trivium disciplines, was caused by the rise of vernacular literacy (reading in languages like English, French, German, Spanish, and Dutch) and the consequent reduction in the importance of Latin. The Roman Catholic Church was the absolute center of Latin learning, so potential reformers were at a disadvantage if they did all their work in that language. The translation of the Bible into vernacular languages and the subsequent explosion of vernacular writings of all kinds changed the Trivium by shifting the focus of grammar instruction from pure Latinity to literacy in general.[28] This was the start of an enormous intellectual change in Western culture, although it took a long time for the full significance of the shift to the vernacular to be appreciated. Latinity was still very important for intellectual work and would remain so until the beginning of the twentieth century. After all, every major text from the past had been written in or translated into Latin, and scholars all over Europe could communicate with each other in Latin even though they had many different native languages. But once the sacred text of the Bible was available in the vernacular languages, there was much less of a sense that every new work had to be written in Latin if it was to be taken seriously.

Also contributing to the decline of the importance of Latin was the fission of Western Christianity into many competing religious sects during the Reformation. The resulting adaptive radiation of Protestantism into

---

[28] As a scholar of medieval literature (and particularly of Old English), I must point out that back in the ninth century, King Alfred was translating Latin texts into the vernacular, although he was not doing so for religious reform reasons but simply because the Vikings had murdered almost everyone in England who could read Latin. See the Preface to King Alfred's translation of Gregory the Great's *Pastoral Care*, in Michael Lapidge and Simon Keynes, eds., *Alfred the Great: Asser's Life of King Alfred and Other Contemporary Sources* (New York: Penguin, 1983), 124-127.

many sects led to fierce competition for believers. The sects that converted the most people were rewarded with greater wealth and power, and this dynamic led to a substantial increase in preaching in vernacular languages. There had always been some preaching in the vernacular, of course, or the vast majority of the population who were not literate in Latin would not have understood their own religion, but the rewards for effective preaching (that which brought in converts or inspired people who already believed not to convert to another sect) were now much larger than they had previously been.[29] Vernacular preaching became an important feature of the intellectual life of Europe for several centuries, so the study of rhetoric was pushed to the center of the curriculum. The better you were at rhetoric, the more powerful your sect became and the more resources it had to reward you. This dynamic produced immense evolutionary selection pressure on the discipline of rhetoric to adapt itself to vernacular languages. Teachers realized that all the rhetorical tricks in the world were insufficient if a preacher could not write and speak effectively in the language of the audience, so the grammar portion of the Trivium began to augment Latin with instruction in the grammars of the vernacular languages, and the discipline of rhetoric evolved to fit the languages in which it was being used.[30] The fundamentals from Greek and Latin were still present, and Aristotle's *Rhetoric* was still the key text, but the specific details of rhetorical practice were more language-specific.

This process continued through the Wars of Religion and into the eighteenth century, which is why that time period is sometimes called "The Age of Rhetoric" (although if you mention this in front of professors of Rhetoric, they will burst out with "*Every* age is the Age of Rhetoric!"). Indeed, up through the 1850s, particularly in the English-speaking world, the most common justification for supporting universities was that these institutions trained people to be effective clerics: they had to go out and

[29] Turner, 44-50.

[30] I think if you had told an educated Roman that people would one day study the grammar of languages that were not Latin or Greek, he would have laughed at you, saying, "But their noises don't have *grammar*. They're just a bunch of barbarians!" The word "barbarian" comes from Greek and Roman writers saying that people who didn't speak Greek or Latin "barbled"—they made noises that sounded like "*bar bar bar.*"

give sermons that were both doctrinally correct and rhetorically effective, so they needed instruction in the specific theology of their individual religions, but they also needed training in grammar, logic, and rhetoric to be able to construct an effective sermon.[31]

It is worth noting that in both England and the American colonies, sermons were a form of popular entertainment. In church on Sunday, people would be excited to hear a long, complex, sophisticated argument that they would discuss for the rest of the week and then write about in letters to their friends and relatives (in some communities this practice continued up through the end of the nineteenth century).[32] A lot of knowledge from the Trivium was on the loose in the culture during this time period, which was one of the reasons that the founders of the United States were so incredibly effective at logic and rhetoric. Yes, a surprising number of them were also geniuses, but they wrote and reasoned and argued so powerfully because they were the beneficiaries of the Liberal Arts. Many knew Greek as well as Latin, and the beginnings of science were starting to enter the curriculum, but the core of their learning was a very deep engagement with the traditional knowledge of the Trivium. In America, to a greater degree than in Europe, this knowledge had broken some of its long-standing bonds to religion, because in America there were so many different variants of Christianity that no single one became dominant. Educated individuals were, for the most part, strongly attached to their own religious denominations, but shared among all of them in the wider culture was the traditional learning of the Trivium, the core of the Liberal Arts.

The great upheavals and revolutions of the eighteenth century demonstrated that grammar, logic, and rhetoric were remarkably effective

---

[31] The oldest institutions of higher education in America, most visibly Harvard and William and Mary, were founded *explicitly* to produce effective, doctrinally correct ministers.

[32] "Sermons outsold novels," Walter E. Houghton, *The Victorian Frame of Mind, 1830-1870* (New Haven, CT: Yale University Press, 1964 [1957]), 21 n. 7. See also Keith A. Francis, William Gibson, Robert Ellison, John Morgan-Guy, and Bob Tennant, eds., *The Oxford Handbook of the British Sermon, 1689-1901* (Oxford: Oxford University Press, 2012).

tools for the emerging leaders of the slowly democratizing European nations. A king who rules by divine right might not technically need rhetoric, as theoretically he can give orders and receive absolute obedience,[33] but leaders of free or relatively free peoples rise and fall through their skills with logic and rhetoric. The democratization of information caused by the development of the printing press in the West amplified the power that individuals could access through logic and rhetoric, making these skills even more valuable. People formulated, evaluated, and communicated their ideas to a large public audience, inspiring others to support them. The Liberal Arts thus became more valuable for individuals than they had been since the time of the Roman Empire, because at many different levels of society the rewards for successful leadership increased substantially.

Successful leadership is the single greatest thing that a human can do to add value to his or her society. A good leader can turn hundreds of confused or non-cooperating people into a force to be reckoned with, and this is why, even though they sometimes frustrate us, we tend to value managers and leaders so highly. No one likes being bossed around (which is what bad leaders do), so good leadership, the kind that *convinces* people, makes a huge difference in the success of any enterprise. Unfortunately, no one has figured out a perfectly effective method of selecting good leaders, and creating them is even more difficult. But the Liberal Arts are a very good foundation, because they teach you how to think about the complicated, messy situations that most benefit from good leadership, situations in which you do not have all the information you need, in which people lie to you or are confused about what is going on, in which your picture of the world is incomplete.[34] Having been trained in disciplining your own mind through logic and in convincing others through rhetoric gives you a great advantage over someone who has not had this training,

---

[33] This is not actually true, as the king always has to gain the assent of those who support him, particularly the powerful nobility, or he will not remain king for very long.

[34] This part of my argument is consistent with that made by George Anders in *You Can Do Anything: The Surprising Power of a 'Useless' Liberal Arts Education* (New York: Little, Brown, 2017).

which is why the rulers of societies have recognized the value in such skills and made certain that their children acquired them.

What about science? The disciplines of science certainly teach people valuable ways to think, as is made evident by the number of current leaders of extremely successful countries (including China and Germany) who were trained as engineers or scientists.[35] In fact, the benefits of science and scientific thinking are so obvious that the teaching of the traditional Liberal Arts is less common today than it was a century ago. As we have seen, fields we recognize as hard sciences—Mathematics, Astronomy, Medicine—were part of Varro's original nine disciplines, and Astronomy and Mathematics were also two of the Seven Liberal Arts. But the slowly growing division between the Trivium and the Quadrivium, plus the new emphasis on theology and religion, especially at the end of the Middle Ages, broke up the coherence of the old seven-part curriculum. After this time, the disciplines in the Quadrivium evolved along different pathways than those in the Trivium. The result was the split between science and the Liberal Arts that we have today, as well as many of the subdivisions within both larger categories. Although I believe that too large a division between the two types of intellectual disciplines weakens both the sciences and the Liberal Arts, the differentiation among the various subdisciplines has produced many benefits. But before lamenting the great separation or trying to repair it, we should understand what happened and why, which is the subject of the next chapter.

---

[35] Angela Merkel, former, long-serving Chancellor of Germany, has a doctorate in Quantum Chemistry. Xi Jinping, President of China, studied Chemical Engineering at Tsinghua University.

Chapter 2

The Split from Science

If we trace the scientific disciplines back to the Quadrivium and then compare these origins with the current sciences, we note an incredible improvement in effectiveness, but when we compare the disciplines of the Trivium to their descendants, we do not see such enormous differences. You could even argue that people educated in the contemporary forms of the Liberal Arts are *less* effective at using grammar, logic, and rhetoric than their predecessors. It certainly seems that one of the biggest differences between the sciences and the Liberal Arts is that the former found a way to produce new results, while the latter remained not very different in effectiveness from that of their ancient ancestors. In this view, which is held by many people today, the sciences pulled away because they *worked*, while the Liberal Arts stayed behind because they did not.

However, as we will see in this chapter, when we trace the historical development of the disciplines on both sides of the split, the story gets a little more complicated. It turns out that some subdisciplines of the Liberal Arts were at times more "scientific" than the sciences, many of which contained much more religion and philosophy than they do now. The big schism between the sciences and the Liberal Arts, C. P. Snow's famous "two cultures" divide,[36] is a relatively recent phenomenon.[37] When you look at the developments historically, you find more similarity than

[36] C. P. Snow, *The Two Cultures and the Scientific Revolution* (Cambridge: Cambridge University Press, 1959).

[37] Our current perception of the division between the sciences and the Liberal Arts is also amplified by contemporary forms of social and political organization in universities. It is in almost everyone's short-term best interests to exaggerate differences, because the more distinct fields there are, the more different professors you need to hire and the less they compete directly with each other for resources. There is a lot of unconscious pressure, particularly among senior faculty, to emphasize the differences rather than similarities among the disciplines.

difference even when you trace the split back to the separation of the Trivium from the Quadrivium.

My thesis in this chapter is:

A science is just a Liberal Art that has gotten itself intellectually organized.

To make that case, I am going to start with the one discipline that everyone —or at least everyone on the outside—thinks is perfectly intellectually organized: mathematics, which Gaus called "the queen of the sciences." One of the great beauties I see in math is that everything fits together so tightly. There are rigorous standards for proof, so we know exactly what we have proved and what we are only guessing or inferring. Absolutely clear, step-by-step logic is required, so an answer is correct regardless of who says it, and there are definite boundaries between the things we know and the things we do not. At least that is how math appeared to me, and, I am certain, how it appears to almost everyone who is not a mathematician. Furthermore, I assumed that mathematics was *always* like this: go back to Zeno or Pythagoras or Archimedes, and you would find rigorous intellectual discipline in which everything thought to be known had been logically proven to be true.

But then one day I was explaining my theory that a science is just a Liberal Art that has gotten itself intellectually organized to my colleague, the mathematician William Goldbloom Bloch. "You *may* be right," he said, "but mathematics as a discipline did not get itself in order until Cauchy. Before that it was an intellectual mess." To me, this was shocking, and not only because I was so ignorant of the history of math that, when Bill said "Cauchy," I heard "Koshi" and assumed that the mathematician was Japanese (this led to many fruitless online searches), but also because mathematics seemed like the one field that would have been intellectually organized since its origin in ancient Greece. But as I began to study the history of mathematics, I learned that my colleague was not really exaggerating: math as a discipline *was* a confused mess until the French mathematician Augustine Louis Cauchy organized it at the beginning of the nineteenth century.[38]

For this, and for much other work, Cauchy is justifiably famous. It is claimed that there are more concepts, theorems, and practices named after him than any other mathematician. The overall effect of his work was to introduce rigorous logical methods into all areas of mathematics and to organize the knowledge of the past in useful ways. Previously disparate observations in seemingly unrelated sub-fields were shown to be connected. After Cauchy, mathematics became much more of what we think of today as a science, with a reasonably clear set of boundaries. You can tell what is outside the field of math and what is inside, and within mathematics itself there is a differentiation of approaches and the classification of information into subfields organized by content.

When mathematics got its intellectual house in order at the beginning of the nineteenth century, it was only imitating what astronomy had done when it became an independent field at the end of the sixteenth, a development that was due in part to the Danish scholar Tycho Brahe. For nearly two centuries, starting with Galileo and reaching a pinnacle with Newton, astronomy included not only the observation of the stars and planets but also what we now see as experimental physics (although the latter field eventually split off).[39]

By the time of Cauchy in the nineteenth century, a process of fission and differentiation had been underway in the sciences for several hundred years, and an alternative power structure within the universities had developed to go along with this new set of intellectual traditions. The disciplines of the Trivium were not entirely excluded, but they were given less emphasis and pushed down to lower levels of education. It was also at the beginning of the nineteenth century that the payoffs from science became so obvious that even political leaders could recognize them. The wealth thrown off by industrialization was enormous and its connection to

---

[38] For the history of mathematics, I have found particularly helpful Dirk Struik's *A Concise History of Mathematics* (Mineola, NY : Dover, 1987 [1948]) and E. T. Bell's *Men of Mathematics* (New York: Simon and Schuster, 1937).

[39] J.L.E. Dreyer, *The History of Astronomy from Thales to Kepler*, 2nd ed. (Mineola, NY: Dover, 2011).

science and technology very visible. Around the time of the American Civil War, in the 1860s, the Powers That Be realized that science and technology could be the difference between winning or losing a war, so the disciplines of science increased in prestige and power. We can infer that leaders still believed in the value of the Liberal Arts because they continued to educate their own children in these disciplines, but the scientific fields now had much more support than they had in the traditional curriculum.

We will pause here, in the middle of the nineteenth century, because it is around this time that certain aspects of the Liberal Arts started to become more like the sciences. But in order to understand how this happened, we need to look at some of the initial subspecializations within the Liberal Arts themselves, going all the way back to the origins of philology.[40] That name should be familiar from Martianus Capella's *The Marriage of Philology and Mercury*. Martianus uses "philology" to mean knowledge that is acquired via reading and writing, but "philology" itself means only "love of words," and words were indeed the central focus of a subdiscipline within the Liberal Arts that was called philology, which would eventually evolve into the current literary disciplines and, more recently, into linguistics.

Philology as a discipline arose because of the good problem of there being too many texts. The great Library of Alexandria had gathered in one place many, many scrolls. The Ptolemies (the family that ruled Egypt) bought, stole, and forcibly borrowed manuscripts. Supposedly, every ship that visited Alexandria was required to hand over any scroll on board, which would then be copied, with the owner receiving the copy and the Library keeping the original. Organizing this massive treasure trove of knowledge generated a new set of intellectual problems. Handwritten documents always contain errors, particularly if the copyist rushes, is sloppy, or does not fully understand the text being copied, and these errors accumulate each time the documents are copied.

---

[40] For this discussion of philology I am indebted to the work of James Turner, whose masterpiece, *Philology: The Forgotten Origins of the Modern Humanities* (Princeton: Princeton University Press, 2014), is the single best book on the history of the discipline.

Zenodotus of Ephesus, who served as the first librarian, invented the practice of organizing the scrolls alphabetically by author. This arrangement enabled the librarians to begin comparing the many versions of the texts they had, and they soon discovered an enormous amount of contradiction and omission, as errors and variations had built up over the centuries. The librarians set out to clean up the mess. They began with the works of Homer, which were extremely culturally important to the Greeks. By comparing many manuscripts to each other, Zenodotus produced the first collated edition of Homer, using his knowledge of language and culture and his aesthetic sensibilities to try to determine which of many variants was the original form that had been miscopied. Thus began the practice of philology.

The goal of the philologists was to produce accurate editions of texts out of the messes that they had inherited. Originally, this meant performing what is called simple collation: comparing all the different versions, line by line, seeing which one made the most sense, and discarding the others. But very quickly it became evident that collation by itself was not sufficient; sometimes *none* of the surviving passages made sense because the language and the culture had changed so much that the scribes had not understood what they were copying, and sometimes both made some kind of sense so that it was impossible to choose between them. Faced with this problem, the Alexandrian librarians began to develop a set of methods of editing and analysis. Zenodotus came up with the idea of drawing a horizontal stroke, called an *obelus*, next to lines that he thought were likely to be wrong or which he did not completely understand. Subsequent scholars devised additional marks, including the asterisk, the accents we still use to help us pronounce words correctly, and graphical indications of how long to pause while reading aloud: the comma, colon, and the period. But even with all of these innovations, many aspects of culturally important texts (like the *Iliad* and the *Odyssey*) remained obscure, so the philologists began gathering information from outside the texts, information they could use to clarify confusing references to history, social customs, religion, and art. Some began to match the references in one text to references in other texts and to those in historical records, eventually producing chronologies of both texts and events. This work was the foundation of the discipline of history.

The works of Homer were important to Alexandrian scholars, but not nearly as significant to them as the book of Hebrew law, the Torah, was to the Jews living in that city, many of whom spoke Greek rather than Hebrew as their native language. Around 300 B.C., the Torah was translated into Greek to make it more accessible to this audience. This translation created a new set of errors, corruptions, and confusions, not only from the process of translation itself, but because the translations were based on various imperfect texts of the Torah.[41] Jewish scholars would surely have sorted out the mess (as they eventually did), but before the text could be fixed, the new religion of Christianity spread the flawed Greek translation throughout the Roman Empire, thus massively increasing the number of imperfect texts and introducing a myriad of new errors. The Christian Bible was not based directly on the Hebrew scriptures, but on a Greek translation, which is called the Septuagint ("the 70" because supposedly 72 translators completed it in only 72 days, and all of the separate versions miraculously agreed with each other).

The textual problems created by all the variations in the translation were emotionally and politically significant to a great number of people. A confusing or opaque passage was not just a difficulty for literary critics, but also a problem in understanding what Christians believed to be the very word of God. Christian scholars, therefore, had good reasons to use every philological method at their disposal to produce a correct text of the Bible. The most useful of these tools was still old-fashioned collation, the comparison of multiple variant readings. Origen, a scholar from Alexandria, produced the *Hexapla*, a six-column edition that enabled different versions of the biblical texts to be compared word-for-word (the six columns were Hebrew, Hebrew transliterated into Greek letters, the Septuagint, and three additional Greek versions of the text). St. Jerome built upon Origen's work, first using the Hebrew texts to correct the earliest Latin text of the Bible (the Vetus Latina), and then producing his

---

[41] William M. Schniedewind, *How the Bible Became a Book: The Textualization of Ancient Israel* (Cambridge: Cambridge University Press, 2004).

own Latin translation, the Vulgate, which remained standard for over 1,000 years.[42]

With the text itself finally stabilized, scholarship became less focused on what the text said and more on what the words *meant*. Although traditionally less important than other methods, this approach had always been a part of philological scholarship. If a passage was unclear, the words might be corrupt, but it was also possible that your understanding was faulty. The practice of reading *allegorically* allowed for such problems to be solved: if the words on the page did not seem to mean what a reader thought they should mean, they were reinterpreted to be consistent with the reader's understanding of the larger meaning of the text (e.g., the actual text of the Bible may have said that God's people must not eat pork, but what the text *really* meant was that God's people should not indulge in gluttony). Most of the time, however, the allegorical interpretation did not contradict the words on the page but instead added new layers of meaning to them. Eventually intellectual attention became focused almost exclusively on allegorical readings; thus it was the dominant form of interpretation for the entire Middle Ages.

Textual philological approaches were reborn, however, when scholars in the Renaissance needed methods for figuring out how to understand the damaged and culturally distant manuscripts that preserved and transmitted the secular Greek and Latin culture that they wanted to revive. At the same time, debates within Christianity about the interpretation of the Bible using allegorical methods had reached an impasse. To try to gain advantages in their arguments (or to produce different arguments than those that had been batted back and forth for centuries), scholars went back to the text itself. The Reformation, the Counter-Reformation, and the Wars of Religion raised the stakes for the interpretation of the Bible, and the efforts to translate it into vernacular languages made philology relevant again.

[42] In a parallel intellectual development, Jewish scholars in Babylonia and Palestine used manuscript collation and other philological methods to produce the Masoretic text of the Hebrew scriptures. This scholarly work was begun in the sixth century and completed in the tenth.

This work, in turn, laid the foundations for a great flowering of philology in the nineteenth century, when scholars such as Jacob Grimm, Rasmus Rask, and Franz Bopp further systemized the methods and created a science of comparative languages and literature, *Vergleichende Philologie* [Comparative Philology], which was as "scientific" as the more obviously scientific disciplines at that time. Grimm discovered "laws" of sound change that explained how ancient languages had evolved to become their modern versions. Subsequent scholars refined and expanded these laws and then used them to reconstruct ancestral languages (and, by extension, lost histories of nations and cultures). Although there were some flaws in the reasoning that are now obvious, and although the early philologists probably claimed too much, you cannot read their work without recognizing immediately that the discipline had become at least as much of a science as chemistry at the time of Lavoisier, biology before Darwin, or even perhaps mathematics before Cauchy. In fact, it is not hard to make the case that *Vergleichende Philologie* was *more* logical and rigorous than the subdisciplines of the physical sciences that had not been fully mathematicized, including geology, biology, and, especially, medicine. Grimm's immediate intellectual heirs thought of themselves as scientists and saw their discipline as a science, believing that it would be further developed and expanded to produce a complete understanding not only of language, but also of mythology and literature.

For a hundred years, literary research was primarily philological in nature. The most famous scholars were philologists, and the most prestigious of these were at German universities, which were the pinnacle of intellectual achievement and power in literary studies. Philology was thus strongly identified as a "German" science, which is why it became less prestigious after World War I, with some British scholars even implying that German intellectual dominance of philology had led to arrogance and thus to the war. Then, after World War II, philology completely fell from grace. Not only were the German universities decimated, but the discipline itself, with its strong focus on medieval Germanic languages and literature, was unfairly and opportunistically blamed for contributing to the barbarism of the German National Socialists. Philology was mostly exiled from the curriculum of literary studies, and the pendulum swung back towards allegorical interpretations—not always recognized as such—of, among other characteristics, politics, gender, sexuality, and race, in the same way that Christian allegorical interpretation had replaced textual philology in the Middle Ages.[43]

But although philology itself was pushed out of English and Modern Language departments, its scientific aspects were not completely expelled from the universities. Even before World War II, a new discipline, linguistics, was being built upon the foundations laid by Grimm and others. Like philology, linguistics was the scientific study of language, but while philology was focused on texts, particularly literary texts, linguistics became centered around speech. The fame of American scholar Noam Chomsky's work gave linguistics an enormous boost in both notoriety and funding after World War II. Departments were founded; professors were hired; and the independence of linguistics became institutionalized. Originally linguistics was not completely separate from its roots in literary studies, but after a series of particularly nasty attacks by literary scholars, and the development of independent sources of funding, most linguists abandoned the study of literary texts, and the discipline evolved to be more like psychology and other social sciences than to literary studies.[44] More

[43] There are a few surviving philologists—almost all of them scholars of medieval literature or classics—but their positions are tenuous, and, especially in the past ten years, they have not been replaced as they retire. There are some positive signs, however: in recent years, scholars of English language and literature in China, Japan, and India have become more interested in philological approaches, perhaps because these methods are similar to the scientific disciplines that are highly valued in these contemporary cultures.

[44] Flush with the success of Chomsky's work, linguists in the 1960s and 1970s began to apply linguistic approaches to the analysis of literary texts. The literary-critical establishment reacted strongly against this perceived intrusion, with high-profile scholars like Stanley Fish and Barbara Herrnstein-Smith leading efforts (mostly successful) to strangle the infant field of literary stylistics in its crib. Since then, most linguists have confined their research to non-literary texts; those who do investigate literature tend to circle warily around the periphery of the literary establishment, like dogs staying just out of range of an angry skunk. See, among others, Roger Fowler, "Studying Literature as Language" in *The Stylistics Reader*, ed. Jean Jacques Weber (London: Hodder, 1995); Stanley Fish, *Is There a Text in this Class? The Authority of Interpretive Communities* (Cambridge: Harvard University Press, 1982); Barbara Herrnstein-Smith, "Surfacing

recently, linguistics research has also become interdisciplinary with computer science, and it has followed psychology in that discipline's evolution into neuroscience, becoming more biology-based and brain-focused.

This long history of the development of philology strongly supports my contention that a science is simply a Liberal Art that has got its intellectual house in order. Philology developed from a loose set of practices into a discipline in which *methods* had been systematized. Over time, philologists identified the techniques that would be most likely to get accurate results, and they devised ways to adjudicate between competing claims. The methods worked to keep the analysis closer to logic than to rhetoric and to focus on evidence rather than on abstraction, so while philology, with its focus on language, has always been conceived of as being part of the Liberal Arts of the Trivium, its operations as a subdiscipline were more like those of one of the sciences. These scientific parts of the field were exactly the parts of philology that were peeled off to form the new discipline of linguistics, and from that new discipline, the more logic- and brain-focused subspecialties have begun to split away from the old historical linguistics and become closer in practice to cognitive psychology, neuroscience, and artificial intelligence research.

If you figure out reliable methods that produce verifiable and testable knowledge, your discipline can become a science, and there are very real material rewards for evolving in this direction. This reward system produces great pressure for disciplines to become science-like (not only to get a share of funding, but also to produce high-quality results that are widely accepted by other scholars). This pressure in turn helps cause the traditional Liberal Arts to further specialize and divide, because the smaller and more specialized a field, the easier it is to devise methods that generate reproducible results. If the field is small enough, the methods can be so thoroughly customized that they generate consistent results even if few of the underlying principles are completely understood.

---

from the Deep," in *On the Margins of Discourse: The Relation of Language to Literature* (Chicago: University of Chicago Press, 1983).

The contemporary Liberal Arts grew out of the Trivium and differentiated into multiple fields, many of which are still considered Liberal Arts, though perhaps not to the same degree as the old core of grammar, logic, and rhetoric. Outgrowths of grammar that formed their own disciplines include literary study in English and other modern languages, classics, art history, music history, and other related disciplines. Outgrowths of logic include, most importantly, philosophy, the fields of religion or theology, and, in part, psychology and history, although these two disciplines also have roots in rhetoric, as does philosophy. Here, too, we see that once a field gets its act together methodologically, it starts to be seen as a science. In fact, the origins of the social sciences are not primarily in the Quadrivium, but in the Trivium disciplines of logic and rhetoric.

Psychology is perhaps the best example. Today, Freudian psychology sounds both quackish and hopelessly fuzzy (because it mostly is), but Freud himself and some of his earliest followers were, among other things,[45] trying to make a science out of a Liberal Arts discipline. In Freud's own time and for a surprising number of years afterwards, Freudian psychology was thought to be scientific. However, if you read some of Freud's major works, you quickly find that the core of his work is much less of a natural science than it is a form of literary study. There is a very deep connection to the allegorical side of literary interpretation (what literary works *mean* to a reader) and far more interest in stories, mythology, art, and culture than in measurement or experiment.

Building upon both Freud and the later corrections to some of his silliest ideas, psychology became first a social science and is now, at least in the subdiscipline of neuroscience, a biological science, perhaps on its way to being a physical one. Sociology and anthropology traveled down a similar road, introducing methods of measurement and experiment. In the early twentieth century, there was a sense among many historians that Marx had turned the Liberal Arts discipline of history—which had evolved in tandem with philology for many centuries—into a new "science" of

[45] First among those other things was the (highly successful) effort to promote Freud, Freudianism, and Freud's disciples to the general public both as part of an end run around scientific gatekeepers and as a very financially remunerative set of lecture tours.

materialist history. That program ended up being unsuccessful, as Marxist historical approaches turned out to fail the tests of prediction and repeatability, but the methodology of history did change to become much less *pre*scriptive and more *de*scriptive, with an emphasis on evaluating information rather than subsuming it to some abstract master-narrative.[46] History also became more subdivided through the same processes of ramification and subspecialization that affected all the Liberal Arts.

For the past 150 years, specialization has paid greater dividends than generalization, as the smaller the field became, the easier it was to make it seem like a science. Not only could very restricted data be synthesized more easily, but small fields could mimic the intellectual consistency of science through social pressure. All the hundreds of thousands of chemists in the world will tell you that table salt is made of sodium and chlorine; all of the contemporary scholars who study Emily Brontë will probably tell you that her work is a response to the oppression of women in her era. The unanimity among chemists is the result of consistent experimental results as well as logic, while that of the English professors arises more from politics and social pressure, but from the outside, both appear to have reached the same state of near unanimity, so it is easy to assume that the processes by which this has happened were also the same.

This system, in which being like a science is a means of gaining rewards and resources, was not fully in place until after World War II. Even in the first part of the twentieth century, the Liberal Arts were still widely recognized as the disciplines most useful for being a free person and leading other free people. As such, they were the focus of the study for the children of the ruling classes. It is sometimes surprising to read the biographies of great twentieth-century chemists and physicists and learn that their parents were often worried that studying the sciences was less helpful than studying the Liberal Arts in preparation for a career in politics, business, or law. Going to "Tech" (i.e., attending engineering school) was not as

---

[46] Although I suppose we will never be entirely free of the "arc of progress" narrative: the idea that, despite temporary setbacks, human culture is inevitably progressing to whatever form of political and social organization that the writer of the history prefers.

prestigious as going to one of the old, East-coast universities that focused on the Liberal Arts. World War II, however, changed everything. At first in America and the Soviet Union, but then all over the world, it became obvious that the future would belong to the nation that had the most effective science and engineering programs, so enormous effort was expended in educating more scientists and engineers.

However, it is impossible to educate a person to be an effective engineer or scientist without *some* traditional Liberal Arts education. You need grammar in order to read and write; you need logic in order to reason; and although naive scientists may think that there is no rhetoric in scientific arguments, there actually is quite a bit, so you need rhetorical training both to convince people and to avoid being tricked into agreement (rhetoric within science emphasizes different aspects of rhetoric than those that are the focus of politics or law, but there is still plenty of rhetoric). The old Trivium disciplines are still valuable, but they are not as central or as prestigious as the specialized disciplines exactly because they have not been made into sciences,[47] including the non-linguistics part of the study of language and literature, the philosophical and metaphysical side of logic, and pretty much all of rhetoric, which have thus far resisted all efforts to make them sciences. Or, more accurately, those aspects of these fields that could be made into sciences were peeled off and developed into scientific or semi-scientific disciplines; what remained were the intellectual endeavors for which no one had yet devised consistently successful methods of analysis.

[47] The absence of agreed-upon methods in these fields makes it difficult to measure the productivity of their scholars and teachers, who have tended to lose out in competitions for scarce resources because things that cannot be measured are usually valued less than things that can be. Even if the measurable discipline only contributes .01 percent to the success of graduates, in the eyes of many administrators, +.01 percent is better than +???%. Not all administrators are stupid, of course, and there has remained enough of a tradition of the Liberal Arts in Western institutions to keep these disciplines from being completely eliminated from the curriculum, but the teaching of the Liberal Arts has often been relegated to introductory courses for undergraduates (or even relabeled as material that high school students should have been taught before college), and their teaching, therefore, has become less prestigious.

That seems like a negative way to define the Liberal Arts, as merely the leftover fields that were unable to evolve into sciences, the disciplines that had no consistent methods or that studied phenomena that could not be measured quantitatively, or those that lacked an agreed-upon set of procedures for determining the truth of arguments. But although the definition sounds negative, it actually should be taken as a great celebration of the value of the Liberal Arts. Lack of method, measurement, and accepted adjudication do not necessarily demonstrate that the Liberal Arts are flawed or fuzzy or childish. Rather, the remaining Liberal Arts have failed to become sciences not because they are too "soft," but because they are too difficult. The Liberal Arts are not the "hard" sciences: they are the hard*est* sciences.[48]

A science is a Liberal Art that has gotten its intellectual house in order. In great part this getting in order comes about because scholars have figured out how to isolate variables and then relate them to each other. That is the genius of the scientific fields: at some point in their histories, scholars saw how to separate out the different variables and study them both individually and then in their interaction with each other. If you are studying gasses, you figure out that there are qualities of temperature, pressure, and volume, each of which is a variable to be studied, and then you see how they are interconnected (giving the ideal gas law). Understanding that variables should be isolated in order to study them, and then finding ingenious ways to do so, is the very core of science.

But in some fields of study, there are so many variables that we do not know how to untangle and isolate them except in very crude terms. Scholars in psychology and sociology, for instance, have to be incredibly clever in constructing problems and situations to try to isolate single variables, and it often turns out that these variables were not as isolated as

---

[48] This aphorism is a modification of something I heard one of my colleagues say in an argument about the relative value of the physical and social sciences. A colleague who was a physical scientist used the term "hard sciences" to describe physics, chemistry, and astronomy. "Well," said the other colleague, "I guess we in sociology, anthropology, psychology, and political science work in the hard*er* sciences." When I chimed in to say that English must then be the hard*est* science, they laughed, as if to say, "Let's not get crazy here." But I was right.

the researchers hoped. For instance, in one famous study, a researcher wanted to see if rats could be trained to choose a particular door based on its relation to other doors (i.e., if the rats could learn that food was always behind the second door on the left). The researcher painted the doors identical colors and put food smell on every door and made the lighting uniform, but the rats still kept going wherever the food had previously been. Finally, he figured out that the rats were hearing the different tiny sounds the floor made when they ran across it and so could tell exactly where they had found the food previously.[49] Even in this very simple experiment, it took enormous effort for the researcher to figure out what the variables were, and he was working with *rats* in a completely controlled environment. Imagine how many more variables there are, and the complexity of their interactions, in *human* behavior in society.

If the variables in the social sciences are this difficult to isolate, the variables in the Liberal Arts are even more so, because they are built by and upon human minds and cultures. Psychologists and sociologists struggle mightily to figure out even something as minor as whether or not the color of clothing people wear can influence how their words are interpreted. There are a large number of interacting variables, including not only the color of the clothing, but multiple characteristics of the speaker (gender, race, age, height, weight, facial appearance, etc.), the audience, and the setting. And this is a much simpler situation than that of a person looking at and having an emotional reaction to a painting, in which the number of variables is gigantic and the ways they might interact almost incalculably vast.

In literary studies, history, art history, music history, rhetoric, and certain kinds of philosophy, the problems are so complicated and messy that we have almost no idea how to isolate variables and perform the kind of analysis at which science excels. Incredibly important aspects of all of these fields happen inside people's heads, and even if you could ethically cut open someone's brain to try to determine what happens when he or

---

[49] I learned of this experiment from Richard Feynman's 1974 Caltech graduation speech, "Cargo Cult Science," published in Richard Feynman, *Surely You're Joking, Mr. Feynman! (Adventures of a Curious Character)* (New York: W.W. Norton, 1985).

she reads a poem by Emily Dickinson or a novel by Toni Morrison, you would not know what to look for.[50] In those fields that remain in the Liberal Arts, we do not know how to measure, or how to isolate, or how to be certain that our beliefs about the phenomena we study are true or if they are just social agreement among researchers. Unable to rely on the proven techniques of the sciences, we are forced to use intuition, rules of thumb, good guesses, and rough approximations. This does not mean that we are completely ignorant, but we are often forced to grope our way through the dark with only vague hints that we are going in the right direction.

The complexity of the Liberal Arts can be daunting to researchers. One way to eliminate the problem is to claim that scientific approaches will *never* work for the Liberal Arts, that we should not even wish for them to do so. Instead, we should celebrate the eternal differences between these fields and the sciences. I reject this conclusion, because the history of the Liberal Arts shows that fields that were once as complex, messy, and intractable as the contemporary Liberal Arts evolved to become sciences.

Even that hardest of hard physical sciences, physics, sometimes has seemed to be a confused mess, even to the field's intellectual leaders. In 1983, the great physicist Richard Feynman gave a series of lectures at UCLA about Quantum Electrodynamics (QED). This theory is the intellectual crown-jewel of twentieth-century physics because it is able to make predictions that are accurate down to the eleventh decimal place. Feynman describes the remarkable degree of precision as "think if you could measure from New York to Los Angeles and be accurate within the length of a human hair." At the end of the final lecture, Feynman goes beyond QED, explaining other research in particle physics in the 1960s and 1970s that produced what is called the "Standard Model." He says:

---

[50] My own theory is that network activation in the brain may be qualitatively different when reading poetry by Dickinson than when reading poems by more conventional poets. Dickinson's remarkable innovation was to "tell the truth but tell it slant," producing rhymes and syntactic constructions that occupy a gray area between the conventional and the grammatically or metrically incorrect, thus producing in her readers a subtle sense of formal unease that may be detectable with technological methods. Collaborative research in this area between English and psychology is in its very early stages.

> So that's everything about the rest of Quantum Physics. It's a terrible mix-up, and you might say it's a hopeless mess physics has got itself worked into. But it's always looked like this! Nature has always looked like a horrible mess! But as we go along, we see patterns! And put theories together! A certain clarity comes, and things get simpler. The mess I just showed you is much smaller than the mess I would have had to make ten years ago, telling you about more than 400 particles. And think about the mess at the beginning of this century, when there was heat, magnetism, electricity, light, x-rays, ultraviolet rays, indices of refraction, coefficients of reflections, and other properties of various substances; all of which we have since put together into one theory: Quantum Electrodynamics.[51]

It is worth taking a moment to reflect on the fact that here Richard Feynman, a winner of the Nobel Prize, is talking about the discipline of physics, the most well-organized and most mathematized of all the sciences, and that he says his own discipline was a mess not in the 1880s, but in 1983! So there is hope that fields of study that also seem to be total messes will get their houses in order and become better at understanding what they study. But I think it is also the case that there will be, for the foreseeable future (and even in the imagined far future), the need for disciplines that can try to explain the phenomena of human culture, art, and behavior without requiring the isolation of every variable. For these fields, we have to think in different ways. Studying the Liberal Arts teaches us how to mobilize the parts of our brains that grasp wholes, that create and intuit, that jump from A to J to Z rather than moving steadily from A to B to C. These mental abilities allow us to synthesize enormously complex and conflicting material into information that we can comprehend and manipulate, converting bewildering data into helpful knowledge that allows us to see truth below the confusing surface.

---

[51] Richard Feynman, *QED: The Strange Theory of Light and Matter* (Princeton: Princeton University Press, 1985).

Chapter 3
The Tools to Rule

Because the Liberal Arts college where I teach is very small, I get to know many of my students pretty well, and sometimes they introduce me to the people who actually pay my salary: their parents. Some of the conversations go something like this:

> Parent: My son loved your classes on *Beowulf*, and Old Norse, and Chaucer, and I'm really proud of how he can now translate these old languages, and how he knows all kinds of really impressive-sounding technical things about manuscripts and sound changes and history. But I have to ask you: What kind of job could he get if he specializes in this field? What could he do with a degree in English focusing on Medieval Literature?
>
> Drout: Be the boss.
>
> Parent: Of what?
>
> Drout: Of anything. Of whatever company or organization he works for.

And then I tell them how my students have succeeded in an enormous variety of careers, including law, medicine, finance, marketing and public relations, teaching at both primary and secondary schools, international sales, politics, journalism, entertainment, writing, publishing, technology, and many different areas of academia.[52] There is such a wide range of vocations my former students are pursuing that it is difficult to identify any common pattern in their career paths, except for one thing: my students, wherever they go, become the boss. They are not only a librarian, but the

[52] I even have a student who went from English major to midwife, another who is a career Army officer, and one who is a professional blacksmith!

Director of the Library; not simply working in finance, but Chief Financial Officer;[53] not merely an administrator, but the Head of Department.

Now, it could be that my students happen to be particularly excellent (this is, in fact, true), or that any student who has specialized in medieval literature must be much smarter than average and so rises to the top of an organization (this is also true), but the pattern seems more robust, as it is also found among the graduates of other Liberal Arts colleges. There must be some contributing factor other than my students simply being smarter than almost everyone (although they are). That factor, I believe, is the effectiveness of the Liberal Arts at giving people the skill to lead others, which is why I call the Liberal Arts "the tools to rule."[54]

The Roman aristocrats who developed the Liberal Arts curriculum were relentlessly practical people. They were deeply concerned with leadership because they cared about power. Remember, they called the arts "liberal" because they saw these disciplines as the appropriate study for free people, and being a free person did not just mean that you were not a slave

---

[53] When I learned that a former student of mine—who had excelled in Chaucer—was the CFO of an investment company, I thought it might be a good idea to have her firm manage my retirement savings. Then I saw what the company's minimum investment was and realized that (a) my former student must be doing incredibly well to be CFO of a firm where the *minimum* is so high and (b) that company probably does not have many English professors among its clients.

[54] Although we reach many of the same conclusions with regard to the value of the Liberal Arts and the desirability of studying and teaching them, Steven M. DeLue makes the argument on somewhat different grounds. Obviously a believer in progressive "arc of history" narratives, he argues that the Liberal Arts enable people to think from a variety of different viewpoints and that this "enlarged thinking" enables autonomy, freedom, and democracy. According to DeLue, if the institutional Liberal Arts are lost, the wellspring of our democracy will be as well. (*How the Liberal Arts Can Save Liberal Democracy*, New York: Lexington Books, 2018.) Coming from, I believe, a different end of the political spectrum, Laurie Endicott Thomas' argument is surprisingly compatible with DeLue's, except that she fears that the wellspring has *already* been lost. Critiquing most non-Liberal Arts educational approaches, she argues that by deviating from the Liberal Arts tradition, American educational institutions (particularly at the primary and secondary level) have intellectually crippled generations of students. The solution to this disaster is to study and teach the Liberal Arts. (*Not Trivial: How Studying the Liberal Arts Can Set You Free*, Leawood, KS: Freedom of Speech Publishing, 2013.)

(although that was essential), but also that you ruled well over others. Perhaps because we are distracted by the existence of the all-powerful emperor at the top, we sometimes fail to appreciate how much distributed leadership was required to make the massive and extended hierarchy of the Roman Empire function. Free Romans all did at least some ruling, over their own households if nothing else, managing money, property, and people. Most were also deeply involved in the many other kinds of political, commercial, and civic work that kept the city and the Empire functioning. Rome needed many leaders; success in leadership at one level often led to increases in prestige and power; and competition among the aristocratic families was fierce. Romans were willing to devote substantial resources towards their children's success in the political and cultural life of the Empire, so there was very strong selection pressure shaping the educational system to focus on the forms of training that helped people rise in the hierarchy. The foremost of these were the military disciplines and associated logistics and road-construction for which Rome is justly famous. The next most important was education in the intellectual disciplines that contributed most to leadership skills: the Liberal Arts, which were exactly what elite Romans thought their children needed to know. It turns out that what worked for the children of Roman aristocrats still works today.

At first glance, this continued relevance and power of the Liberal Arts might be surprising, since the disciplines were organized for a particular purpose in a specific time and place, and we are separated from the Romans by nearly two millennia of cultural, social, political, and technological change. But perhaps human social behavior has always been and will always be fundamentally the same, so that what the Romans (and the Greeks before them) discovered about the tools necessary for leadership will always be true. Or, it could be that the richness and complexity of the Roman Empire happens to be a perfect match for our current exceptionally complex, extended, global society, so that the same skills are applicable. I think the first statement is more likely to be true because, as we saw in Chapter 1, the rulers of societies continued to be educated in the Liberal Arts long after Rome fell. But there is probably some truth in the idea that the Liberal Arts are more important in a complex and sophisticated culture than they might be in other circumstances (such as the warrior-culture of the Migration Period in the early Middle Ages). In either case, the study of the Liberal Arts prepares individuals for success, power, and leadership.

We already touched on some of the ways in which the Liberal Arts provide tools for ruling. The applicability of the Trivium disciplines of grammar, logic, and rhetoric is obvious. In our culture, and the culture of the West for a millennium, to succeed in leadership of any kind of complex organization you must be able to read and write, and you must be able to be *articulate*,[55] to speak in such a way that people understand you, so you therefore need grammar. This discipline changes the way you think by teaching you to understand the multiple variables that affect speech and writing and to control them for your benefit.

Next in the Trivium is logic (dialectic). The application of logic to leadership is so obvious that I almost could skip over it, but I think it is worth taking a little time to be absolutely clear about what "logic" means. The discipline is, at its heart, an understanding of the discrete steps of thinking you must make in order to be certain that a statement or a set of statements about the world is true. This sounds very simple but turns out to be quite difficult because human brains are only naturally logical when reasoning about certain limited types of phenomena. The discipline of logic teaches us how to extend this reasoning into areas in which we are not naturally logical. For example, humans often have a difficult time separating correlation from causation. If something happens, and then something else happens, our brains naturally conclude that the thing that came first *caused* the second. In many instances, of course, this is true: dropping the glass caused it to shatter. But other times, there is no relationship at all between correlation and causation. I will give you a personal example that perhaps will strike a chord, since many people, it seems, do similar illogical things.

[55] The word "articulate" means "to cut up into joints or segments." As applied to speech or grammar it means that the boundaries of the natural segments of speech are clear to a listener, so that an articulate person pauses at the logically and syntactically appropriate places, pronounces sounds so that they are not confused with similar sounds, and chooses words with maximal semantic relevance to a given situation.

When my wife and I were first dating, Michael Jordan and the Chicago Bulls were playing the Lakers for the NBA championship. We were watching one of the finals games in my tiny studio apartment in Palo Alto. The Bulls were losing when I decided to get a drink and so took the one step from the living room area to the kitchen area. As I did so, Michael Jordan hit a three-point basket and then stole the ball, dribbled down the court, and dunked for another score. "Stay out there!" my wife-to-be, a big fan of Michael Jordan, ordered. So in order to help the Bulls win, I watched the rest of the game from the kitchen (which, to be fair, was about five feet from where Raquel was sitting). This was obviously silly, as there was no possible way that a tiny difference in my position could have affected a basketball game that was being played a couple hundred miles away, but the human mind very easily interprets correlation as causation, and such links are only broken with substantial intellectual effort: it is much easier to be superstitious.

Logic provides a method for separating out correlations from causes, allowing us to break spurious links and determine when indeed one thing has caused another. Logic also allows us to reason in much more sophisticated ways even if all we have at the beginning is a simple causal link from one thing to another. If we know that if P is true, then Q is true, we also know that if Q is not true, P is not true (this relationship is called the *contrapositive* of a statement). If something is a fish, then it lives in water, and therefore if something does not live in water, it is not a fish. We can also determine, through logic alone, that some other relationships between P and Q will not necessarily be true. The negation of both sides of the original statement, which is called the *inverse,* is not always true: if something is not a fish, we cannot conclude that it does not live in water: octopuses are not fish, but they are aquatic. Likewise a statement constructed by reversing the arrangement of P and Q (call the *converse*) is not necessarily true. The statement "if something lives in water, it is a fish" is not true because squid, turtles, and whales—none of them fish—all live in water. Thus a single true statement can be used to construct other kinds of knowledge about the world by allowing us to know the truth or falsity of some statements through logic alone: the contrapositive will always be true, but the inverse and the converse do not have to be.

In addition, if we have a set of true statements that are all related, we can often join them together in certain ways to extend our knowledge of the world. So if we know that if P is true, then Q is true, and we also know that if Q is true, then R is true, we can conclude that if P is true, then R is true (if an animal is a fish, then it lives in the water; if an animal lives in the water, then it cannot live on the top of Mt. Everest; therefore, if something is a fish, it cannot live on top of Mt. Everest). The chain of logical statements, called a *syllogism*, is the foundation of all deductive reasoning. Link together enough syllogisms, and you can eventually draw very complex and sophisticated conclusions about the world, even about things that you cannot directly measure, and you can be certain that your conclusions are correct. For example, you can prove logically that the square root of two cannot be represented precisely by any ratio of two numbers even though you can never possibly test all possible pairs. You can prove that matter cannot travel faster than the speed of light in a vacuum without ever being able to perform such an experiment.

We tend to think of this kind of logic as belonging to mathematics, but in fact it has always been an essential part of the Liberal Arts. However, purely abstract logical reasoning—formal logic—although immensely powerful, is also limited. This type of thinking is successful in math or physics because those disciplines have matched the phenomena they study to the kinds of abstract claims that can be proved using formal logic. Even in these very restricted situations, formal logical reasoning is very difficult. It is even harder when we are not dealing with abstractions but instead with the actual complexities of the living world, and it can be nearly impossible when we are trying to use purely logical reasoning to understand the social and mental worlds in which we also live. For these sorts of problems, although formal logic is an excellent check against confusing correlation with causation or making other kinds of basic errors, it is not enough.

Faced with this difficulty, we do not abandon logic altogether, but instead adapt it not only by developing systems of informal logic, but by finding more general patterns, tendencies, and rules of thumb. We learn to reason about possibilities and probabilities, and we identify variables that have blurry, permeable boundaries. We reason by analogy, trying to shift problems into forms that are a better fit for the ways our brains work. Doing this can create what the philosopher Daniel Dennett calls "intuition pumps," ways of reconceptualizing problems so that they are more easily engaged by the brain's strengths rather than its weaknesses.[56] If we think that water "wants" to go downhill, we can more intuitively grasp the ways it will flow, and we can then use *that* conceptualization in trying to understand other phenomena. For example, when thinking of the behavior of electricity in circuits, it is often helpful to imagine the electricity flowing through the wires the same way water flows through pipes.[57] By studying the Liberal Arts, you gain access to a large set of intuition pumps, partial analogies that you can apply to new situations. Having seen a model for a phenomenon in one area of inquiry, you can adapt it to help solve whatever problem is at hand.

This is the kind of adaptable logic that helps leaders succeed in novel situations. Studying what people have previously done gives you a rich hoard of examples, counter-examples, and analogies. From these you can both synthesize general principles (by recognizing the abstract categories that might underlie seemingly different surface phenomena) and apply your natural intuitions to new situations. For example, from your study of the Napoleonic Wars and World War II, you might conclude that invading Russia in the winter is unlikely to lead to military success. Or you might develop a rule of thumb: "Do not invade when your supply lines are long and your troops are suffering from the elements." Or you might conceive of an even more general principle that greedily trying to conquer too much rather than consolidating your gains leads eventually to your downfall. You could then take appropriate measures to avoid this fate. The core of logic is the abstract reasoning of <u>if P, then Q</u>, but the Liberal Arts

[56] Daniel C. Dennett, *Intuition Pumps and Other Tools for Thinking* (New York: W.W. Norton, 2014).

[57] "All you need to know about plumbing," a plumber friend once told me, is that "the hot's on the left, the cold's on the right, and water runs downhill." There are worse approximations.

version of logic also includes a very large set of parallels, related problems, and historical data. The more you study such material, the better you can synthesize it, the richer your mental model of the world will be, and the more likely you will be to make correct decisions.

The third part of the Trivium, rhetoric, certainly requires both grammar and logic, but it also goes somewhat beyond both of these disciplines. Rhetoric expands your ability to think and influence others in the social world. Unfortunately, rhetoric often has a bad reputation, as there is the sense that it is a kind of trickery and that if we lived in an ideal world, we would make all our decisions based on logic (dialectic) rather than rhetoric. But it is impossible to separate logic from rhetoric when we are dealing with other humans. Rhetoric takes into account the fact that there can be great differences among perceptions and values and that, except in a few rare cases, it is very difficult to separate out our individual values and desires from our evaluation of arguments. We think we are being logical, but so does the person who disagrees with us.

Rhetoric is so essential to human endeavor because it can help produce cooperation among competitive individuals with different desires, ideas, and values. The ancient Greeks studied rhetoric so intensely because the small city-states in which they lived were governed by the decision-making of many individuals who had to find some way to cooperate. The founders of philosophy, therefore, had experience participating in the decision-making processes of medium-sized, semi-democratic groups. They observed that some arguments were effective, while others, which were logically similar, were not. Eventually they synthesized some general principles that became the foundations of the discipline of rhetoric. Aristotle noted that the problem of differing values and perceptions can sometimes be solved rhetorically by finding at least some area of agreement, no matter how small, and then building a series of syllogisms from this shared origin. The foundational premise, which must be general enough to be agreed to by both sides of the argument, is called an *enthymeme*. It is a starting point, sometimes as vague as "we can at least agree that we want our city (or family or country) to prosper," but the tiny point of agreement that the enthymeme creates is the foundation for successful persuasion.[58]

The Greeks also recognized that it was not always possible to find an enthymeme and then reason together, so they also studied the techniques by which someone could win an argument not by logic, but through the manipulation of the emotions. There were certain ways of speaking that were more effective than others at convincing an audience to take the speaker's side of an argument. Teachers of rhetoric trained their students how to use their voices as well as what to say with them, systematizing the different ways people had discovered to amuse the audience, attack opponents, and counter these same techniques when they were used against them. In time, the discipline of rhetoric accumulated an enormous amount of knowledge about how to convince others and thus how to rule.

But although the knowledge of the ancients—particularly that taken from Aristotle and from the Latin orator Cicero—was at the heart of the Liberal Arts discipline of rhetoric for centuries, study of the ancients was not in itself sufficient to bring about consistent success in rhetoric for two major reasons. First, if you could learn rhetorical techniques, so could your opponents. A counter-attack was developed for each rhetorical move, and both sides came to know all the same tricks. Second, a psychological tendency called *habituation* ensures that even the most novel phenomena become less stimulating as they are repeated. An audience may be surprised or amused by the first instance of a rhetorical innovation, but their interest rapidly trails off with repetition. When it comes to a rhetorical trick or a joke, as the science fiction writer Robert A. Heinlein once said, "Once, you're a wit; twice, you're a half-wit." The audience's interest decays exponentially.[59] Thus when one particular rhetorical strategy becomes widely popular, the phenomenon of habituation creates opportunities for speakers who do something different. An example from American political

[58] Aristotle, *Rhetorica: The Works of Aristotle Volume 11*, trans. W. Rhys Roberts (Oxford: Clarendon Press, 1924).

[59] Robert A. Heinlein, *The Moon is a Harsh Mistress* (New York: G.P. Putnam's Sons, 1966).

rhetoric, in which I managed to be wrong in both my original analysis *and* in my correction (and will possibly be shown to be wrong in my correction to the correction), illustrates this point.

In 2006, I recorded an audio course "A Way with Words: Rhetoric, Writing and the Arts of Persuasion," in which, as part of my discussion of political rhetoric, I used the then-recent example of a speech given by former Mayor of New York Rudy Giuliani at the 2004 Republican National Committee. This speech supporting the re-election of President George W. Bush was enormously powerful in part because it did not seem that Giuliani was using a prepared text but instead was simply speaking to the audience about the terrorist attacks of September 11, 2001 and the heroic response of police and firefighters to the tragedy. Like everyone who watched the speech, I thought Giuliani was improvising; perhaps he had some memorized notes, but he was definitely not reading a formal speech. The emotional power of that particular address at that time (and, to be fair, in contrast to many other truly awful speeches given by the other politicians) was so great that I predicted that other politicians would imitate Giuliani and that the future of political speech would be more like "reality" television—rather than being scripted word-by-word, it would be improvised around a certain set of ideas. Such oratory, I thought, would sound more authentic than even the most artfully constructed script and would therefore replace traditional political speech for all but the most formal occasions.[60]

I could not have been more wrong in my prediction, which did not anticipate President Barack Obama's arrival on the political scene and his incredibly effective use of traditional, formal oratory. The habituation of Americans to informal, folksy, and highly simplified speeches had created an opportunity for the success of a different kind of rhetoric, one which happened to be a perfect fit for the remarkable oratorical skills of Obama, whose speeches were characterized by a highly literate formality, blending

[60] I have since learned that I was not quite right about what had happened. A cameraman who was in attendance at the convention listened to my audio course and contacted me to say that Giuliani actually had a script on the teleprompter, but, on the spur of the moment, he ignored the written text and spoke informally. His improvisation was not planned in the way that I thought it had been.

classical rhetorical figures with vocal effects and cadences from the tradition of African-American preaching, all tied together with a controlled, calming, mellifluous, and deep voice. Suddenly the seeming authenticity of informality was out, replaced by high-culture oration. Therefore, in the 2013 audio course on the Liberal Arts that was the antecedent of this current book,[61] I confessed my error and changed my prediction: American political rhetoric, I said, would likely follow the path of Obama's speeches, returning to a more formal and elaborate form in imitation of his success.

I said that my first prediction could not have been more wrong, but, sadly, this second prediction, even though it was the opposite of my first prediction, was at least as wrong (and is probably more wrong). I had failed to anticipate the power of the rhetoric of President Donald Trump,[62] whose syntactically fragmented, discursive, and even rambling speech patterns are *much* more informal than Giuliani's improvisational speech. Transcripts of Trump's speeches read almost exactly like the transcriptions of informal conversations among friends that linguists use to study conversational dynamics.[63] While most people adjust their syntax for even slightly more formal occasions, in nearly all contexts Trump retains all the characteristics of free-flowing, casual speech, including the practices of interrupting one clause to insert another, stringing multiple clauses together without completing a grammatical sentence, interjecting short evaluative phrases ("So great!" "The best!"), and looping back from the end of one sentence to link to a syntactic structure started much earlier but then dropped.

Like Giuliani's improvisations, Trump's speech patterns conveyed a sense of authenticity, but of a slightly different kind: Giuliani convinced his

[61] *How to Think: The Liberal Arts and their Enduring Value* (Prince Frederick, MD: Recorded Books, 2013).

[62] To be fair, so did, well, everyone, especially putative "experts" in politics, media, communication, and government.

[63] For an explication of some of the sophisticated though unconscious rules of how conversations work, see Deborah Tannen, *Conversational Style: Analyzing Talk Among Friends* (Oxford: Oxford University Press, 2005 [1984]). Tannen is most famous for her work on the differences between male and female speech in contemporary culture, but I think this earlier work is just as enlightening.

hearers that he was presenting to them his true, personal feelings about something he had deeply considered and that he was experiencing those feelings while speaking and recalling the tragedy and heroism he witnessed. Trump created in his hearers a sense that they were hearing whatever came to mind. Trump also communicated that he was expressing his real feelings, but with far greater sense of spontaneity and therefore even less artifice, or even, perhaps, careful consideration. His monologues felt no more planned-out or focus-grouped than your Uncle Louie's when he had gotten to rambling at the Thanksgiving dinner table after a big meal and a few drinks—the only agenda appeared to be him speaking his mind, saying whatever he felt in that particular moment. In a media ecosystem that constantly, overtly, and archly tries to manipulate hearers by meticulously tailoring messages to the various demographic, ideological, and emotional qualities of a given audience, Trump stood out by giving the impression that he was not using workshopped talking-points or calibrating his words for each separate subsection of his audience. This made his speeches *feel* more honest than those of his competitors even when, in factual terms, they might not be. Trump's rambling and seemingly unplanned remarks conveyed the impression that there was no team of writers and consultants carefully crafting remarks for him to memorize and that he was putting no effort into trying to trick or manipulate his audience; he was just talking to them. This rhetoric then constructed an audience that, instead of being divided into smaller and smaller intersectional categories, was pulled together as one momentarily homogenous group because the speaker was, it seemed, talking to all of them at once rather than shifting his attention from one sub-group to another. It is perhaps ironic that the most recent previous politician to accomplish this rhetorical feat was President Obama in the set of very formal speeches that culminated in his inaugural address in January 2009—speeches that were massively different from Trump's in nearly every way *except* their effects on the audience.

In hindsight, my original prediction—that with the rise of unscripted speech throughout the media landscape, informality would be more rhetorically effective than traditional oratory—might have been correct, and President Obama's approach was a shocking deviation from the evolutionary path.[64] Perhaps going forward, political rhetoric will be more improvisational (or, more likely, improvisational *seeming*) than formal. But I am now getting out of the prediction business except to say that eventually audiences will become habituated to President Trump's informality in the same way they became habituated to President Obama's soaring oratory. Whatever follows will likely be a contrast rather than a continuation of style, but how that contrast will be manifested is an idea I will keep to myself in order to avoid further embarrassment.

The larger point that I hope is illustrated by these examples is that, despite millennia of study, there is no single formula that humans can use to create successful rhetoric. Rhetorical power is an always-moving target, as both audiences and opponents change and react. That is why the Liberal Arts, even more broadly construed than the disciplines of the Trivium, are so valuable for those who need to convince and lead others. Studying a manual of rhetoric, even Aristotle's *Rhetoric* itself, and being able to use some figures of speech and identify some arguments as logical fallacies, is extremely helpful (far more helpful than those who have not tried using it can know), but it is not sufficient. To become a master of rhetoric, a speaker or writer needs not only the general principles, but the specific instances. The more examples speakers have encountered, the more mental models they have constructed of rhetorical situations, the larger their intellectual toolkits, and thus the more effective rhetoricians they will be.

In grammar, logic, and rhetoric—in every field, really—the deeper and wider a mind's knowledge, the richer and more sophisticated mental models of the world it can create. If a person's mind contains many models and also includes some general principles that can be used to choose between or modify these models, then that mind is more likely to create an effective rhetorical strategy in a novel situation. For example, if your reputation is that of an overly rigid, somewhat intolerant mayor of New York City, you seize upon the chance to speak utterly informally about the generosity, bravery, and heroism of ordinary people. Or if you are a relatively unknown junior senator from Illinois, you employ a soaring

[64] The elections of 2020 and 2024 provide no meaningful data due to the bizarre circumstances of candidates avoiding speaking to the public as much as possible.

oratory that makes you appear to be immensely better educated and culturally sophisticated than your competitors.

Rhetoric is the art of choosing effective forms to fit the content that will accomplish a speaker's or writer's purposes. Although its foundations are in public speaking, rhetoric is not limited to speech or even to language. The very font in which a document is written can have significant rhetorical power by communicating emotion or authority. The typeface Helvetica, which was designed in 1957, is very familiar, partly because millions of computers come with it pre-installed, but also because it has been used consistently in certain kinds of authoritative documents. The United States 1040 income tax form (the most widely used by individuals) is printed in Helvetica, which is also the font used by NASA on the space shuttle. Helvetica is also used for the signs in public transportation systems in New York, Chicago, Philadelphia, Madrid, and Washington, D.C., and it appears on the products of many large businesses, including General Motors, 3M, BMW, Verizon, Skype, Panasonic, Jeep, Target, and Texaco.[65]

Helvetica is a type of font called "sans-serif" because it lacks small tags at the ends of letter-strokes. Sans-serif fonts are associated with modernism and industrialization. They were considered forward-looking when they were developed, and they were adopted by organizations that wanted to associate themselves with the new, the modern, and the powerful. Helvetica implies the authority of immediate power rather than that of old tradition. My students are always shocked when I show them that the famous sign over the gates of the Auschwitz death camp, "Arbeit Macht Frei," is not in a complex, prickly, old-fashioned Gothic-style typeface, but is cast in a modern-looking sans-serif font that looks much like Helvetica and would not be very stylistically out of place on a hospital, school, or other modern government building. With their choice of font, the Nazis who built the death camp were trying to communicate that they were scientific, progressive, and modernist—that they were the future. Thankfully they were wrong, but their font choice does illustrate the

[65] A film about the font, entitled simply *Helvetica*, directed by Gary Hustwit, was distributed in 2007.

rhetorical power of typography, a knowledge of which is another tool useful to those who rule.

Indeed, sometimes typography can tell us more about the people who use it than they want their readers to know. Returning to Germany for another example, we find that up to the interwar period, it was traditional to use the Gothic-looking *Fraktur* script to print books on what were thought to be on "German" or "homey" subjects—family, home-life, the outdoors, love, and romance. Scientific, philosophical, and classical topics—the serious and rigorous intellectual pursuits—were printed in Roman type (what the Germans called *Antiqua*). Nationalist Germans usually preferred *Fraktur*, while internationalists and cosmopolitan intellectuals used *Antiqua*. Yet despite his reputation for nationalism and his belief that German was the greatest of national cultures, in 1941 Hitler ordered the country to abandon *Fraktur* and switch entirely to *Antiqua*. He desired the prestige and power of the latter rather than the warmth and loving personal bonds among people indicated by the use of *Fraktur*.[66]

The founder of Apple, Steve Jobs, certainly recognized the importance of fonts. Helvetica is pre-installed on so many computers because Jobs had taken a calligraphy course in college and had learned about fonts: how they are constructed, how the letters must be fit together inside a word, how far above and below the lines they must go, the difference between serif and sans-serif scripts. He recognized before anyone else that the ability to choose among different fonts would be as valuable a tool for individual computer users as it had always been for publishers. He was right. One of the great advantages of the Macintosh was the ease with which users could switch between fonts.[67] This particular tool for ruling thus has its ultimate origin in a Trivium subject (you had to learn

---

[66] See Geoffrey Samson, *Writing Systems*, 2nd ed. (Sheffield: Equinox, 2015), 126-29.

[67] When this capability first became wide-spread, in 1986, we students were so excited by the novelty that we would sometimes turn in papers in which each paragraph was in a different font or effect (such as outline, shadow, underline, or bold). One of my professors at Carnegie Mellon was so frustrated that he forbid the use of any font other than Courier (which looks most like a typewriter font), complaining that the paper of a certain student (who shall remain nameless) looked like a kidnapper's ransom note constructed from random words cut out of magazines.

handwriting along with grammar), and it has evolved and expanded over time whenever technology or social change made its use particularly valuable. There are ongoing efforts to study the effects of fonts, colors, and document layouts in more scientific ways,[68] and perhaps one day the study of typography will follow the path of other Liberal Arts that have gotten their acts together and become sciences, but for now the field of graphic design is still very much more an art than a science.

As with fonts in documents, so too pitch and intonation in speaking, sentence-length or complexity in writing, and a myriad of other techniques can be employed to help convince listeners and readers. Taken together, all of these small features of speech or writing can be seen as creating *styles*. We recognize intuitively that some styles are more effective than others, depending upon who is speaking, who is listening, and what is being said in what circumstances. Unfortunately, at the present state of our knowledge, we have great difficulty in explaining style in logically rigorous terms (some of my technical research is on this topic, so I know how much work remains to be done to even develop shared terminology, much less deep understanding). We have many good observations and examples, and we have collected and organized historical information, but we do not yet understand the underlying principles except in the broadest and most general terms. This does not mean that studying rhetorical style is useless, but it does mean that we have to study it differently than we would in a mature scientific discipline. Rather than beginning with abstract principles, we need to assemble a large collection of instances and then allow our brains to extract patterns from these and make useful generalizations.

The best way to study rhetorical style and other similar phenomena —things that we know are important but which we do not yet fully understand—is an iterative approach of exposure, classification, generalization, and testing, all of which culminate, we hope, in some kind

---

[68] See, for example, Edward R. Tufte, *The Visual Display of Quantitative Information* (Cheshire, CT: The Graphics Press, 1983); *Envisioning Information* (Cheshire, CT: The Graphics Press, 1993); and *Visual Explanations* (Cheshire, CT: The Graphics Press, 1997).

of synthesis. First, we expose ourselves to many instances of the phenomenon of interest. We read and listen, building up a body of specific knowledge based on many individual examples. Then we try to put those examples into different categories so that members of a category have more features in common with each other than they do with the entities outside the group. From these groupings, we try to extract some rules of thumb or general guidelines. We then loop back to reading and listening, but this time we do so with our categories and general rules in mind. If the phenomena fit, we develop some confidence in our preliminary conclusions. If not, we adjust the categorizations and rules. We repeat the process until eventually our general guidelines become a limited synthesis.

In order for this approach to work, we need a collection of materials, an archive, and in order to construct an archive, we need a knowledge of the history of the phenomena we are hoping to explain. A knowledge of history also allows us to identify approaches that have worked previously and to understand the context in which they worked. The philosopher Heraclitus said that you never step into the same river twice.[69] Similarly, information, art, or culture from one time period is never a perfect analogy for that from another, but nevertheless, we can use the past to develop a better idea of the full range of possibilities and to begin to recognize patterns.

For this reason the discipline of history, although it is not one of Martianus's seven liberal arts or Varro's nine disciplines (in part because it was assumed to be an important part of grammar, logic, and rhetoric), is utterly essential to the Liberal Arts. Historical materials provide essential background and context, and the study of history shows why institutions and cultural practices are the way they are. The study of history also provides us with what psychologists call *schemas*, pre-tested ways of doing things so that we do not always need to create ideas out of nothing in the moment they are needed. Having knowledge of a wealth of historical

---

[69] "You cannot step into the same river twice, for other waters and yet others go ever flowing on." P. Wheelwright, ed. and trans., *The Presocratics* (New York: Odyssey Press, 1966), 70-71.

examples thus improves our cognitive processes, making us better at thinking and more likely to make good decisions.

The humorist P. J. O'Rourke once joked that although the eighteenth- and nineteenth-century British upper classes studied almost nothing except Latin and Greek, the young men thus educated climbed aboard ships and rapidly conquered more of the world than Alexander the Great.[70] They had read Homer and the Roman historian Livy's histories and perhaps Thucydides' *The Peloponnesian War* as school texts, so when they arrived in India or Australia, they possessed rich and sophisticated templates for understanding human behavior. Studying Homer, Virgil, and other classical authors taught them how to reason effectively, how to communicate, and how to persuade.[71] And because these men had made the intellectual connection between themselves and the Greek and Latin literature they had read,[72] they could intuit how people would act in new situations, even people with very different cultures and backgrounds. Studying the works of Homer and Virgil (as well as Dante and Shakespeare) was extremely valuable because these texts gave great insight into human perception, behavior, and emotion, insights that could be adapted to the unfamiliar cultures that they now encountered.

---

[70] P.J. O'Rourke, *Age and Guile Beat Youth, Innocence and a Bad Haircut* (New York: Atlantic Monthly Press, 1995).

[71] Their education also trained them to trust one another and, because the education of all young, aristocratic men was very similar, to have a good idea of what other members of their social class would be thinking and doing in a given situation.

[72] In 1843, General Sir Charles Napier, who was in command of the East India Company's Bombay Presidency Army, not only defeated the Muslim rulers of Sindh (present-day Pakistan) as he had been ordered, but also conquered the entire province—which he had been explicitly told not to do. Upon his victory, he telegraphed a single word, *peccavi*, which in Latin means "I have sinned," thus making a punning reference to his controlling the province ("I control Sindh"), and also admitting that he had failed to follow his orders. That Napier was confident those receiving the telegram would not only recognize the word but would also understand the first person singular past-perfect form of the verb beautifully illustrates how widely and deeply classical learning was shared among the British ruling class. The only flaw with the entire story is that the punch-line is invented: Napier never sent the one-word telegram; a woman named Catherine Winkworth submitted the pun to the magazine *Punch*, which then printed the story about the telegram as a factual report.

I know scholars of Classics who assert that you can learn everything you need to know about human nature from the works of Homer. That is a large claim, but I have never been able to find an easy way to prove it wrong. The underlying idea is that the characters in the *Iliad* and the *Odyssey* present every single fundamental human personality type and demonstrate how these types interact. If you have read these texts carefully, you will have in your mind a set of models—the Achilles type and the Cassandra type and the Hector type and the Helen type and the Stentor type and the Ajax type and the Agamemnon type—that you can use to understand and predict the behavior of real people both as individuals and in groups. True, only a few of our contemporary workplaces are as violent as Bronze Age Greece, and it is unusual to witness arguments, even in English departments, being settled by gifts of tripods or sacrifices of cattle,[73] but the emotions and interaction are fundamentally the same as people experience today. Homer's larger-than-life epic dramatization only serves to make them more memorable, not qualitatively different.

However, in order to read and understand the *Iliad* or the *Odyssey*, or even the works of Shakespeare (which are so many centuries closer to our time), we need teaching and guidance: the tradition of scholarship and interpretation that has evolved alongside these works. Even the most famous and familiar of the great texts require context that is not contained in the text itself. For example, even *Hamlet*, a play so popular and frequently imitated that it sometimes seems like it is constructed entirely out of clichés,[74] makes more sense when we have some background knowledge that can only be acquired through scholarship.

The character Hamlet traditionally wears black, a costuming choice that is consistent with theories of emotion in Shakespeare's time. Human personality, it was thought, depended upon the balance of four liquids in

[73] Given how intractable personality clashes and permanent animosities can be in English departments—and elsewhere in academia as well—gifts of tripods and even animal sacrifices (or at least large feasts) might be worth a try. They would probably be less expensive and more effective than "communications coaches" and "dispute mediators." Anyone who sets up a Homeric dispute-resolution mechanism: please contact me and tell me how well it works.

[74] Shakespeare said them all first.

the body. A surplus or deficit of one of these four humors—blood, phlegm, yellow bile, and black bile—could cause disease.[75] Hamlet calls himself "melancholy," a word that comes from the Greek *melaina chole* 'black bile.' Although melancholy is now simply another word for sad, to Shakespeare and his audience, it was a medical term, reasonably equivalent to our term "depressed." Hamlet is not merely sad at the loss of his father: he suffers from an inability to decide or act, a general lack of energy, and feelings of hopelessness. Today we might recognize these behaviors as symptoms of clinical depression or bipolar disorder.

As the scholar D. W. Robertson explains, the black costume was not merely a representation of Hamlet's emotions; it was also a way of making the character instantly recognizable to audiences of his time as being part of a tradition going back to the medieval Mystery Plays: black-clad characters represent the sin of sloth (the animal is named after the sin, not vice versa).[76] Today we might think of sloth as laziness and lack of effort, but in the medieval Christian tradition, these features of the slothful person are the result of the underlying cause: *wanhope* (pale or insufficient hope), a type of despair in which a person believed that he or she had already committed so many sins that there was no point in trying to atone for them. The person consumed by wanhope stopped trying to be better, and in the worst cases became arrogant and malicious, looking down upon those who tried to do the right thing.[77]

Robertson argues that the early audience of *Hamlet* would recognize the young prince of Denmark as a sloth-figure the moment the

---

[75] The surprising similarity of this system to that of traditional Chinese medicine was one of the many things I learned from reading and studying *The Dream of the Red Chamber* (see Chapter 8).

[76] D.W. Robertson, "A Medievalist Looks at Hamlet," in D.W. Robertson, *Essays in Medieval Culture* (Princeton: Princeton University Press, 1980), 312-331.

[77] Wanhope was a sin in medieval Christian culture in part because it was interpreted as a mere mortal asserting that there were limits to the infinite power of the deity to heal or forgive. In other words, to think you had done something so terrible that God could not forgive it was both to set limits on God's power and also a failure to understand that no human could ever do enough good to deserve eternal salvation, which was why forgiveness of sin was a gift of grace rather than something earned—which nevertheless did not excuse the sinner from putting forth an effort to repent.

character appeared on stage, not only by the black costume, but from the way he interprets his uncle's usurpation of the Danish throne in terms of how it makes him (Hamlet) feel. Hamlet visibly lacks the *fortitude* that spiritual treatises, like Chaucer's *The Parson's Tale*, saw as the remedy for sloth: stop focusing on how things make you feel, and instead do your duty to others, no matter how painful it is, and the sloth will be defeated (easier to recommend than to do, of course). A Shakespearian audience would recognize Hamlet as a sloth-figure, Robertson argues, and would therefore not see him as some kind of hero, flawed or otherwise, but as a tragic person whose repeated failures were direct results of his spiritual weakness, which manifested itself in his unbalanced humors, which caused his behavior.

The character's humoral imbalance could be a consequence of his spiritual flaws or his spiritual flaws could arise from his distribution of humors. That the Shakespearean audience believed in one did not make them stop believing in the other. Indeed, combining the medical interpretation (overabundance of black bile) with the spiritual (sloth without countervailing fortitude), we not only get a better understanding of the play, but of human nature as well. Anyone in such a terrible situation would feel sorrow, as Hamlet does, but the difference between grief and melancholy—between normal sadness and clinical depression—is that the person overcome by too much black bile cannot get better without some kind of external intervention to rebalance the humors: a shift in diet, being bled by a physician, taking purging medicines, or changing his physical location to a warmer or drier place.[78]

But Hamlet's weakness of character—too much sloth, not enough fortitude—prevents him from taking any steps to restore the balance of his humors. His wanhope causes him not only to interpret his basic situation as hopeless, but also to invent new obstacles as an excuse for inaction. Even though he has heard Claudius confess to the murder, he decides not to

[78] The fundamental difference between sadness and depression—to the frustration of generations of sufferers—is that depression is by definition the state in which people *cannot* follow the well-intentioned advice of friends and family to "just cheer up" or "get up and get moving and you'll feel better": the inability to change the feelings of sorrow is what makes it depression.

avenge his father at that time because, he convinces himself, doing so might send his fratricidal uncle to heaven (an interpretation of Christian doctrine that Shakespeare's audience would have known to be bogus).[79] Hamlet has no moral objection to killing. He does not hesitate to stab Polonius behind the tapestry, and his substitution of the letter leads to the unnecessary deaths of Rosencrantz and Guildenstern. But his slothful character leads him to choose easy victims, tormenting and harming those weaker than him, and eventually leading to the bloody tragedy of the play's conclusion.

In Hamlet's alternation between brooding introspection and frenetic, sometimes violent, action, we may think we recognize the characteristics of mental illness triggered by trauma. Freud thought he saw the effects of repressed sexual desires. Shakespeare and his audience probably saw both humoral imbalance and moral failings. And all of us can also recognize that Hamlet (and then those around him) suffer from the "Angwissh of troubled herte" [Anguish of troubled heart] that comes from losing hope. In order to understand such a complex text, in which no single piece of evidence is definitive and in which it is difficult to separate out the effects of multiple variables, we need to read it as a thing itself, in terms of its culture *and* in light of the traditions of reading and scholarship that have grown up around it. When we do so, the rewards can be enormous, for in its full context, *Hamlet* gives us great insight into the complex and unexpected ways that circumstances, personality, moral character, and (possibly) mental illness interact with each other, producing behavior that might not be understandable in purely rational terms.

People educated in the Liberal Arts place into their minds *Hamlet* and many other sophisticated depictions of human behavior. The brain's pattern-recognition abilities can then extract general principles from these models, and logic can be used to evaluate their applicability and modify them to fit other circumstances. When these abilities are coupled with skills in communication, the result is a person who can understand new situations both rapidly and in depth and can therefore make good decisions and convince others to help carry them out. The most powerful

[79] At worst it would have sent Claudius to Purgatory, which was where he was going anyway, regardless of when he was killed, as long as he had genuinely repented of his sins.

tool in the history of the world is the trained human mind, and the most adaptable and powerful minds, for millennia, have been those that have been educated in the tradition of the Liberal Arts.

Student Success Stories:
Finding the Best Job in the World

My student A, whom I taught in a First Year Seminar on fantasy literature, was the second member of her family to attend Wheaton. Her older sister had been a superstar in international relations, and A, who was also flawlessly bilingual, planned to follow in her footsteps. But towards the end of her sophomore year, when it was time to declare her major, A came to my office hours and suddenly burst into tears. It turned out that she really did not like any of her international relations classes and was, for the first time in her academic career, finding it impossible to motivate herself sufficiently. I told her that this was not an impossible situation and, as I normally do in these circumstances, asked her what her best classes had been each of her four semesters.

"That's the problem, Drout!" she said. "The classes I love are all in philosophy! What am I going to do with *that* as a degree?"

So I gave her the talk about how graduating with an A-average in philosophy is much better than graduating with a C-average in something else (or not graduating at all). She declared her philosophy major later that day and went on to excel (as I knew she would).

About six months after her graduation, I sent her an email to see how things were going.

"I'm temping," she wrote. "Mostly office work but sometimes some event-planning, and I'm thinking of trying to start my own business doing that."

I will admit my heart sank, as I wondered if A and her parents now hated me for encouraging her to pursue the major that she had found meaningful rather than something that might have led to a more prestigious job.

Eighteen months later, A popped up on my Facebook, and she had a job title: Wish-Granter for the Make-a-Wish Foundation. Because granting wishes to sick children is obviously one of the best jobs one could ever hope to get, I suddenly felt much better about my advising.

I felt even better when, a number of years later, my daughter and I met up with A in Chicago for a "quick dinner" that turned into a three-hour conversation. I was immensely proud as I listened to A's amazing stories about working with celebrities and sports stars to grant wishes to critically ill children (you should have seen the names she had in her phone's contacts!), and I was prouder still when she explained the ethical complexities of her job and how she met the challenges of synthesizing sometimes conflicting values. And I was happier still to learn that it was A's philosophy degree that had helped her get the initial interview with Make-a-Wish. She stood out from hundreds of other applicants with her philosophy major, and also, and perhaps more importantly, because the people who hired her knew that being a Wish-Granter required the ability to think carefully through ethical and moral issues and to solve complex problems. Then, in her interviews, A's ability to communicate clearly in both speech and writing (and in two languages!) made her stand out even more. And once she had the job, her intelligence, work-ethic, compassion, and insight made her remarkably successful.

The point of this story is not that "majoring in philosophy will allow you to get one of the best jobs that exists," although in this particular case it did. True, A's remarkable personal qualities—intelligence, energy, moral conviction, compassion—were obvious from the day I met her and are certainly more relevant to her success than her college studies. But she developed her rigorous thinking and effective communication by studying the Liberal Arts, and majoring in the particular Liberal Arts discipline that she found most rewarding, allowing her to put the maximum energy into her studies and therefore get the maximum learning out of them. All of this means that the lives of hundreds of children and their families over almost two decades have been made better: they have been given a glimpse of light in their darkest moments because A has put all her formidable talents and her gigantic heart into helping them.

Chapter 4

Does Studying the Liberal Arts Make You a Better Person?

As we saw in the previous chapter, the Liberal Arts are tools to rule. The ways of thinking that they teach empower individuals both to make effective decisions and to convince others. But the Liberal Arts are not the only intellectual disciplines that can train people how to think. The institutions of the military, religion, and business also possess long traditions of training rulers, and, more recently, the ways of thinking encouraged by education in science and engineering have contributed to the success of many leaders around the world. Tools are not moral or immoral: only humans are. However, the specific capabilities of different tools do seem to encourage certain behaviors in the humans that use them. Over time, the tools can shape their users even though the users create the tools. Cultures with strong military traditions, like ancient Sparta, tend to put an emphasis on hierarchical decision making, obedience, and physical bravery. Those that are very good at trade and commerce, like ancient Athens or Renaissance Venice, tend to emphasize distributed decision-making, individualism, and finesse. Just as an education in the military or religion or commerce will predispose a person towards certain worldviews and approaches, so too does an education in the Liberal Arts.

We who teach the Liberal Arts like to think that our sort of education is morally better than that provided by other approaches, that people who study the Liberal Arts will be more likely to make good moral choices, leading to greater happiness for themselves and those they are leading. We want to believe that there is an automatic moral component to the study of the Liberal Arts, so that merely by studying them, you *become* more good in addition to gaining the ability to *do* more good with the power given to you by these ways of thinking. Supporters of other intellectual disciplines surely believe that their own approaches are better. Supporters of the military could reasonably argue that people educated in their tradition will be better leaders because they will be self-disciplined, strong, brave, and loyal. Supporters of religion would similarly argue that being educated their way will lead to moral, kind, and generous decisions. This chapter is far too short to adjudicate among these possible claims, and I do not know enough about education in the military, religion, or business to treat these disciplines fairly, so it is entirely possible that they may be better than the Liberal Arts—although I do not concede this point. My goal in this chapter is narrower: simply to determine whether or not education in the Liberal Arts leads to morally good results both for individuals and the societies around them.

Even this more limited claim turns out to be difficult to prove because the historical evidence is somewhat mixed. For example, free Romans produced a society and culture that for centuries dominated the lands surrounding the Mediterranean Sea and brought about enormous advances in technology, civil engineering, architecture, art, literature, commerce, communication, medicine, and transportation. Many of these accomplishments can be traced directly to Varro's Nine Disciplines and the later Seven Liberal Arts, and even those that do not have a named discipline of their own are built upon the effective social organization and leadership enabled by education in the Liberal Arts (although many Romans were also trained by their military service). But the glory of Rome also had a darker side. The very same people, families, and institutions that built and maintained the great civilization could be brutal, cruel, and tyrannical. The rich and sophisticated culture of Rome did not prevent the violence and injustice of Nero or Caligula or Diocletian and all the free men who carried out their orders. The decadent and corrupt elites who helped bring about the Fall of Rome were educated in the same Liberal Arts traditions as the great and humane emperors Trajan, Hadrian, and Marcus Aurelius. The historical evidence is equivocal, so we must rely on some other data.

We can identify four major arguments in favor of the idea that the Liberal Arts makes its students better people, good in themselves and more likely to lead others to good ends:

1. *The argument of truth*. The Liberal Arts help people see the world—especially the human world—as it really is, and knowing the truth about the world helps a person be right and therefore good.
2. *The argument of empathy*. Literature, art, and music help people imagine what it would be like to be in other situations and thus understand the experiences and viewpoints of other people. Such empathy makes the people exercising power more benevolent.
3. *The argument of discipline*. Studying the Liberal Arts (like studying a science or pursuing athletics, music, or martial arts) requires self-discipline. Students end up learning how to think by rejecting pleasing but incorrect ideas. They learn how to focus, to eliminate irrelevances, and to control their bad desires. Self-discipline and rationality make people more likely to lead society to good results.
4. *The argument of doubt*. Studying the Liberal Arts, in contrast to the sciences, forces students to recognize how incomplete and provisional our knowledge is and how we often must rely on very imperfect approximations for decisions. Understanding the many good reasons to doubt makes leaders more self-critical and less likely to impose their will on others without having very good reasons for doing so.

There is truth in each of these arguments, but, as we will see, each has problems as well. None by itself is completely sufficient, though perhaps as a group they are reasonably convincing.

The *argument of truth* goes all the way back to Plato and his battle with the Sophists, his competitors. The Sophists paid close attention to the workings of persuasion in political matters, and, from their observations, they developed ways of teaching people to be better persuaders. Questions of the morality of arguments were irrelevant to them. They offered to teach their students the techniques that worked to *win*, regardless of whether the winner was wrong or right. Plato rejected the Sophists, arguing that finding the truth was more important than winning the argument and that the truth was itself a rhetorical tool—perhaps the most powerful of all. Although he did recognize that sometimes things that the Sophists said would be more appealing to listeners, Plato maintained that there were eternal truths and that eventually people would be convinced of the right path of action because the truth was the way the world actually worked. Boiling things down to absolute essentials, the Sophists said, "We will teach you how to win arguments!" while Plato said, "I will teach you how to find the truth, and as a byproduct you will win arguments."

The battle between these points of view has continued for more than two thousand years. The intellectual heirs of the Sophists believe that there is no absolute truth, only opinion and ideology, so that winning arguments is everything, because winning arguments gives power, and power *produces* "social truth." Platonists counter that people can, through reasoning and investigation, discover at least an approximation of eternal truths. The disciplines of the Liberal Arts have never been able to settle this argument completely, although the discipline of Logic may help to clarify the details of the disagreement.

When an argument has bogged down for a long time, it is sometimes helpful to reverse your thinking to see where a new perspective might lead. If you are interested in proving a particular idea, assume that its opposite is true, and then reason from that assumption, taking this line of reasoning as far as you can. If you end up with a contradiction, then your original idea is likely to be correct. Plato's idea is that knowing the truth about the external world will make you a better person, so let us assume the opposite, that knowing the truth about the world will make you worse. If that is true, then society would be better off if you learned and believed falsehoods about the world because believing in specific lies would improve individuals and the societies in which they live. However, falsehoods are inaccurate, so they will generate in their believers an inaccurate understanding of the world. Inaccurate or incomplete knowledge is more likely than accurate knowledge to lead to mistakes, so leaders who believe in many falsehoods are more likely to make mistakes that harm either themselves or their followers.

You can see where this argument goes. If we assume that learning falsehoods about the world is better than learning the truth about the world, we end up with a logically tangled mess, because while learning wrong things about the world might make you a better person in some ways or in the short term, incorrect knowledge is more likely to lead to bad decisions in the long term (there are many ways of being wrong and only a few of being right, just as there are vastly more ways of being dead than there are ways of being alive).[80] For example, if people really are evil, but you falsely believe they are good, you may be more likely to be kind and benevolent (good things), but many of your other decisions will not lead to the results you hope for since people will not act as you would expect. If the argument that it would be better to believe falsehoods about the world than to know truth leads to contradictions or ridiculous results, then the opposite of that argument is more likely (but not certain) to be true. Thus the argument for truth is logically superior to the argument for not knowing the truth, and this argument supports the contention that the study of the Liberal Arts can lead to good outcomes. However, as an argument for favoring the Liberal Arts over other fields, it is much less convincing, since other disciplines—particularly the sciences—could certainly claim that they lead as much or even more surely to the truth than the disciplines of the Liberal Arts.

The *argument of empathy* does not have quite as long a pedigree as the argument for truth, but there nevertheless is a tradition of inferring that studying the Liberal Arts increases a person's ability to understand and sympathize with others.[81] One of the most powerful summations of the idea was made by the philosopher Iris Murdoch, who said that "The purpose of literature is to show that other people really exist."[82] History and our own observations show us that humans are not particularly good

---

[80] Richard Dawkins, *The Blind Watchmaker: Why the Evidence of Evolution Reveals a Universe without Design* (New York: W.W. Norton, 1986).

[81] The argument of empathy (though not explicitly labeled as such) is at the core of DeLue's case for the Liberal Arts in *How the Liberal Arts Can Save Liberal Democracy.*

[82] Iris Murdoch, *Under the Net* (London: Chatto and Windus, 1954); Iris Murdoch, *Existentialists and Mystics: Writings on Philosophy and Literature*, ed. Peter Conradi (New York: Penguin, 1995).

at believing that other people have an inner life that is as complete or sophisticated or fully human as we ourselves possess. As soon as we find someone who disagrees with us or behaves differently than we would, we start believing this person to be stupid, or depraved, or faulty, or evil (otherwise they would agree with us and do what we are doing). Literature and art help counteract this tendency by allowing people to experience imaginatively what other people might feel and think, to see through other people's eyes. Such an experience can help to bridge the gap between ourselves and others.

This power of literature and art has long been recognized. When President Abraham Lincoln met Harriet Beecher Stowe, the author of *Uncle Tom's Cabin,* he supposedly said, "So you're the little woman who wrote the book that made this great war!"[83] Stowe's book never argued for war itself, but Lincoln was acknowledging that the empathy for enslaved African Americans engendered by Stowe's *Uncle Tom's Cabin* had persuaded many Americans that the institution of slavery was too evil to be allowed to continue in America.[84] Stowe had done this not by preaching about the war or making logical arguments, but by depicting characters in such a way that readers felt their suffering and so recognized emotionally that slaves could have the same sorts of inner lives as free white people.[85] Because of this empathy, many people were willing to make the great personal sacrifices necessary to end slavery.

William Faulkner's *The Sound and the Fury* helps us try to understand perspectives even more divergent than those between slaves and free people by showing us how the world might be perceived by someone

[83] There is no definitive documentary source for this quotation, which is based on Stowe family tradition. It seems unlikely that President Lincoln, who correctly viewed the Civil War as a tragedy, would say something like this. Nevertheless, the apocryphal quote does accurately represent the massive influence of *Uncle Tom's Cabin*.

[84] Harriet Beecher Stowe, *Uncle Tom's Cabin* (Mineoloa, NY: Dover, 2005).

[85] When we read *Uncle Tom's Cabin* today, we see the characters as crude stereotypes, which is one reason why calling someone an "Uncle Tom" is a serious insult in the African American community. At the time, however, Stowe's depiction of slaves as good, honest, and noble was revolutionary, and the book really did help convince the American public that the institution of slavery was evil.

who is severely mentally handicapped.[86] Charlotte Perkins Gilman's "The Yellow Wallpaper" makes us experience the onset of mental illness along with the story's protagonist.[87] Other works of literature can expand our circle of empathy even beyond humans, making us feel as if we have shared experiences with and can understand the points of view of intelligent robots or aliens or even animals. Richard Adams' *Watership Down* makes readers care deeply about the lives of mere rabbits,[88] and the power of literature can make even the striving of *moles* emotionally engaging (and they cannot even *see* inside their underground tunnels).[89] Literature and art have the power to make leaders and rulers imaginatively experience what the weak, the sick, the exploited, the oppressed, and the hopeless feel. Such leaders, it seems, would be more likely to be kind, supportive, and benevolent than those who had not experienced such an emotional connection because they would be able to apply their emotional intuition as well as their logical reasoning to their decision-making.

There are, however, some significant problems with this argument. First, even if we accept the premise that literature, music, and art can make leaders more compassionate, we cannot prove that such empathy will be sure to lead to better decisions. In some cases, works of the imagination can be *too* powerful at manipulating our emotions. It is easy to find art, literature, and music that, while causing us to have empathy for some characters, also generates feelings of hatred and contempt towards others. When brought out of the text and into the real world, these sorts of emotions can have negative effects. The film *Braveheart,* for example, was so emotionally powerful that it seems to have played a part in reanimating a long-dormant hostility towards England among the Scots.[90] One of the causes of the warfare that occurred with the breakup of Yugoslavia was the cultural significance of the city of Kosovo and the battle of the "Field of

[86] William Faulkner, *The Sound and the Fury,* 3rd ed. (New York: W.W. Norton, 2014).

[87] Charlotte Perkins Gilman, *The Yellow Wallpaper and Other Stories* (Mineola, NY: Dover, 1997).

[88] Richard Adams, *Watership Down* (New York: Scribner, 2005).

[89] William Horwood's *Duncton Wood* (New York: McGraw Hill, 1980) and its sequels are an epic fantasy series whose main characters are, yes, moles.

[90] Lin Anderson, *Braveheart: From Hollywood to Holyrood* (Edinburgh: Luath Press, 2004).

Blackbirds" in Serbian literature and culture. So although it at first seems obvious that the increased empathy that can be generated by literature and art will have beneficial effects, we cannot simply assume that happy conclusion. There are even circumstances in which we can imagine literature and art creating empathy for evil and thus potentially weakening the social order. The film *Dead Man Walking*, for example, makes the audience empathize so completely with the killer who is to be executed that we find ourselves forgetting his victims, who are not present to stimulate our sympathy. The film was so emotionally powerful that after seeing it, many viewers reconsidered their previous firm beliefs in the morality of the death penalty.[91] We can see the power of art to create such empathy as being socially valuable, since it might convince us to inflict less suffering upon a person—even a guilty person—than we might be willing to countenance if that person were invisible and anonymous. But it is also possible that the same empathy could be socially destructive, for example, by convincing us to value the killer's life more than the lives of the people he slaughtered, or by causing us to sympathize with invaders or oppressors as much as their victims. Perhaps there are situations in which too much empathy is as bad as too little.

The American novelist Don DeLillo creates such a scenario in his novel *Running Dog*, the plot of which centers around the search for what is thought to be the most pornographic film in the world, filmed in Hitler's bunker as the Russian and American armies were advancing on Berlin.[92] When this (imaginary) film is finally viewed in the novel, the reader is surprised that there is no sexual behavior in it at all. Instead, the film shows Adolph Hitler trying to cheer up terrified young children by imitating the actor Charlie Chaplin's clownish mockery of Hitler himself. The Hitler in the film performs an act of kindness that indicates both a self-awareness and a self-deprecating modesty that is horrifying both to the character in the novel who sees the film and to us, the readers of the book. People have a visceral revulsion to the idea that a monstrous person responsible for

[91] The power of the film was such that it provoked sympathy even in viewers who were fully aware that it was intended to manipulate their emotions.

[92] Don Delillo, *Running Dog* (New York: Vintage, 1989).

millions of deaths could act this way. We may know intellectually that history's greatest villains are likely to have been more complex in real life than our imagined caricatures of them, but for the most part we avoid engaging emotionally with the implications of this idea unless forced to by the power of art. It is possible to argue that being made to feel empathy even for a monster could be good, and that doing so helps us reconsider unexamined assumptions and reflexive judgments,[93] but our intuition, which DeLillo harnesses so brilliantly, is that there is something wrong with feeling sympathy for Hitler. We reasonably fear being manipulated through our empathy into accepting or supporting evil, and there is no obvious way to constrain this power so that literature and art only lead us towards good things.

The argument of truth, however, is a potential solution to this problem. If study of the Liberal Arts does lead us towards the truth, then we should be able to use that knowledge to determine whether or not we should be more or less empathetic in a given situation. For instance, if there really existed a film of Hitler comforting frightened children, we could still use logic to reason that a small act of kindness cannot make up for monstrous evil that killed millions, and so while we might *feel* our emotions being engaged, we could counteract them with our intellects. Potentially negative outcomes of increased empathy would thus be mitigated by the disciplined *study* of literature and culture. In fact, even if we accept neither the argument of truth nor the argument of empathy, we can recognize that studying the Liberal Arts helps us to be more conscious of the ways that works of art and literature can manipulate our emotions. We can therefore engage with artworks intellectually as well as emotionally, using both logic and rhetoric. After all, if the increase in empathy caused by exposure to literature, art, and music were an unequivocal good, we could simply read more literature, view more art, and listen to more music. But because increases in empathy can be positive or negative, we need the discipline of formally studying the Liberal Arts.

[93] DeLillo's choice of Hitler is deliberately shocking and is perhaps so effective because to most contemporary readers, Hitler is the single historical figure with whom people cannot (and do not want to) empathize.

This point is closely related to the *argument of discipline*, which claims that the kinds of intellectual effort required to study the Liberal Arts trains a person in methods of thinking that are beneficial in other aspects of life. In itself, this does not seem like a very controversial conclusion. Hard, disciplined study, especially when chosen deliberately rather than being imposed from outside, cultivates virtues of focus, dedication, and persistence that are the foundation of both personal success and effective leadership.

The weakness in this argument, however, is that the same claim could be made for almost any other approach to education. If studying the Liberal Arts provides beneficial intellectual discipline, so does studying the sciences, social sciences, business, religion, or the martial arts. In fact, many people would probably assume that the sciences require *more* discipline, since they are tied more closely to logic and are founded upon mathematics. The social sciences may be less mathematical and logically rigorous than the natural sciences, but they still appear to require at least as much discipline as the Liberal Arts. However, my goal in this chapter is not primarily to argue that the Liberal Arts are better than other sets of disciplines, only that they can help an individual to become good, or a leader to do what is right, and the argument of discipline does support this contention.

Finally, and perhaps most controversially, we come to the *argument of doubt*. Studying the Liberal Arts forces a student to realize how tightly entangled our intellectual conclusions are with our emotions and desires and how difficult it is to be sure that we really know anything. The more we learn about the complex and intellectually messy phenomena we study in the Liberal Arts, the more we realize that we cannot isolate all the relevant variables and that we often lack clear and rigorous principles to explain their interaction. We learn that even seemingly basic facts are a lot more vague and contradictory than we had thought. We discover that there is a great deal of contingency and luck in history, that actual events are far more complicated and ambiguous than we had assumed, and that the events are depicted in ways—even in many scholarly and sophisticated sources—that advance one agenda or another. At certain points in a

Liberal Arts education, the more you learn, the less confidence you have in your knowledge.

From some perspectives, this doubt could be beneficial if it prevented leaders from imposing bad ideas upon those who follow them. If, because of the doubt engendered by the study of the Liberal Arts, you are not entirely sure of the correctness of your ideas, you are less likely to force others to carry them out, thus preventing the implementation of bad decisions if your ideas happen to be wrong. Doubt helps prevent premature decisions and allows for the correction of errors. Doubt leads to the humility that is essential in a person who has responsibility.

But doubt can have negative effects, as well. "The best lack all conviction, while the worst / Are full of passionate intensity," writes William Butler Yeats, in his poem "The Second Coming," indicting the culture of early twentieth-century Europe.[94] People who doubt are often less emotionally prepared to stand up to people who are certain, but if those overly certain people are both wrong and ineffectively opposed, the results can be very bad indeed. For example, people who are devoted to a particular religion or ideology are often passionately sure that their approach is right and so are willing to expend a great deal of energy trying to impose their preferred order upon society. People educated in the Liberal Arts, who have enough historical knowledge to doubt categorical claims, could potentially also doubt their own doubting and so might not resist as strongly as they could have. Also, just as the empathy generated by works of literature and art is not equally distributed to all members of society, so too the doubt created by the study of the Liberal Arts is not, in any given moment, evenly applied to every phenomenon studied. The "confirmation bias" inherent in human nature makes us more likely to believe things that are consistent with our desires. We notice phenomena that support our conclusions but do not recognize conflicting data or, if we do notice it, strongly doubt information which conflicts with our preferred hypotheses, so even our doubt is biased. The argument of doubt, therefore, cannot on its own convince us that the Liberal Arts can make you a good person and leader.

---

[94] William Butler Yeats, *Michael Robartes and the Dancer* (Dublin: Cuala Press, 1921).

As we noted above, the argument of empathy is bolstered by the argument of truth. We can also see how the argument of discipline helps explain why we can expect that students of the Liberal Arts resist being manipulated too much through empathy. The argument of doubt in turn balances the argument of truth. The four major arguments, therefore, are not entirely independent, though they are not perfectly integrated either. Taken all together, the arguments for truth, empathy, discipline, and doubt provide some support for the contention that studying the Liberal Arts can make you a better person and leader, but not enough support for us to consider the case proven.[95] The Liberal Arts are tools for ruling and, as such, empower people to exercise power over others at the same time that they are, perhaps, channeling that exercise of power into pathways more likely to lead to good results. But there is no guarantee that study of the Liberal Arts will lead only to positive things. The Liberal Arts probably do make us better people, but that is not the most compelling reason to study them. Rather, as we will see in the next chapter, the best reason for studying the Liberal Arts is that they teach us how to think in ways that are particularly valuable for solving complex and ill-defined problems, and they transmit these thinking abilities across generations.

---

[95] That Alexander Hanan, after working his way through similar chains of reasons in *Reimaging Liberal Education*, adds explicitly religious and moral ideals to the Liberal Arts supports my conclusion that the study of the Liberal Arts alone is not sufficient to *ensure* that a person will be morally good.

Student Success Stories:

His ideal career combined loving books and fighting monsters. He settled for loving books and doing good.

J was a student in the very first course I taught at Wheaton, an English 101 called "Writing About a Wonderful Life." An English major, J worked on an interdisciplinary project with me to recreate medical remedies from the Anglo-Saxon period. In the process, J traveled around England interviewing various experts in disciplines ranging from literature to archeology. He then learned to home-brew wine so that we could make sure our reconstructed remedy would not contain any modern preservatives.[96]

It was towards the end of his very successful college career that J came to my office hours to ask for advice.

"I've enjoyed being an English major," he said. "And I've learned a lot. But what am I going to do next? Everyone else in English seems to be going into editing or publishing or journalism, but I don't think those things are for me."

I asked him to tell me what his dream job would be.

"Giles the Librarian from *Buffy the Vampire Slayer*," he replied without hesitation.

That was early in my career, so I did not have enough former students that one of them might be able to facilitate a connection, and even now I don't know if even my most remarkable former students could get a new college graduate a job doing research for a Vampire Slayer to support her

---

[96] I am going to skip over the details of how he turned his home-brewing skills into a profitable business by making beer and cider for his friends in the dorms. J was discrete enough—and a certain Provost kind enough—that I didn't learn about this entrepreneurial work until after the statute of limitations had run out.

work fighting demons, monsters, and other supernatural entities (though stranger things have happened).

"Well, I don't know about the killing monsters part," I said. "But what about graduate school in Library Science?"

"Is that even a real thing?" he asked.

Yes, it was a real thing, and fortunately one of the best programs in that discipline was at a school in Boston, and fortunately J took my advice, went there, and excelled. And then even more fortunately, just as he was graduating, Google, Yahoo, and other tech companies were hiring away experienced librarians from their jobs, which opened up opportunities for new graduates. J raced up the ranks of librarians first at universities and then at local libraries. A few years later, he emailed me to say that he was now a head librarian and was pioneering letting people use 3D printers, drones, virtual-reality headsets, and other high-tech equipment in libraries —it turned out that not only were such things popular in themselves, but their presence increased the number of people who checked out books!

One Halloween, J sent me a picture of a display he had set up at his library: "How to Survive the Zombie Apocalypse." He had combined books about zombies with books about wilderness survival, "prepping," and emergency response.

"So you *have* managed to become Giles the Librarian from *Buffy the Vampire Slayer*," I wrote back.

"OMG I had forgotten about that conversation until you brought it up," he wrote. "I guess I have."

And, like Giles, J did not merely preserve and spread knowledge (though that would certainly be enough); he went beyond his regular duties to do good in the world.

Although J's major at Wheaton was English, and he was as fully in the literary side of the Liberal Arts as anybody, because he knew how to learn, when his library had an opportunity to buy a 3D printer, J taught himself how to use it (and just as importantly, how to fix it, as the 3D printers in 2005 broke down a lot more than they do now). J would print complex shapes and display them around the library so that patrons could see what they might be able to create with the printer.

One day, a 3D-printed model of a human hand that J had sitting on his desk caught the eye of a library patron. “Could you make one of those for someone?” she asked.

“You could make it yourself; I’ll show you how,” said J.

But the patron was really not interested in learning how to use the 3D printer herself. Instead, she needed a hand for a man who was staying with her while he received medical treatment.

A resident of a remote and poor part of Guatemala, this man came to the Boston area every few years for treatment for the severe burns he had suffered as a child (he was having his thirtieth surgery at Shriners Hospital for Children). Because the geometry of his finger stumps changed with each surgery, it was difficult and expensive to get prostheses, and these often broke when he was at home.

J did some fast research, found a community of 3D-printer enthusiasts who had worked to develop inexpensive but effective prostheses, downloaded the design, and then worked to customize it to the man’s hand. It took three attempts to get a perfect fit, but when it came time for the man to return to Guatemala, J had a box of spare hands for him to take home.

“Realistically it took me a week to get the design right and customized for him,” J said. “And it takes three hours to print each one. But it’s only $11.00 of materials, so it was really no big sacrifice for us to print him enough hands to get him through to his next visit to Boston, when we’ll have more waiting for him.”

Maybe it’s not slaying monsters and researching how to close portals to demon-dimensions, but there is more than one way to do good in our world, and knowing how to learn opens up more possibilities.

Chapter 5

Best Reasons for Studying the Liberal Arts I: Solving Complex Problems

In the previous chapter, we tried to determine if studying the Liberal Arts can make people more inclined to be good and thus more likely both to be happy in their lives and better leaders of others. If this notion is true, then when taken along with our demonstration that the Liberal Arts provide intellectual skills that increase an individual's ability to lead or rule, it would be a compelling argument for studying the Liberal Arts, because the power granted by this kind of study would automatically be channeled so that it was used for good purposes. However, although the idea is plausible and intuitively appealing, we can only say that it is *likely* that the study of the Liberal Arts will lead a person to be good. This in itself might be a sufficient argument for their support, but, as we will see, there are two much stronger reasons we should highly value the Liberal Arts. The first of these arguments is the effectiveness of the ways of thinking taught by the Liberal Arts at solving complex, ill-defined problems (the subject of this chapter); the second is that the tradition of the Liberal Arts preserves and transmits the cultural accomplishments of previous generations so that others can build upon them (the focus of Chapter 6). Taken together, these arguments show that the Liberal Arts are valuable not only to individuals, but to society as a whole because they enable us to progress towards the solution of problems so complex that they require more than one lifetime of creativity, intelligence, and effort.

Multivariate, poorly understood, messy problems that are not easily attacked by the isolating methods of physics and engineering are exactly the sort of problems that most trouble our culture. This is not a criticism of the science-based disciplines, whose powers were painstakingly developed over centuries and which have done so much to improve the lives of all people. We must not underestimate the difficulty of old problems simply because they have now been solved. To study the history of physics from Newton up through the end of the twentieth century is to be awed by how much has been accomplished in such a short time—even if we set aside the massive technological accomplishments and focus only on the intellectual triumph of understanding how the physical world works. Saying something is "just an engineering problem" or "just a physics problem," while it sounds dismissive on the part of the speaker, is actually an acknowledgment of the massive achievements of engineering and physics. These sorts of problems only sound "easy" because many great minds over many years built the intellectual tools to solve them.

Nevertheless, many of our most intractable problems are not able to be solved by purely technical approaches, for if the problems could easily be solved that way, they would have been. If, as we argued previously, a science is just a Liberal Art that has developed an effective methodology, it makes sense that those fields that have not become sciences are those that focus on the kinds of problems that scientific approaches are not (yet) good at solving. Where we have many different inputs that are not easily measured; where interactions are extremely complex and non-linear; and where individual perceptions, values, and interpretations are important components of phenomena, the scientific approach usually cannot provide answers. Likewise, in areas of inquiry where we have trouble determining facts, where all the data is biased, ambiguous, or poorly understood, scientific approaches are not usually successful.

The Liberal Arts are very good at dealing with these kinds of situations. For example, let us imagine that you are leading a business and are considering extending its operations into an unfamiliar part of the world. You think there might be a good market for your product or service, but you also need to evaluate the risks, costs, possible profits, and potential dangers that would come from expanding. If you have gone to business school, you surely know how to create a business plan, and you have acquired formulae, decision-trees, and rules of thumb that help you make such plans. But you have a fundamental problem: all of your sources of information are flawed in one way or another (sometimes in many ways).

The published information is both incomplete and biased, and it was compiled for different purposes by people or institutions with agendas that you do not know or understand. Some of the information you have was recycled from still other unfamiliar institutions, and some of these organizations may not even exist anymore, so it is difficult for you to find out what their capabilities and agendas might have been. You know that your individual informants are sometimes prejudiced and often not fully knowledgeable, and you cannot be sure that they are not self-dealing or simply misunderstanding you. You also do not speak the language of the new market, and the nuances of the culture are very difficult for outsiders to interpret. You cannot discount *all* of your sources of information as untrustworthy (or you will have no information at all), but you cannot take *any* of them at face value either. So you must evaluate imperfect information by seeing how it correlates or conflicts with larger patterns and in relation to other knowledge you have about similar situations. You evaluate quality in terms that are subjective, but not so subjective that you cannot map them onto the actual world. You assemble a tentative model of the situation and then adjust that model as you gather more information. You make judgments based on experience, principles, and the data you have evaluated.

With all due respect for the good work done in business schools, the Liberal Arts teach this kind of reasoning better than any other discipline. In fact, much of business-school education is based around "case studies," in which students investigate particular instances of problem-solving and decision-making. Although the name itself comes from social science and medical research, case studies are really a Liberal Arts approach; they are the equivalent of studying an individual historical event, literary text, artwork, or musical composition in great detail and using the knowledge thus gained to recognize some patterns and derive some general principles. Business schools use case studies exactly because business leadership is really a specific, focused application of Liberal Arts skills rather than a completely separate science of its own.

In the study of almost all human activities and creations, we have to deal simultaneously with different levels of understanding—even though our focus will shift, depending upon exactly what we are hoping to understand. Sometimes we concentrate on the surface level, trying to figure out what exactly the text says, what the painting is representing, what happened in that particular battle. Other times, we need to set the phenomenon in some wider historical or cultural context, recognizing that a seemingly strange feature of the text (for example, a monster fleeing the smell of garlic) is actually an example of a genre convention that the audience would have recognized,[97] or that a seemingly absurd attack on a politician (insulting him by saying that his mother has no nose)[98] is part of a cultural tradition. Other times we have to account for biases: one historian might have celebrated the qualities of an ancient king not for their own sake, but because they contrast with the characteristics of a contemporary ruler; a second historian might want to curry favor with this ruler and so would emphasize different aspects of the past. For example, the Roman historian Tacitus was more interested in criticizing the aristocratic Romans of his own day than he was in precisely documenting the actual behaviors of the Germanic peoples, so we can never be sure if he is accurately describing Germanic customs or inventing things in order to make a political point.[99] Faced with these kinds of challenges, we have to find ways to synthesize small and potentially conflicting fragments of information into some kind of coherent whole.

That is a somewhat general description of the kinds of problems that are faced in the Liberal Arts and how these disciplines go about trying to solve them. It is perhaps easier to understand this process when it is presented more concretely, so to this end we will investigate in some detail

---

[97] The tradition of vampires hating garlic comes from Bram Stoker's novel *Dracula*. Stoker chose one plant of the many that in various folk traditions have repelled vampires and other supernatural creatures, but because Stoker's novel was a source for so many other vampire novels, the garlic tradition was amplified so widely that it is now an expectation of twentieth- and twenty-first-century audiences that vampires cannot tolerate garlic.

[98] An anthropologist who has done field research in Mongolia has told me that many of the most offensive insults in the traditional culture he studied were based around hinting that a person's relatives suffered from syphilis, which in its untreated, late-stage form can cause the bridge of the nose to collapse.

[99] There is further discussion of Tacitus' *Germania* below in Chapter 6.

how the disciplines of the Liberal Arts could help us understand why a set of sophisticated cultural artifacts—Michelangelo's famous paintings in the Sistine Chapel—are the way they are.[100]

We begin simply by looking. This may sound obvious, but looking, reading, or listening are often neglected skills even in the disciplines of the Liberal Arts. Professors and students often rush too quickly to use their powerful tools of analysis and so neglect the equally important work of perception (the disciplines of art history and music history, however, *are* particularly good at training students in perception). So the first step is to look carefully at Michelangelo's paintings on the ceiling and the far wall of the Chapel, trying to understand what we are seeing. In one place towards the center of the ceiling, we see a bearded figure reaching his hand towards a young man. If we are participants in Western culture, we will know almost immediately that this picture is a famous depiction of the biblical story of God's creation of Adam, the first man. This recognition shows that even at the very beginnings of analysis, viewers of the paintings are doing the kind of work that is at the heart of the Liberal Arts: interpreting the painting not only as a thing in itself, but also in light of information that comes from outside the artwork, information learned elsewhere. Art historians have collected a great deal of data about *iconography*, the tradition of associating certain images with certain meanings, and they can use this accumulated knowledge to identify the images in the Sistine Chapel paintings, matching the scenes to specific characters and stories in the biblical tradition. We can then compare Michelangelo's depictions to the stories themselves.

Such comparison, however, turns out to be harder than it sounds because, as we noted in our discussion of philology, the biblical text itself was not always the same through space and time. We therefore must determine which particular version Michelangelo would have known. Only then can we try to read that text and figure out, from the language and the cultural context, how Michelangelo may have understood it. Thus we need either to learn to read the language in which the text the artist could have

[100] For more details on the discussion that follows, see Loren Partridge, *Michelangelo: The Sistine Chapel Ceiling* (New York: George Braziller, 1996).

read was written (Latin) or know enough about the scholarly tradition to know which translations we can trust before we can have some confidence that we will be able to use the text to help us understand the painting.

Even then, the text itself might not be enough—we may need to engage with scholarship *about* the text or its cultural contexts. For example, although the Sistine Chapel ceiling contains many scenes from Old Testament history, and Moses is one of the most important characters in the Old Testament, Michelangelo did not paint a figure of Moses on the ceiling.[101] Moses does appear in the Chapel, however, in a wall fresco by Sandro Botticelli. In that painting, beams of light are depicted as shining from Moses' forehead. But when Michelangelo created a statue of Moses for the Tomb of the Medici, the sculptor did not carve beams of light or a halo, but instead depicted the Hebrew lawgiver with two stubby, cow-like horns poking out of the top of his skull.

Why was Moses horned in this statue, which was carved five to seven years after the Sistine Chapel ceiling was completed, and not in Botticelli's fresco, which was completed even before Michelangelo began painting the ceiling? As the scholar Ruth Mellinkoff explains, the iconography of the horned Moses has its origin in a mistranslation of the Hebrew word *karan*, which St. Jerome, the early editor and translator of the Bible, thought was related to the root *keren*, which does mean "horned." *Karan*, however, actually means "shining" or "giving off rays of light." Nevertheless, Jerome's mistranslation became standard and was incorporated into the Latin translation of the Bible, so for centuries, Moses was depicted as having horns, and this is the tradition that influenced Michelangelo.[102] However, the translation error had been corrected in the Latin Bible well before Michelangelo carved his Moses in 1513-1515, and we can infer that even non-scholars would have known the more accurate translation of "rays of light," because that is how Botticelli had depicted Moses in his fresco three decades before in 1481-1482. Michelangelo's

[101] Instead of an image of Moses himself, Michelangelo depicted the Israelites surrounding the bronze serpent that God had told Moses to erect in order to heal any people who had been bitten by poisonous reptiles.

[102] Ruth Mellinkoff, *The Horned Moses in Medieval Art and Thought* (Berkeley: University of California Press, 1970).

decision to put horns on his Moses sculpture, therefore, cannot simply be the result of the sculptor having followed a textual mistranslation but instead must represent a deliberate choice to follow an iconographic tradition even when that was no longer believed to represent the biblical story.[103]

We do know that Michelangelo's particular artistic choices were influenced by his immediate political and historical context. The Sistine Chapel ceiling was probably originally blue with gold stars, but Pope Julius II, a warrior Pope, decided to have the ceiling painted with figures, so Michelangelo was responding to the desires of a powerful patron. There are also technical reasons why the figures are the colors and shapes that they are. Michelangelo sometimes transferred drawings onto the plaster, using a grid to enlarge smaller drawings, but in other places he seems to have drawn directly on the ceiling. The technique of fresco painting required him to paint on damp plaster, which in turn limited the amount of work that could be done in a day and the amount of time that could be taken with a portion of any single figure or scene. The geometry of the ceiling, which itself was shaped both by the architect's vision and the physical limitations of the techniques and building materials, influenced not only the general layout of the paintings but the arrangements of many scenes and figures that had to fit into areas defined by architectural features. Taking all of these factors together and figuring out how much weight to put on any one piece of evidence requires a scholar to have internalized an enormous amount of information gathered from many sources.

All of this information has also been processed through the minds of previous scholars, who in turn were influenced by their own cultural contexts as well as the histories and intellectual traditions of their disciplines. For example, over the centuries after Michelangelo painted his masterpiece, the carbon from candles and lanterns accumulated on the Chapel's ceiling, darkening the paintings. The degree to which the original

[103] I am unconvinced by the arguments that Michelangelo's horned Moses is connected with the folk anti-semitic trope that Jews have horns (or tails), which seems to be a straightforward development of medieval devil imagery, especially because in all the images I have found, those horns are curved and thus goat-like, completely unlike the stubby cow horns on Michelangelo's statue.

colors had been changed by the overlay of soot was not recognized by all scholars, and for many years it was thought that Michelangelo had deliberately used muted colors to produce a particular chiaroscuro effect. When the great work of restoration began towards the end of the twentieth century, the brilliance of the colors of the cleaned frescoes shocked many art historians and required these traditions of interpretation to be revised. Thus, if we identify some other work of art that has been influenced by the Sistine Chapel ceiling, we need to be aware that the later artist might have believed that the colors were partially obscured, and so he may have built upon a misconception, or, like Michelangelo sculpting a Moses with horns, he may have deliberately ignored the correction and decided to maintain a visual tradition.

To figure out how to interpret the images Michelangelo painted, we need to learn to "read" them the way he and other educated people in the Renaissance would have. A common method of interpretation was the allegorical reading (discussed briefly above), in which a story is thought to have multiple levels of meaning. First, there is the *literal* level of an allegory, which is simply the story being told. Second is the *typological* level, which relates that one story to some other story. For example, in the Christian tradition, Abraham's willingness to sacrifice his son Isaac as an offering to God (he is only stopped by the intervention of an angel) is interpreted as a *type* of the story of the crucifixion and death of Jesus: both are seen as following the same fundamental pattern, so telling one invokes the idea of the other. Third, there is a *tropological* level of meaning, in which a story is seen as imparting a lesson in morality. The Sacrifice of Isaac would be interpreted as teaching people that they will be rewarded for unquestioning obedience to God. Finally, there is an *anagogical* level of meaning, in which a story reveals some universal truth about spiritual life, some pattern that can be found in many stories—in this case, the Christian idea that absolute faith in God's benevolence leads to an ultimate heavenly reward.[104] It is possible to read Michelangelo's figures at all four levels.

[104] Technically, the anagogical meaning is that which "climbs upwards," interpreting the text to be expressing a truth about the soul's progress through the world and to eternity.

There is also a second kind of typological reading that may be particularly applicable to Michelangelo's work in the Sistine Chapel, in which we recognize that some features of an artwork can be references both to widely known cultural traditions and to specific incidents in the artist's life. For example, among the figures in the fresco of the Last Judgment on the wall of the Sistine Chapel, which the artist created about twenty years after he completed the ceiling, Michelangelo painted an image of a man with donkey ears. These ears indicate that the figure is Minos, who in classical tradition was one of the judges of the dead in the underworld. But the figure's face is not one taken from classical depictions of Minos, but is instead from Michelangelo's life: it is a portrait of Biagio da Cesena, the Pope's Master of Ceremonies, who had objected to the nudity of the figures in Michelangelo's paintings. The image thus implies both that the classical traditions are subsumed under Christianity (Minos exists, but in the Christian hell) and that Biagio was a jackass.[105]

We see, therefore, that in order to understand something as complex as the Sistine Chapel ceiling (or even one or two small parts of it), we need to correlate many different kinds of information, and the only way to do this is to be able to evaluate not only the individual pieces of data but also the various syntheses that have been made by previous scholars. We cannot start from nothing because we cannot even begin to understand the meaning of any complex human creation without having a substantial amount of background knowledge, but that background knowledge itself needs to be evaluated, which can only be done by looking at individual phenomena, which only make sense in the context of background knowledge. This dilemma of circularity cannot easily be resolved using the scientific approach of isolating individual variables. The ways of thinking that have been developed in the disciplines of the Liberal Arts, however, handle the problem of circularity by repeating, with slight variations,

[105] Supposedly when De Cesena complained about being depicted with donkey ears, the Pope said, "I am not in charge of hell," and so did not force Michelangelo to change the portrait. I think this story is too good to be true. In the same fresco, Michelangelo painted his self-portrait as the flayed skin of St. Bartholomew. See Norman E. Land, "A concise history of the tale of Michelangelo and Biagio de Cesena," *Notes in the History of Art* 32.4 (2013): 15-19.

processes of approximation and tentative model-building. We look at the data, try to synthesize it, reexamine the data in light of the synthesis, integrate more data, and repeat the process.

The study of the Liberal Arts relies heavily on the intuitive abilities of the mind. These capabilities, which the study of the Liberal Arts cultivates, are often effective in situations where pure logic is not. Metaphorical or analogical thinking, in which we temporarily equate one phenomenon to another (Biagio da Cesena is a jackass; King Louis the XIV is the sun that shines on everything; the American political system is a never-ending clown-fight) in order to better understand it, is a strength of the Liberal Arts. The biologist Stephen J. Gould once wrote that he was delighted to discover that moving vans in Greece and luggage carts at the Athens airport were labeled "metaphora," which emphasized to him that a "metaphor" is something that makes it easier to carry a thing (or an idea) from one place to another.[106] All intellectual disciplines use metaphors, of course, but the Liberal Arts disciplines are particularly effective at evaluating and improving those metaphors, making them better both at describing the world and at being understood by our minds. Metaphors serve as Daniel Dennett's "intuition pumps," allowing us to apply our natural and unconscious understanding to a larger range of situations.[107] Science uses intuition pumps, for instance, when we say that a negatively charged atom "wants" to combine with a positively charged atom, or when we envision the different degrees to which organisms are adapted to their environments as abstract landscapes. Since humans are very good at intuiting how desires would affect behavior and at visualizing landscapes, we can more easily understand the scientific phenomena if we think about them in these terms rather than trying to reason with purely abstract logic.

Metaphors we develop in the Liberal Arts are usually complicated and multidimensional, so they can be used to understand ambiguous or chaotic situations. If the arrogance of one person leads to a cascading series of failures, we can interpret the chain of events by metaphorically equating

[106] Stephen J. Gould, "Four Metaphors in Three Generations," in *Dinosaur in a Haystack: Reflections in Natural History* (New York: Harmony Books, 1995), 442-457.

[107] See Chapter 3 above.

them to a "Greek tragedy," or we can see an evil adviser as being like Iago in Shakespeare's *Othello*. This process of metaphorical identification allows us to understand a complex situation not merely in terms of an oversimplified schema, but as being similar in important ways to some other complex situations with which we are more familiar or that we understand better, such as the plots of *Hamlet* or *To Kill a Mockingbird*. Liberal Arts thinking helps us recognize that objects, phenomena, and institutions operate on multiple levels of meaning and authority, and the Liberal Arts approach helps us to determine which level is relevant for a particular inquiry.

This great strength of the Liberal Arts, however, is counterbalanced by a weakness: the very flexibility of metaphorical thinking makes it difficult to recognize when the metaphor is leading us astray, when the two things being equated are so different that knowledge about one does not provide useful knowledge about the other. As the physicist Richard Feynman said, "The first principle is that you must not fool yourself—and you are the easiest person to fool."[108] The sciences have developed effective methods to avoid fooling yourself: repeated experiment, determination of statistical significance, and insistence upon logical rigor. These techniques are not as well developed in the Liberal Arts tradition, but they do exist, and we know they can be applied since they are used to different degrees in different Liberal Arts disciplines.

Philosophy, for example, puts great weight on the value of rigorous, logical thinking because philosophers believe that it is possible to reason so effectively that one does not need to perform experiments or their equivalents. Conclusions stand or fall on the basis of the chains of reasoning that led to them. Unfortunately, outside of the very disciplined, restricted forms of discourse in philosophy (and sometimes within them!), it is very easy to assume an incorrect premise or make an early mistake in a long chain of reasoning and not recognize this flaw until the reasoned conclusion comes into conflict with the physical world. Philosophers recognize this problem but see repeated evaluation of the chains of reasoning as being—eventually—an effective solution. The physical

[108] Richard Feynman, *Surely You're Joking, Mr. Feynman!*, 345.

sciences solve the problem by regular experimentation. No matter what the pure reasoning, or even the mathematical calculation, says, if the abstraction is inconsistent with the experiment, then it is wrong.

The rest of the Liberal Arts operate on a model somewhere between that of philosophy and that of the sciences, except that history and tradition take the place of experimentation (which is difficult to do in many Liberal Arts disciplines). If historical facts or the development of traditions contradicts the predictions of the theory, then the theory should be understood to be incomplete or wrong.[109] Each field has developed its own ways of testing conclusions derived from reasoning: its own *epistemology* or method for determining truth and authority. A big part of becoming educated in the Liberal Arts is learning what these methods are and the reasons they are used. The beginning student learns first *what* and then *who* is authoritative; the advanced student tries to figure out *why*.

The Liberal Arts give us sophisticated models, methods for evaluating messy data, and techniques for synthesizing information. These allow us to understand ourselves and the world around us better and thus make better decisions. The most complex problems only have a chance of being solved if we use all the different capabilities of our minds, which is the kind of thinking that we develop by studying the Liberal Arts.

[109] The actual practitioners and institutions of the Liberal Arts, sadly, do not always live up to this ideal.

Student Success Stories:

People who can solve the messy problems are valuable.

My daughter went off to college determined to become, like her grandfather, a medical doctor. At the time, this seemed almost pre-ordained. When R was six years old, we brought her to a faculty holiday party at Wheaton. One of my good friends, a professor of mathematics, politely asked her what she would be doing over the winter vacation.

"We are going to New Jersey to see my grandparents," said R. She then volunteered, "My Grandpop is a *doctor*!"

My friend, intending, I'm sure, to give a nice compliment, said, "Well you know, both of your parents are doctors, too."

R gave him a withering look (or as withering a look as a six-year-old holding a large candy cane can give). "No," she said. "My Grandpop is the kind of doctor who can *do something* for you."

(I always use this anecdote to explain, in part, why I do not want to be called "Dr. Drout" because the only people I would ever call "doctor" are MDs, not PhDs.[110] Also, to borrow an expression from Crush the turtle in *Finding Nemo*, "Dr. Drout is my father, dude.")

So none of us were surprised when R spent a big portion of her senior year in high school shadowing a famous orthopedic surgeon and sitting in on more than forty operations, or that she declared herself pre-med as soon as she arrived at Princeton.

---

[110] In graduate school I came up with "Drout's Laws of PhDs," the third of which is "You can be pompous and force civilians to call you 'Dr. _____' for as many weeks as you spent years in grad school, but then you must get over yourself." Recently I have had conversations with colleagues in the UK who strongly object to Drout's Third Law. They argue that a PhD ranks higher than an MD, and so they have at least as much claim to being called "doctor." I will never accept that a PhD outranks an MD, but that is almost certainly because I am the former and my father was the latter.

And it was a surprise when, a year later, she called to tell us that she was changing her major from pre-med to art history.[111]

"I hope you're not upset, Daddy," she said.

I was not, and I told her so, wondering if perhaps my rant about how foolish it was of President Obama to mock majoring in art history (as he did in 2014) had made an impression on her in some way. I remembered saying then that art history required all the erudition, insight, and cultural knowledge necessary for studying literature, and it *also* required you to understand visual representations and their effects on human minds. "Art history professors are some of the smartest people I know!" I had yelled.

"I am not upset at all, sweetie," I said. "I'm proud of you, and I'll be even prouder when some day you are a professor, too."

It should not be possible to hear a withering look, but that's what happened.

"A professor?" she said. "That's a *terrible* life! I'm not going to do *that*!"

This, as you might expect, did lead to further conversation, and I learned that R wanted to have a much higher salary than any professor anywhere makes and not to have to take the chance of her job being in "East Nowhere University." I bit my tongue and did not repeat Obama's mistake of saying that a major in art history might not be the most obvious first step on a path to a highly compensated job in a cosmopolitan city.

And I'm glad I kept my mouth shut, because almost a full year before her graduation, R had secured a job at a management consulting firm in New York, a job that, yes, compensated her substantially more than she would have been paid as a professor (and yes, substantially more than if she were to replace her father in his job).

Among the reasons she got that position—in addition to her hard work of preparing for a remarkably rigorous interview process—was that majoring in art history showed her employer that she was both intelligent

[111] Though in retrospect we should not have been surprised. R had a truly gifted first-grade teacher who loved art and brought paintings, sculptures, and stories of artists into many of her lessons on other topics. The first time we brought R to the Museum of Modern Art she rushed over to "Broadway Boogie Woogie" and announced "That's *my* Mondrian!" She was eight years old.

and sophisticated, that she could understand and solve very complex, ill-defined problems, and that she could communicate effectively. Or, as we say in Massachusetts—“Majoring in art history shows you’re *wicked smaht*!”

(And honestly being a professor is not in any way “a terrible life.” That was just hyperbole on her part. At least it doesn’t *seem* like a terrible life, not really. And no, I am not fully over this…)

Chapter 6

Best Reasons for Studying the Liberal Arts II: Preserving and Transmitting Culture

We cherish the idea of a single gifted individual putting forth maximal mental effort and finding the solution to some enormous, previously intractable problem, so much so that we often compress an extended process of approximation and refinement into a single mythologized "Eureka!" moment. But even a truly instantaneous breakthrough, like Augustus Kekulé's discerning the structure of benzene after having a dream of a snake biting its tail,[112] would be impossible without centuries of work by other minds that built up the immense base of knowledge upon which the later work depends. Fortunately, we have a system by which the energies of multiple minds can be applied to enormously challenging problems over long periods of time: by preserving and transmitting culture, we allow people to stand upon each other's shoulders so that those coming later can see further. The value of this coordination of minds and construction of knowledge across the generations is the other great argument for the Liberal Arts.

My specialization within the field of English is the study of the literature and culture of the Middle Ages (approximately AD 500-1500), the era between the collapse of the Western Roman Empire and the Renaissance. If you study this period at all, you become acutely aware of how easily the continuity of culture can be broken. As a result of the Fall of Rome and the barbarian invasions, the transmission of knowledge and culture from generation to generation that had held through the Roman

[112] There are some minor disputes about when Kekulé would have had his dream and whether or not it is an ex post facto explanation for his breakthrough. For discussion, see Albert Rothenberg, "Creative Cognitive Processes in Kekulé's Discovery of the Structure of the Benzene Molecule," *American Journal of Psychology* 108.3 (1995): 419–438.

Empire was interrupted, resulting in a general decline of Western European civilization that took centuries to reverse.

That the collapse of the Roman empire was really a collapse and not merely a shift in cultural preferences (as some revisionist historians have suggested in recent years) is evident from the long-term decline in the population of Britain, which did not return to the Roman level for a millennium and a half! As Bryan Ward-Perkins demonstrates from his analyses of pottery remnants, the living standards of middle-class and lower families dropped substantially and in effect permanently, and the changes cannot be explained away as mere cultural preferences. For over 300 years, no one in Britain used a wheel to throw pottery![113] The Anglo-Saxons did not live in abandoned Roman villas—despite their stone walls being superior to anything that Anglo-Saxons could build—because no one in Britain was able to manufacture clay roof tiles.[114] Skills that had once been common did not just become rare or specialized (like, say, harness-making or blacksmithing are today)—they were completely lost.

When a society loses the ability to manufacture such essentials as building materials and tableware, it is no wonder that other kinds of cultural continuity are broken. The traditional name for the five centuries after the collapse of the Western Roman Empire, the "Dark Ages," was originally a reference to the lack of written historical information from the period, as few texts were written or copied, and much culture was lost forever. Great works of art, literature, philosophy, and science are now only known to us from entries in catalogs or brief references in other works. Although the Wars of Religion, the various revolutions, and the two twentieth-century global wars did great damage, even these cataclysms—combined!—were less culturally destructive than the Fall of Rome.

---

[113] Pottery was still being made and used; it was just distinctly inferior to that of the Roman period, and this is not a mere aesthetic judgment. The pots broke more easily, were limited in size, and were irregular enough to create measurement and storage difficulties.

[114] Bryan Ward-Perkins, *The Fall of Rome and the End of Civilization* (Oxford: Oxford University Press, 2005), 87-137. This is the most interesting book about broken pottery that I have ever read (and yes, I have read more than one).

Much culture was lost because its preservations relied upon an unbroken chain of transmission across time. Lessons need to be re-taught, songs re-sung, buildings repaired, and books copied anew in each generation if they are to survive the centuries. The story of the works of the Roman historian Tacitus shows how easy it is for even an important and popular text to be lost. Tacitus' books are of interest in part because he describes the cultures of the Germanic tribes before they had acquired the technology of writing, so his *Germania* is one of our only sources of information about the people living in the northern part of Western Europe at this time. But although Tacitus wrote *Germania* around the year AD 98, the oldest copy we possess is a single manuscript that was copied in the ninth century and only discovered in a monastic library in 1425.[115] If that single manuscript had been destroyed (as have all others) at any time between AD 900 and the first printed edition of the text, Tacitus' *Germania* would be lost to us forever.

All human creations are worn away by time, and even long preservation is no guarantee of continued survival. Books and artworks are always vulnerable to being destroyed by nature or accident: many unique copies of medieval English texts were lost in the 1731 fire in the Cotton Library that damaged *Beowulf*; the unexplained collapse of the City Archive at Cologne, Germany, in 2009 destroyed irreplaceable documents; and the 2018 fire in the *Museu Nacional* in Brazil was even more culturally catastrophic. The most well-protected monuments of civilization can be wiped away by earthquakes, volcanoes, and floods.

But, sadly, the greatest danger to culture is people. The ancient giant statues of Buddha in Bamiyan were blown up in 2001 by the Taliban, and they and their ideological allies continue to destroy architecture and artifacts throughout the Middle East. Nor is our own society immune to spasms of cultural destruction, as evidenced by the spate of politically motivated statue-toppling in 2020. The idea of starting over, building

[115] Brought to Italy and eventually becoming the source for our editions of Tacitus, the manuscript itself disappeared from the historical record for nearly five hundred years until it was rediscovered in a private library in 1902. In 1936, the manuscript was almost stolen by Hitler's SS troops, but its owners hid it in a cellar. Damaged by flooding in 1966, the manuscript is now held in the National Library in Rome.

everything "from scratch," may sound superficially appealing to those who do not think it through, but as the Khmer Rouge discovered in their monstrous attempt to begin society anew at a putative "year zero," such practices set culture back to the Stone Age, if not to the level of chimpanzees.[116] "To be ignorant of the past is to be forever a child," wrote Cicero.[117] Every human being inherits the fruits of millennia of culture, and every human society can only survive in the long term if it allows its new generations to build upon the work of the old.

Cultural artifacts may be preserved by hiding them in caves or mines, but even that solution is temporary, as hidden materials can be found and stolen or forgotten and lost. Knowledge does have a better chance of being preserved if it is spread widely, although even this approach is not guaranteed to work. After World War II, scholars and political leaders, who had seen so much of the common cultural inheritance of Europe destroyed in a few years, decided that the best way to preserve the knowledge of Anglo-Saxon manuscripts was to publish a series of photographic facsimiles that could be kept in libraries all over the world. Having so many copies of the texts increased the odds, it was thought, that at least one copy could survive a great war or a disaster. In recent years, however, the project was terminated for lack of money and interest, demonstrating that the problems of preserving culture are not merely technical but also rely upon the more general transmission of knowledge, culture, and values across generations.[118] If the sense of valuing a particular cultural artifact is not bequeathed to a new generation, that generation is

---

[116] The Khmer Rouge were communists who seized power in Cambodia in 1975 and ruled until 1979, slaughtering almost a quarter of Cambodia's population. Claiming that they were creating a new Cambodian society that would have no connection to its earlier form, they declared the date of their taking power "Year Zero," asserting that all previous Cambodian history was irrelevant. See Ben Kiernan, *The Pol Pot Regime: Race, Power, and Genocide in Cambodia under the Khmer Rouge, 1975-79* (New Haven, CT: Yale University Press, 2008); Loung Ung, *First They Killed My Father: A Daughter of Cambodia Remembers* (New York: Harper Perennial, 2006); and David Chandler, *Voices from S-21: Terror and History in Pol Pot's Secret Prison* (Berkeley, CA: University of California Press, 2000).

[117] "Nescire autem quid ante quam natus sis acciderit, id est semper esse puerum," Cicero, *Orator ad M. Bruto*, Ch. XXXIV, Sect. 120.

not likely to expend resources to preserve it, so over time, chances increase that the artifact will be neglected and eventually lost or destroyed.

Loss of artifacts and knowledge damages human culture because so much of what we accomplish is built upon the work of previous generations. One of the most remarkable powers of books, paintings, and sculpture is that they do not have to be transmitted continuously in order to survive but can be ignored, forgotten, or disliked for long periods of time until, like long-dormant seeds, they can come to life to instruct and inspire later generations. But for this to happen, the objects must not only survive physically; their users must also have the ability to read and understand them. They therefore require the presence of a cultural matrix, which can only be kept alive through a tradition of history, scholarship, interpretation, and understanding. Without the accumulation of the knowledge of previous generations, human culture is not very impressive.

By itself this is certainly a very strong argument for libraries, museums, and other institutions that preserve culture but not—at first glance—an argument for the study of the Liberal Arts. However, artifacts (even books) without a continuous tradition of study that transmits information about how to understand them can become opaque and, eventually, incomprehensible to viewers or readers. The problem of language is obvious: if the language has become extinct or has changed sufficiently over time, we cannot read the book (the very name of Egyptian hieroglyphs means "secret writing" because no one could read them for millennia). But even if we can still read the language, and even if language is not necessary to engage with an artwork (like a painting or a sculpture), we can rarely understand a cultural work in splendid isolation—we need context, and, since no work contains its context (by definition, context is outside the work), without an unbroken line of general cultural transmission, that context is lost.

[118] There are ongoing efforts to preserve culture by digitizing it and distributing it across the internet, but no one knows if such preservation will be more effective in the long term than preserving physical copies of books in libraries. Some digitization projects that are less than twenty years old have already become unusable or have disappeared from the internet.

Preservation of a cultural matrix sufficient to allow later people to understand books, art, music, and other human creations is no easy thing. Rust never sleeps; time grinds down even the highest mountains; and the cultural matrix is fragmented both so slowly that the people living through the change do not notice that it is happening and so rapidly that there is not time to preserve all the essential knowledge. Poets often do not bother to provide information that they believe everybody in their culture already knows, things so common that an audience would be bored listening to them described. For example, no one bothered to write down how Vikings got on and off their ships: was there a set boarding order and assigned rowing seats, or was it first-come, first-served? Did fights break out when someone tried to cut in line? How exactly did one travel with a band of warriors in an open boat across the Baltic Sea? In line 226 of *Beowulf*, we read that when the Geatish ship arrives in Denmark, the warriors step onto the shore and "syrcan hrysedon, guðgewædo," "rattled/shook the mail-shirts, the war-clothing." Scholars for many years have taken this to be merely a simple description of the sound that coats of mail would make when warriors were walking. But, fifteen hundred years before the invention of stainless steel, did the warriors wade through salt water *wearing* their steel mail-shirts? (Every single ring would have to be filed free of rust at some point.) Or did they, as I believe, transport their chainmail rolled up (perhaps wrapped in oily wool) in the sea chests that they sat on to row, carry the rolled-up corselets to land draped over their shoulders, and then shake them out in order to make the rings hang properly? Is this the sound being described? Is the point of the description that Beowulf's men are not part of an amphibious landing and so do not need to be wearing their armor in order to fight their way to shore, and so that the shaking-out is able to be done on the land and in unison rather than on ship and one at a time? The poet does not bother to explain, presumably because everybody in the audience knew something so obvious, just as the audience undoubtedly knew who the character Yrmenlaf was, even though that name appears in one line of *Beowulf* alone and nowhere else in all of English literature. When Grendel's Mother kills King Hrothgar's most trusted advisor, the king laments "Æschere is dead, Yrmenlaf's older brother!" and that is all. It seems almost certain that the poet and original audience knew who Yrmenlaf was so that any explanation was unnecessary or even superfluous.[119]

Not only do we need external context to make sense of works of art and literature, we need additional knowledge specifically *about* the works themselves in order to understand them. When all we possess is an artwork, with no parallel knowledge about the ways in which people understood it, we have no way of knowing what features of a cultural creation are *salient* (convey meaning) and which are trivial. It is impossible for a work to carry within it metadata about which of its features are salient, and without this knowledge, we cannot be sure that what seems important to us was important to the person who created (and the people who first engaged with) the work.[120]

A helpful example of the problem of identifying salient features is the reproduction of Hebrew alphabets in Anglo-Saxon manuscripts. Although the first Jews did not arrive in Britain until after the Norman Conquest of 1066, Christian scholars could piece together the Hebrew alphabet because in St. Jerome's Vulgate translation of the Bible each verse of Psalm 118 starts with a Hebrew letter. Because they had no first-hand experience with Hebrew, Christian scribes occasionally confused a Hebrew letter with one from the Roman alphabet or thought a decorative flourish in a letter was a significant feature. In the manuscript London, British Library, Cotton Vitellius a. xii., the scribe mistook the Hebrew letter Resh for a Latin U and so created a word, "Vres," that was not in the original source. In Durham, Cathedral Library B.II.11 (no. 230), the Hebrew alphabet is written neatly and mostly correctly, but *backwards*, left to right rather than right to left, and a decorative serif on one letter has been

[119] Perhaps the fate of Yrmenlaf was as well-known to the original audience of *Beowulf* as the fate of the *Titanic* is to us. It is easy to imagine readers in the distant future missing the point of a reference like "Why do you think their marriage was unlucky?" "They went on a cruise for their honeymoon—on the *Titanic!*" Explicitly stating that the ship sank would eliminate any tiny bit of humor in the joke.

[120] This phenomenon is discussed in detail in my *Tradition and Influence in Anglo-Saxon Literature: An Evolutionary, Cognitivist Approach* (New York: Palgrave, 2013), 18-35, and elsewhere *passim*.

converted to a distinctive feature.[121] If you read Hebrew, then the difference between ח and ה is obvious and significant, but if you do not, and you are merely copying the visual form, it is impossible to know if the small gap on the left-hand side is salient or merely decorative. Readers who doubt the difficulty of detecting salient features and who do not read Chinese are encouraged to copy some characters and then show what you have written to someone who reads Mandarin—you will find that when you do not know which features of a character are salient, it is remarkably easy to produce unintelligible text even when you are trying to make an exact replica of your exemplar: letters or characters in multiple scripts or fonts are "invariant" only when we have learned the writing system.[122]

The same problems of salience occur with poetry: if you do not know what a sonnet is, you cannot extract the poetic pattern from a single instance of a sonnet, as it is not obvious which features (the meter, the rhyme-scheme, perhaps the theme) are essential and which are optional (the subject, the imagery, perhaps the theme). Likewise, the *conventions* of visual artworks, which cannot be transmitted in any single artwork,[123] shape our understanding of them. If you do not know the conventions that evolved over centuries, much European art is totally incomprehensible. Why is one of the women in the picture holding a plate with two eyeballs on it?[124] Why does a man have horns coming out of his head?[125]

---

[121] Much of this paragraph is drawn from material in Damian Fleming, '*The Most Exalted Language,': Anglo-Saxon Perceptions of Hebrew*, PhD dissertation, University of Toronto, 2006.

[122] See Stanislas Dehaene, *Reading in the Brain: The Science and Evolution of a Human Invention* (New York: Viking, 2009), 137-39.

[123] Something cannot be a convention unless it occurs more than once. Art historians will say that a particular convention was invented by a certain artist in a certain work, but if we are being precise, the convention did not arise until a second work was created on the model of some feature of the first work.

[124] Because she is Saint Lucy, who gouged out her own eyes so that she would not have to get married and lose her virginity. When her father allowed her to stay a virgin, God caused her eyes to grow back (hence the eyeballs in her head as well as the eyeballs on the plate). Thanks to her eyeball-regeneration abilities, Lucy is the patron saint of those who suffer from ocular diseases.

Thus we need not only the physical preservation of artworks and books, but also the parallel preservation of information about them, information that tells us which features are salient and which are not and explains how any individual work fits into the larger culture of which it is a part. In our current culture (and for the past 800 years), we rely upon the tradition of the organized study of the Liberal Arts in the college and university system to preserve and transmit all the parallel information that allows us to understand the books, art, music, drama, and other cultural creations that make us who we are.

This institutionalized tradition of the Liberal Arts is the best way we have discovered of preserving and transmitting culture across generations. This is not an attack on the sciences, which obviously have built upon the accumulation of previous research so that current scholars see further by "standing on the shoulders of giants,"[126] but there is a fundamental quality of the Liberal Arts that makes their preservation and transmission more essential than that of the sciences. Even if a cataclysm wiped out most of human knowledge and survivors had to start rebuilding human culture from almost nothing, the truths of science would eventually be rediscovered because they are facts about the physical universe. Our descendants might use different words to describe a positive charge or a helium atom or the principle of least action, but the facts and relationships that they discovered would be identical to those known to current science. The same is *not* true for accomplishments of literature, art, music, and the other kinds of culture that we study in the Liberal Arts. If we lose the only copy of a book or a painting or if we stop speaking a language, it is gone forever and will never be reconstituted in precisely the same form. There are simply too many interacting variables for the same exact book ever to be written twice even if we were to try to recover it from

[125] He is Moses. See Chapter 5 above for a discussion of why he is often depicted as having horns.

[126] Isaac Newton, *The Correspondence of Isaac Newton: 1661-1675*, ed. H. W. Turnbull, vol. 1, (London: Royal Society, 1959), 416.

a description, reference, or catalog entry.[127] What we study in the Liberal Arts, therefore, is priceless because it is utterly unique.

Creations of culture are thus intrinsically precious, and they are also invaluable because they help us attack problems so difficult that only the combined efforts of generations of minds can have some hope of solving them. Because such problems are so large and complex, we can never know in advance what previous intellectual work may turn out to be relevant to their solution, so we need to preserve as much of that previous work as we can so that by studying that work, learning from it, and bringing it to life in many different contemporary minds, we greatly increase the chance that we can identify and build further upon any particularly useful parts. There are many examples in science of long-neglected work suddenly becoming essential—Mendelian genetics for biology, Lie algebra for particle physics—but there are far more examples of works in the Liberal Arts created in previous centuries being rediscovered and used to solve new problems. The very name of the "Renaissance" ("the rebirth") invokes the return to the long-abandoned accomplishments of previous civilizations. Stories, images, architectural styles, political philosophies, and guides for successful living can all be brought back to life by later generations, who benefit from the efforts of their ancestors.

The two most powerful arguments for the value of the Liberal Arts—that they teach us how to solve complex problems and that they preserve and transmit culture—turn out to be different facets of the same underlying quality because the solutions to complex problems can only be found in the matrix of sophisticated culture that has been transmitted

---

[127] In Jorge Luis Borges' story "Pierre Menard, Author of the *Quixote*," a twentieth-century Frenchman sets out to write *Don Quixote* word for word, but without copying Cervantes' text. Menard attempts to produce in himself states of mind that in the twentieth-century will produce the same words that came from Cervantes' pen in the seventeenth. At his death, only Chapters IX and XXXVIII and a part of Chapter XXII of Part I of *Don Quixote* have been completed, but although these are identical, according to the narrator of the story, Menard's version—having been written in the context of the twentieth century—is "almost infinitely richer." Jorge Luis Borges, "Pierre Menard, Author of the *Quixote*," in *Collected Fictions*, trans. Andrew Hurley (New York: Penguin, 1989), 88-95.

across generations. Add to this the arguments for truth, empathy, discipline, and doubt, and the case for the benefit of studying the Liberal Arts becomes very strong. The Liberal Arts give their students the tools to lead others, promote good tendencies in leadership, and give societies that use them the best possible chance to solve their most difficult problems. They are worth all that they cost and deserve any veneration they receive.

Student Success Stories:
A winding path to success and happiness

I first met N when I was a guest judge for a *Lord of the Rings*-themed costume contest at an event in New York City. Before the contest, I had given a lecture on the influence of Anglo-Saxon literature and culture on Tolkien's work, pointing out that the Rohirrim (the "horse lords" of Middle-earth) speak Old English and the place-names in Rohan are often simple descriptions rendered in that language. So, for instance, Edoras, where King Theoden lives, is Old English for "the courts"; the building where he dwells is Meduseld, which means "mead-hall"; the Firien Stream is the "stream that comes from the mountain." Additionally, the names of the kings of Rohan are almost all words that simply mean "king," so King Théoden son of Thengel is "king king the son of king."

N was 14 at the time. With her mother, she sat through my lecture and asked some very insightful questions about the language. She was wearing a beautiful Éowyn costume, much of which she and her mother had hand-sewn. I told her that "Éowyn" meant "Horse-joy" and that Éowyn's brother Éomer's name meant "Horse-fame."

Two years later, I got a call from N's mother that they would be visiting Wheaton on their tour of possible colleges, and during that visit I had lunch with them and discussed the various projects my students were engaged in. The following fall, N enrolled at Wheaton, and for the next four years she was my student, editorial assistant, and, eventually, research partner. She and four other students traveled with me to Dublin to present our research to the International Society of Anglo-Saxonists at their bi-annual conference (and she got to meet Seamus Heaney, who autographed her copy of his *Beowulf* translation). N created a self-defined, independent major in Medieval Studies, wrote a superb honors thesis on *Beowulf*, and upon graduation from Wheaton, was accepted into the University of

Toronto's graduate program in Medieval Studies (the best on this side of the Atlantic Ocean).

There she also excelled, but something else happened as well: for reasons I have never learned, N became absolutely fascinated with ice hockey and began writing freelance articles about the sport. And not just enthusiastic appreciation, either: N became an expert on the most advanced and technical statistical analyses of hockey, explaining new measures of performance and comparative advantage that were only recently developed (and are incredibly complex—though she explains them well). So, after completing her degree in Medieval Studies, instead of seeking a professor job—I hope that she, too, didn't think it would be a terrible life...I am afraid to ask—N decided to write professionally about hockey, which led to her moving to Salt Lake City, Utah, where she did public relations for a local minor-league team, continued to write about NHL hockey, and also developed expertise in other areas. Word of her ability to explain even the most complex and esoteric subjects got around, and her freelance writing and editing career took off.

Technically, most of what she writes now has nothing directly to do with the medieval literature she studied, but in fact much of her success arises from the generalizable skills she developed in her years at Wheaton and then at Toronto studying the Liberal Arts. N knows how to learn, so whether it is high-end statistical analysis of ice hockey, understanding and explaining medical terminology, editing history texts for high-school students, or writing fantasy literature, she rapidly orients herself to the requirements of the job and produces such high-quality work that, unlike many freelancers, she has a backlog of clients wanting to hire her. And it all started with some translations of Old English names from *The Lord of the Rings*.

Chapter 7
The Richness of the Liberal Arts Tradition: *Beowulf*

My academic advisees are sometimes shocked when I tell them that I do not think it matters which major they choose as long as they devote themselves intensely to its study. They do not believe I am being sincere and are certain that there must be one subdiscipline that would be better (in some way) than all the others. Although I would love to be able to tell them that English literature is the best of all possible Liberal Arts majors, I know from experience that what really matters to students' intellectual development is that they engage deeply with some individual discipline, not which subdiscipline it is. As long as they learn the details of how specific knowledge is produced, evaluated, and synthesized within a discipline, they will learn how to think, and that ability will enable them to adapt rapidly to any other discipline and to any career.

"A little learning is a dang'rous thing," wrote Alexander Pope. "Drink deep, or taste not the Pierian Spring." Interpreters always focus on the first line in the couplet, but, as Stephen Jay Gould argues, the imperative in the second line is the really important point.[128] Learning in

[128] This line, from "An Essay on Criticism," is regularly mis-quoted (as "A little *knowledge* is a dangerous thing") and even more frequently misunderstood. Pope's point is that superficial learning is worse than no learning at all because such shallow engagement tricks people into believing that they know more than they really do. John Butt, ed., *The Poems of Alexander Pope* (New Haven: Yale University Press, 1963). I had the privilege of having this line and its misinterpretation pointed out to me by the late Stephen Jay Gould, who, on a visit to Wheaton, generously discussed the issue with me and the student referred to above as J. Stephen Jay Gould, "Drink deep, or taste not the Pierian Spring. (Musings on the Teaching and Learning of Science)," *Natural History* 106.8 (1997):24-25. This same idea underlies the term that has been used for the second year of college since 1680: sophomores [wise fools], particularly at the beginning of the year, are thought to believe that they are already well educated, when in fact their learning has just begun. The

depth is absolutely essential, and depth is only acquired by mastering at least one discipline, understanding not only *what* its knowledge is, but *how* that knowledge is created and evaluated. Depth is necessary because, although general abstract reasoning is a key tool for understanding the world, abstraction alone has too great a risk of compounding error. An abstraction is by nature a simplification. When you make a map, you have to leave out a great deal of information about the territory. You may mark the general location of a river, but you generally do not put on the map the specific color of its water, the day-to-day fluctuations of a sand-bar, or the colors of the leaves on the trees overhanging the bank. That information, however, may be relevant for some purposes, so if later work is built solely upon the map, there is a good chance that the conclusions drawn will be partial or incorrect. Small mistakes are amplified if they come at the beginning of a long chain of arguments. To avoid this problem, it is often helpful to examine specific examples in order to determine if they are in their details consistent with the abstract theory, to re-explore the territory to see if the map is correct, and then, if need be, improve it.

In this chapter, therefore, we are first going to investigate a particular cultural artifact in detail so that we can see some specific ways that knowledge is produced, evaluated, and synthesized, determining if the actual workings of a discipline are consistent with the general conclusions we have drawn about the ways the Liberal Arts teach us how to think. That specific artifact is the Old English poem *Beowulf*. This choice is obviously somewhat arbitrary, in that any sufficiently complex artifact or phenomenon would allow us to perform our comparison of the abstract with the specific, but there are good reasons for selecting this particular

---

infamous "Mount Stupid" in pop psychology is another representation of the same idea: after acquiring a little initial information on a topic, many people overestimate their mastery of the subject and are extremely confident about the correctness of their judgments. Mount Stupid is followed by the "Vale of Despair" in which the acquisition of additional knowledge makes the learners' confidence drop steadily before eventually, slowly climbing with long-term study and eventual real mastery. For more discussion, see David Dunning, "The Dunning–Kruger Effect: On Being Ignorant of One's Own Ignorance," in *Advances in Experimental Social Psychology*, vol. 44, ed. Mark Zanna and James Olsen (Cambridge, MA: Academic Press, 2011), 247–296.

poem. First and most obviously, its study is my research specialty, so I can explain the ways the discipline works in some detail and also provide behind-the-scenes, insider knowledge. But it is also the case that *Beowulf* richly rewards closer study and is often taught poorly by non-specialists, so even if this "case study" did not contribute very much to the general purposes of this book, it would still, I hope, educate and enrich the minds of readers.

Many people educated in English have at least heard of *Beowulf*, perhaps from a 2007 film in which the actress Angelina Jolie, enhanced with computer-generated effects, performed the role of a seductive water-demon; perhaps from the popular translation made by Nobel-prize winner Seamus Heaney; or perhaps because the poem is regularly assigned in high school and college surveys of literature. Some readers will have learned that *Beowulf* is the oldest poem in the history of English, that it contains two troll-like monsters, and that the hero is killed by a dragon. But when we try to figure out where even this minimal knowledge comes from, how our teachers knew to tell us these things, we are immediately plunged into a history that goes far beyond the text itself.

Everything we know about *Beowulf* depends upon a single, unique object, a manuscript that is now in the British Library in London. If at any time between the year 1000 and 1815, that manuscript had been lost or destroyed, we would have no knowledge of the poem at all. A manuscript is a text hand-written on preserved animal skin ("parchment" or "vellum").[129] Because human handwriting is always variable, each manuscript is unique (even if it is a copy of another manuscript, something about it will be different).[130] Therefore, instead of using a universal library cataloging

[129] Parchment is made from the skins of sheep, vellum from those of cows—usually calves (an easy mnemonic is vellum:veal). However, there is some inconsistency in the scholarship, so that sometimes *vellum* is used to describe any high-quality animal-skin writing surface regardless of the specific animal from whence it came.

[130] That every manuscript is unique is so consistently true that medieval book-lists and catalogues identified their manuscripts by the first line on the second leaf: all copies of a given work start out the same, but even by the second leaf there were enough accumulated divergences that the first lines in two different copies were not the same—even if no errors

system to locate manuscripts, we label each manuscript with what we call a *shelf-mark*, which tells us precisely where in the world a given manuscript is physically located. The shelf-mark of *Beowulf* is "London, British Library, Cotton Vitellius A.xv." which means that that the manuscript is in London, United Kingdom, in the British Library, and is part of that institution's "Cotton Collection," a group of manuscripts originally assembled in the eighteenth century by Sir Robert Cotton.[131] In Cotton's original library, the various book-presses were decorated with busts of Roman emperors; *Beowulf* was kept in the bookcase under the bust of the emperor Vitellius on the top shelf (A) and was the fifteenth (xv) manuscript from the left.[132]

From catalogues of the collection, from an inquest that was held in the eighteenth century, and from the condition of the manuscript, we know that *Beowulf* was fire-damaged and very nearly destroyed in October 1731, when a fire broke out in the unfortunately named Ashburnham House, where Cotton's library was then located. The manuscript was charred on three sides but was saved, perhaps by being thrown out of a window, by a hero-librarian. The partially burnt edges of the pages were crumbling away when scholars handled the manuscript, so in the middle of the nineteenth century a conservator at the British Museum carefully made paper frames for each page, obscuring some letters, but halting further destruction.

Where the manuscript was before it became part of Robert Cotton's collection is harder to determine. In the middle of the sixteenth century, the antiquarian Laurence Nowell wrote his name on the first page,

---

were made, differences in spacing and letter-forms would lead to differences in the first line of the second leaf.

[131] All shelf-marks begin with the city and library, but every library has its own system for cataloging manuscripts. The British Library has multiple collections named for the people who assembled them (Harley, Cotton, Sloane), where they were physically located (Stowe), or who donated them (Arundel, Lansdowne). The Bibliothèque nationale simply numbers its manuscripts in order of their acquisition (manuscript number 1 is the Bible of Charles the Bald).

[132] The *Beowulf* manuscript is sometimes on display to the public among the treasures of the British Library.

but we do not know how, from where, or when precisely he acquired it. From the handwriting and the language of the manuscript itself, we can tell that it was copied around the year 1000, but what happened to it for the next five hundred years is a complete mystery. We can probably assume that it was plundered from a monastic library as a result of King Henry VIII's dissolution of the monasteries in 1539, and that whichever collector saved it from being discarded or destroyed did so for reasons other than its contents, since no one in England could read Old English,[133] the language of *Beowulf*, at this time.

Beowulf might still be one of many old manuscripts preserved, but not often read, in the British Museum if in the eighteenth century it had not come to the attention of Scandinavian researchers. In an effort to compile a list of all the ancient manuscripts held in libraries in Britain, the English clergyman George Hickes asked the scholar Humfrey Wanley to inventory all the Anglo-Saxon texts. Wanley's inventory was published as part of Hickes' massive *Linguarum veterum septentrionalium thesaurus grammatico-criticus et archæologicus.*[134] (They liked long titles in the eighteenth century—the title of Wanley's catalog was even longer.) Since very few of the texts in the manuscripts themselves had formal titles, Wanley gave brief summaries of the contents, but he had difficulty understanding the language of *Beowulf* and so described the poem inaccurately: "In this book, which is an excellent example of Anglo-Saxon poetry, it seems that there are wars described which a certain Beowulf, a Dane sprung from the royal race of the Scyldings, waged against the princes of Sweden."[135]

The Scyldings (Skjǫldungar) were a legendary Danish royal family, so scholars in Denmark who read Wanley's description became excited

[133] The terms "Old English" and "Anglo-Saxon" are interchangeably used to identify the language spoken in England from approximately 500 to 1200. The term "Anglo-Saxon" can also be used to describe the people of that time period, just as "English" can be used to identify a language or a nationality.

[134] *A Grammatico-Critical and Archeological Treasury of the Ancient Northern Languages* .

[135] The original text is in Latin: "In hoc libro qui Poesos Anglosaxonicae egregium est exemplum descripta videntur bella quae Beowulfus quidam Danum ex regio Scyldingorum stirpe ortus gessit contra Sueciae regulos."

about the possibility of an old poem that seemed to be about their ancestors. In 1786, an ambitious researcher named Grim Jónsson Thorkelin, who had social connections to the Danish court, convinced a wealthy patron to support his production of a modern edition of the poem, which seemed likely to shed new light on Danish history. Unfortunately, Thorkelin was better at social climbing than at scholarship, and so the first edition of *Beowulf*, which was published only in 1815 after many years' delay, was full of errors.[136] But Thorkelin nevertheless did scholarship the great service of having the poem copied. He hired a scribe to make a transcription as well as making one of his own, and these copies preserve information about many letters that were lost from the crumbling edges of the manuscript before it was protected by the paper frame in 1845.

Thorkelin's edition, inept as it was, got other scholars interested in *Beowulf*. Danish researchers thought the poem could give them important information about the history of their country, while German-speaking scholars believed that the poem would illuminate their own peoples' history. After the British scholar John Mitchell Kemble's 1834 edition of the poem became a surprise bestseller, *Beowulf* entered the syllabus of English literature. The poem has been taught and studied ever since, experiencing periods of both popularity and neglect in the wider culture. The association of *Beowulf* with J.R.R. Tolkien—who, long before he became famous for *The Lord of the Rings,* was professor of Anglo-Saxon at Oxford and studied *Beowulf* intensely—brought new public attention to the poem in the later part of the twentieth century, as did various film adaptations. The translation by the poet and Nobel Laureate Seamus Heaney, published in 2000, gave contemporary teachers of *Beowulf* a beautiful, poetic version in Modern English, invigorating the teaching of the poem. The immense popularity of Peter Jackson's *Lord of the Rings* films generated further interest in the poem, as a global audience discovered Tolkien's work and its influences.

[136] Thorkelin claimed that his draft of his edition was destroyed during the bombardment of Copenhagen by the British in 1807. His house was burned, but somehow Thorkelin managed to save his transcriptions of the poem without saving the draft of his edition itself. It seems unlikely that these two manuscripts would have been far separated if they ever both existed.

Other historical information surrounds each of these facts. *Beowulf* ended up in the hands of collectors because King Henry VIII dissolved the English monasteries, expelling the monks and confiscating their property. Books from monastic libraries were looted or destroyed, and a small portion ended up being purchased by "antiquarians," collectors who valued old materials almost purely for their age and rarity, since they could not easily read them.[137] The king had dissolved the monasteries for political reasons: they were rich and powerful institutions that were aligned with the Roman Catholic Church, so Henry saw them as a threat to his new position as the head of the Church of England he had newly created. Seizing monastic property also allowed him to reward his supporters with the confiscated wealth. Henry had broken from the Roman Church in part because the Pope would not grant him a divorce, and he wanted a divorce in part because his first wife had not produced a male heir, thus creating a political crisis. Henry's actions were also entangled in the rise of Protestantism during the Reformation, and some of his intellectual supporters found that texts taken from the monasteries could be used to support their arguments in religious disputes. Thus the survival of the *Beowulf* manuscript occurred in a context of very high-stakes political and religious conflicts.

The Danish scholars of the eighteenth and nineteenth centuries who were particularly interested in *Beowulf* were also engaged in a very intense argument with important political implications. They were trying to establish whether certain parts of southern Denmark—called Schleswig and Holstein—were originally Danish or German. *Beowulf* was an important piece of evidence in this long-running dispute, which is one reason why significant scholarly resources were put towards understanding the poem.[138] Jacob Grimm—now known primarily for his and his brother's collection of fairy tales, but more famous in his own time as the founder of the discipline of *Vergleichende Philologie* (comparative

[137] The academic study of Old English really began when a few antiquarians decided that they wanted to be able to read the manuscripts they had collected.

[138] Perhaps one reason why Thorkelin misread the poem is that he wanted *Beowulf* to be more closely connected to Denmark. In the title of his edition he called it "a Danish poem in the Anglo-Saxon dialect." There is no such thing as an Anglo-Saxon dialect of Danish.

philology, the foundation of modern linguistics)—was so respected that the Frankfurt National Assembly, the first elected parliament for all of Germany, had reserved a special chair in the center of the auditorium for Grimm so that he could definitively answer any questions about what was or was not "truly German."[139] *Beowulf* became an important piece of evidence in a long-running and intense political argument about which people in Europe were really Germans, and thus which places should belong to Germany.[140] For nearly a hundred years this debate had been carried out through snippy articles published in philological journals, until in 1914 and then again in 1936, Europe decided to settle the argument with guns and bombs.[141] *Beowulf* thus ended up, through no fault of its own, entangled in high-stakes European politics.

Because the majority of the leading philological scholars were German, there was a backlash against the discipline immediately after World War I, to the point where J.R.R. Tolkien was moved to write that some professors seemed to think that philology itself had contributed to the war by increasing German "arrogance."[142] The situation in academia became even worse after World War II. Nazi enthusiasm for an imaginary pagan past ended up contaminating by association all things Germanic,

---

[139] Joep Leerssen, *National Thought in Europe* (Amsterdam: Amsterdam University Press, 2006).

[140] Like Modern German, Old English is a *West* Germanic language, while Old Norse and its descendant Danish are *North* Germanic languages. German scholars asserted that *Beowulf* being set in Denmark proved that the people living there were speakers of a West Germanic language and therefore the ancestors of Modern Germans, and so Schleswig and Holstein should belong to Germany. Among the (many) problems with this interpretation is that all the characters in *Beowulf* are depicted as speaking the same language, so the poem could just as well serve as evidence that the ancestral language of the Swedes (definitely North Germanic) was the same as that spoken in Denmark. But having the Danes, Swedes, Geats, Frisians, and perhaps even the Franks all speaking the same language seems much more like a convenient literary convention than historical, political, or legal evidence.

[141] They would have been better off letting the philologists continue the debate with grumpy essays.

[142] In some quarters, philology was being treated as something "that the late war was fought to end." J.R.R. Tolkien, "Philology: General Works" in *The Year's Work in English Studies*, vol. IV, issue 1, 1924, 20–37 at 36-37.

including the study of early medieval literature, leading to a rapid decline in the study of Old English (and thus *Beowulf*) in the English-speaking world, a decline that has only been partially arrested.[143]

From this very abbreviated history of *Beowulf*, we can see how the production of knowledge in the Liberal Arts is often a tangled, confusing, and somewhat irrational process. Cultural artifacts are studied not only for their age or intrinsic interest (which, in the case of *Beowulf*, we have not even discussed yet) but for reasons ranging from individual reputation to nationalistic pride and political desires. Knowledge is produced not only by the individual scholars who read, transcribe, edit, and publish a poem, but also by subsequent researchers who critique that original work, reinterpret the poem in light of other kinds of information, and teach the text to students by putting it into syllabi and creating translations and adaptations. There are errors, conflicting interpretations, and revisions to knowledge, all of which are shaped both by the work itself and the ways it fits into multiple historical contexts. For *Beowulf*, these contexts include those of the Anglo-Saxon period in which it was copied, the sixteenth-century dissolution of the monasteries in which it was collected, the eighteenth-century fire in which it was damaged, the formation of Danish and German nationalism in which it was edited, and many subsequent

[143] The Nazis had no great interest in *Beowulf* itself, which is a Christian rather than a pagan text that does not uncritically celebrate conquest and which implies that the Nazis had the name of their favorite Germanic hero, Siegfried, wrong. If *Beowulf* is correct, then the dragon-slaying son of *Wæls* (*Völsung* in Old Norse) is not *Sigurd* (Old Norse *Sigurðr*, Middle High German *Sîvrit*, Modern German *Siegfried*), but his father, *Sigmund*, thus implying that the dragon-killing deed of the father had, in the later epics, been mistakenly given to his Burgundian-marrying son. Since *Beowulf* is by far the oldest of the texts that mention this hero, the Old English poem would, presumably, have more authority. None of the most famous German *Beowulf* scholars were known to have aligned themselves with the Nazis (several of the more significant became expatriates), perhaps because the analytical rigor of philology militated against the extreme and unscientific claims of the Nazi propagandists. In the immediate post-war period, however, professors who coveted the prestige and institutional resources that had been controlled by scholars of Germanic Philology in the pre- and inter-war eras used the well-known interest of certain Nazis in "pagan" and putative "Aryan" Germanic culture as a pretense for implying that the study of *Beowulf* and other "Germanic" works was politically and morally questionable.

political, social, and cultural developments in which it has been read, revised, adapted, criticized, and taught.

All of this historical material explains, at least to a degree, why we are studying *Beowulf*, but it does not explain *how* we read the poem. For that, we turn to my own discipline of English and its many sub- and cross-specialties. Paleography, the study of old writing, is one such sub-field. Paleographers study the ways writing has changed across time and space so that they can not only read old manuscripts but also figure out where and when they were written. In Chapter 3, we discussed printed fonts and the ways that they communicate meaning. For hand-written texts, the equivalent of a font is a *script*, a particular way of writing the letters. All the rhetorical effects of fonts that we discussed above are also applicable to scripts.

Paleographers learn to recognize scripts both by comparing multiple manuscripts and by learning how to write the scripts themselves: when I teach paleography, I start by giving my students a calligraphy pen and some parchment paper so that they can learn the *ductus* of a given script, the particular order of strokes used to make each letter. Understanding the ductus helps scholars recognize similarities among and differences between the scripts in different documents. To date and localize texts, paleographers compare the script and the *hand* (the individual scribe) in the document whose date is unknown to those in documents whose dates or locations can be determined by their contents, such as wills, charters, laws, or letters. Over one thousand different scribes have been identified by their handwriting in manuscripts written in England in the tenth century.[144] Experienced paleographers can identify individual scribes and often determine when and in which locations they were working, which is called the *provenance* of the manuscript. Paleographers also study the size and layout of manuscript pages and investigate how they are bound together into books—this particular field of study is called *codicology*—so that they can identify places where pages are missing or have been rearranged. Sometimes the physical proportions of a page, the number of

[144] Donald Scragg, *A Conspectus of Scribal Hands Writing English, 700-1100* (Woodbridge, Suffolk: D. S. Brewer, 2021).

lines per leaf, and the quality of the parchment can provide clues to the date and the provenance.

The *Beowulf* manuscript was copied by two different scribes sometime between the years 975 and 1015—most scholars say "around the year 1000." The first scribe, conventionally called A, copied the first two-thirds of *Beowulf*, from lines 1-1939. His handwriting suggests that he was younger than the second scribe, called B, who took over in the middle of line 1939 and copied out the rest of the poem. Scribe B also went back and made corrections to Scribe A's work. That two scribes split up the copying of the poem between them is not as unusual as it might sound, because copying was slow and tiring work and therefore was often divided up among multiple scribes.[145] From the careful study of the manuscript and its handwriting alone, therefore, we are able to reconstruct some information about when and how the poem was produced—even before we have read a single word. Unfortunately, there are no undisputed connections between Vitellius A. xv. and any other Anglo-Saxon manuscripts: neither scribe's hand has been identified elsewhere, and although some scholars think that the size, color, and ruling of the parchment in the *Beowulf*-manuscript is similar to that in Princeton, Scheide Library, MS 71 (the "Blickling Homily manuscript"), other scholars disagree, and in any event, no one knows where the Blickling Homily manuscript was copied, either.

To read the text of *Beowulf* that is preserved in the manuscript, we need to turn to another discipline for help, our old friend philology. We are fortunate that many texts in Old English are translations of Latin works (primarily Christian works, including multiple books of the Bible), and Anglo-Saxon scholars also compiled multiple glossaries of Latin words with the meanings given in Old English, so we can match unfamiliar words with their Latin equivalents so that we figure out their meanings.

However, there are many words for which we do not have Latin equivalents (these words are especially prevalent in *Beowulf*). For the

[145] We therefore cannot conclude that Scribe A died or was exiled from the monastery in the middle of his work on the poem and that Scribe B took over the copying to honor the memory of his younger colleague. It's a nice, dramatic story, but we have no reason to believe it is true.

meanings of these words we use techniques based on the pioneering work of Jacob and Wilhelm Grimm, Franz Bopp, Rasmus Rask, and other nineteenth-century scholars, who formulated a set of rules of sound-change that explained how the Germanic languages had evolved from their common origin—now called Proto-Germanic—to their modern descendants. We can apply certain laws of sound-change to words in *Beowulf* to see what their Modern English descendants are, and we also can use our knowledge of the various sound-changes across the Germanic-language family tree to identify related words in Old High German or Middle Dutch or Old Norse—in effect identifying an Old English word by comparing it to its foreign cousins. Thanks to the patient work of philologists, by 1834, when John Mitchell Kemble published his edition of the poem, English scholars could read *Beowulf* even though it was written in a language that had not been spoken in their country for over 600 years.

The discipline of philology even allowed scholars to correct errors in the text of *Beowulf*—sometimes without having seen the manuscript itself![146] For example, in line 2186 of the poem, we are told that King Hrethel of the Geats is "Dryhten wereda" [Lord of Hosts]. But this phrase is the standard Old English translation of a Latin phrase used in Christian prayers to describe God: *Dominus Deus Sabaoth* [Lord God of Hosts]. This does not make sense in the context of the poem, since King Hrethel is the leader not of the Troops of Angels in Heaven, but of a Germanic tribe. Indeed, Hrethel is not even Christian. But the people he leads, the Geats, are often nicknamed the "Weders," and clever philologists noticed that "Dryhten we**r**e**d**a" is an easy error to make for "Dryhten we**d**e**r**a"—the scribe accidentally transposed the <d> and the <r>. This error also suggests that the copyist was a Christian who was more familiar with the phrase "Lord God of Hosts" than with "Lord of the Geats," so when he saw something very similar in the manuscript, he converted it to the more familiar form. This knowledge, in turn, tells us that *Beowulf* is at least a

[146] The terrifyingly brilliant N.F.S. Grundtvig printed corrections to Thorkelin's edition of *Beowulf* even though Thorkelin had worked closely with the manuscript and had based his edition on his transcription, while Grundtvig *had never seen the manuscript* and only read Thorkelin's edition.

copy of another document, and other aspects of the manuscript show that it is most likely a copy of a copy (at least). The composition of the poem, then, must have occurred some time before the manuscript that we have was copied around the year 1000.

The Liberal Arts subdisciplines of paleography and philology combine to allow us to start reading *Beowulf*, but immediately we are faced with other problems. The poem begins by praising the achievements of the Spear-Danes, celebrating a great king, Scyld Scefing, who conquered all his enemies and made them pay tribute. When he dies, his people honor him by placing his body on a ship filled with treasure, which they set adrift on the sea. Scyld's son, the manuscript says, was named Beowulf, but it turns out that this is *not* the Beowulf who is the hero of the poem: the eponymous main character is two generations younger; comes from an entirely different people, the Geats, who live across the sea from the Danes; and is not introduced into the poem for nearly two hundred lines. Because the Danish Beowulf is never mentioned again after these few lines, most scholars think the name in the manuscript is a copying error that occurred when the scribe saw the name "Beow" in his example text and thought it was an abbreviation for the name of the hero he knew the poem was about. This is all very confusing, as is the overall historical and geographic background of the events in the poem, and we therefore must turn to other Liberal Arts disciplines to try to clarify the situation.

From Latin histories of the early Middle Ages, we learn that the Danes were indeed a powerful tribe who subjugated many other peoples. They began their conquests in southern Scandinavia, moved across northern Germany, and finally settled in the Danish archipelago and the Jutland peninsula that make up present-day Denmark. The royal family called themselves the "Scyldings," which does seem to link them to the character Scyld, and some lists of kings state that Scyld's son was named Beow, whose son was named Halfdan, which is consistent with the genealogy given in the poem.

Also from the disciplines of history and philology, we learn that one of the characters in *Beowulf* is probably based on a historical figure. The great scholar N.F.S. Grundtvig realized that Hygelac—Beowulf's uncle and the king of the Geats, whom, the poem says, was killed in a raid into Frisia—is the same person as a Germanic leader who was killed, according to the historian Gregory of Tours, while on a raid into Frisia in the year 524. Although the name Gregory uses, Chlochilaicus, does not superficially look like Hygelac, it is exactly the form philologists would expect from a Frankish historian trying to render a Germanic name in Latin. Because *Beowulf* mentions Hygelac's fatal Frisian raid several times, we can conclude that the poem must have been written after 524. References to nations—the Swedes, Danes, Franks, Frisians, Geats, and others—and kings combine with the historicity of Hygelac's raid to lead us to the conclusion that, despite the presence in the poem of a fire-breathing dragon, a pair of trolls, and some sea-monsters, *Beowulf* is set not in a mythical place like Fairyland, Middle-earth, or a Galaxy Far, Far Away, but in the sixth century in the lands around the North Sea.

At the beginning of *Beowulf*, the Danes have built an enormous hall that they called Heorot. Various historical and literary sources tell us that in its early years, the Scylding dynasty was headquartered in a place called Hleithra, which in Danish legend is equivalent to King Arthur's Camelot in British mythology: the greatest court of the greatest king, populated with heroes and champions. The poem describes Heorot as a hall "greater than any previously known to the children of men," and recently specialists in medieval archeology, a discipline that was originally an offshoot of the Liberal Arts but is now usually considered a social science, have discovered the remains of several gigantic halls—larger than any previously known to archeologists—near the present-day town of Gamol Lejre. Although there is still much archeological work to be done, it seems that Lejre was once a center of worship of the pagan fertility god Freyr. What appears to be a large altar made of cracked hearthstones[147] is surrounded by many pits filled with pig bones, and the pig was the animal

[147] Anyone who has been camping and experienced the shock of a stone in the fire-ring splitting as it cools down in the middle of the night can understand intuitively why people might think that the cracking of a hearthstone was a signal from or a request by a supernatural figure.

associated with Freyr.[148] That the site of the Danes' great hall was perhaps once a cult center could explain the names of some of the characters in *Beowulf*, including the Danish king's brother Halga, which means "Holy One," or possibly "Priest" [of Freyr?], and the king's daughter Freawaru, whose name means "Protected by Freyr." The first Danish king's name can be translated "Shield" and his father's name as "Sheaf" (a sheaf is a bundle of grain), and we learn from folklore studies that this genealogy could be interpreted as indicating that military power is derived from success in agriculture, which is why the Danes might credit their military success to the fertility god, Freyr, honoring him by building their great hall at his cult site. We start to see, therefore, that *Beowulf* is a rich and complex mixture of mythology, legend, folklore, history, and the imagination of the poet.

At this point, we are perhaps ready to read the poem and see if we can make sense of it in light of all this background information. Once we sort out the various digressions, the plot is reasonably simple. As soon as King Hrothgar holds his first feast in the newly built hall of Heorot, a monster named Grendel, angered by the happy sounds coming from within the hall, attacks. King Hrothgar's warriors are powerless against the monster, and after many men have been eaten, the Danes abandon their ceremonial hall, which stands blood-stained and vacant for twelve years.

Across the sea in the land of the Geatish people, a young warrior named Beowulf, the nephew of the king of the Geats, hears of this situation. Because King Hrothgar once helped his father, Beowulf decides to rid the Danes of the scourge of Grendel. He and his men sail to Denmark and receive permission from the king to spend the night in Heorot. Grendel attacks and eats one of Beowulf's men, but the hero then seizes the monster and wrenches off its arm. A mortally wounded Grendel flees to a swamp, where he presumably bleeds to death. There is much celebration. Beowulf and his men are richly rewarded, and the Danes hang Grendel's arm from the roof of the hall to signify their triumph.

But that very night, while the Danes are sleeping in their long-vacant hall and Beowulf and his men have been put up in other housing, a

[148] In Old Norse mythology, Freyr rides a flying golden boar named Gullenbursti, "Gold-bristles."

second monster, Grendel's mother, attacks Heorot, takes back the arm, and kills one of Hrothgar's men. When informed of the attack, Beowulf vows to destroy her as he destroyed her son. Hrothgar and his men lead him to the haunted mere beneath which the monsters live, and Beowulf swims down through the serpent-infested waters to reach the cave where Grendel and his mother have their lair. When Grendel's mother and Beowulf fight, the hero's sword fails him, and the troll-woman almost kills him with a knife. But fortunately there happens to be a giant sword hanging on the wall of the cave—a sword so large that only a man with the strength of thirty men (which Beowulf, conveniently, possesses) can wield it. Beowulf seizes the weapon and beheads Grendel's mother. He then finds the body of Grendel, which he also decapitates, and he carries the male monster's head (presumably because it is a larger and thus more impressive trophy) back to Heorot. Upon Beowulf's return, there is more celebration, and Beowulf and his men take rich gifts back with them to their home in Geatland. There, Beowulf loyally serves his uncle Hygelac until that king's death in a raid against the Frisians. He is also a faithful retainer for Hygelac's son, Heardred. But when this young king is killed after backing the losing side in a civil war among the Swedes, Beowulf becomes king of the Geats.

His rule brings fifty years of peace and prosperity until a trespassing thief wakes a fire-breathing dragon from its sleep in a nearby barrow. The dragon burns down Beowulf's hall and ravages his lands. Beowulf swears to kill the monster in single combat and attacks it, but the flame-spouting beast is too strong. Beowulf is losing the battle when one of his warriors, a young man named Wiglaf, disobeys the king's order to stay behind and joins Beowulf in the fight. The two heroes kill the dragon, but Beowulf receives a poisoned wound and dies. The poem ends with his funeral and the Geats lamenting that, now that their leader is dead, they expect to be conquered and enslaved by neighboring peoples.

From even this short summary, we can see that although the poem may be set in a particular historical time and place, *Beowulf* contains a great deal of fantastical material. The hero is celebrated for defeating monsters rather than for ordinary human accomplishments (although he does defeat human foes as well, including a Frankish champion whom he squeezes to death with a bear-hug). Furthermore, in addition to its legendary and historical background, *Beowulf* is also set in a matrix of Christian religious tradition. The poem states that the two Grendel-monsters are "of the kin of Cain," who committed the first murder when he killed his brother Abel. The Anglo-Saxons were fascinated by this story of the first fratricide because in their pre-Christian, Germanic culture, killing within one's family was the one sin that could never be forgiven or expiated.[149] They therefore thought it completely reasonable that monsters would be descended from Cain.

But the link between the monsters that trouble the Danes and the sin of brother-killing goes beyond the biblical story of Cain and Abel. Multiple literary texts from medieval Scandinavia suggest that the Danish royal house had a traditional history of kin-slaying, that the murder of relatives for political gain was the great flaw in the Scylding dynasty. Grendel may therefore not only be a good plot element for the hero to fight but also represent the continuing cycles of destruction that an incident of kin-killing brings to a family. All of the Danish military and political success is undermined by this violent sin, which can never be settled by anyone inside the family group. Only an outsider, like Beowulf—who is not on either of the contending sides—could "cleanse" the hall of Heorot from the sin of fratricide. The attack of Grendel's mother, then, may represent another way that the evil of kin-slaying keeps returning even after the original killer has himself been eliminated. The family members of a murder victim will always want revenge, but any revenge-killing they perform will wrong their victim's relatives, who in turn will want their own vengeance. The cycle of killing will therefore not stop until everyone on one side or the other is dead.[150] One way to look at Beowulf's destruction

[149] All other killings could be settled by a payment of *weregeld*, "man-price," but weregeld could not be paid within a family any more than you can pay yourself compensation for stubbing your own toe by taking money from your left pocket and paying it to your right pocket.

[150] This cultural dynamic of unending revenge is vividly dramatized—and without any distracting supernatural monsters—in *Njal's Saga*, which is considered to be the greatest of the Old Norse sagas. See Robert Cook, trans., *Njal's Saga* (New York: Penguin, 1997).

of both Grendel monsters is that the Anglo-Saxon audience understood that the hero has to kill even the women and children of the hostile family (Grendel's mother and her monstrous son) to put an end to the cycle of violence and revenge.[151] We recover some of these resonances of *Beowulf* from the literature that surrounds the poem not only in Old English, but also in Old Norse, Latin, and Old High German.

But if the attacks of the Grendel-monsters are motivated by things that the Danes have done, the attack of the dragon is quite different. That beast has slept for three hundred years coiled around the treasure in a barrow until a slave or servant accidentally disturbs it by stealing a single cup. Beowulf and his people did not commit any aggression against the dragon: they did not even know that it was there, but the monster nevertheless burns Beowulf's hall, ravages his lands, and kills his people. If Grendel and Grendel's Mother represent the destruction caused by crime, sin, or (even justified) vengeance, the dragon represents the evil that appears for no reason, the catastrophe that was not motivated or deserved. The nature of human civilization is that it can be undone by its own flaws *or* by unexpected outside forces, and we see both of these dramatized in *Beowulf*. By depicting these situations using heroes and monsters, the poem allows us to engage emotionally with the implications of these two kinds of evil, using our intuition as well as our logic. We can read one story in terms of another story (or in terms of our own lives) and recognize the patterns.

This is Liberal Arts thinking at a high level. It also seems to be, in comparison with scientific reasoning, quite impressionistic. *Beowulf* certainly *could* mean these things, but no single piece of evidence definitively proves that it does. This situation, however, is not really that different from many real-world problems people are called upon to try to solve. We often lack determinative evidence and instead must rely upon approximation and revision, making educated guesses to start and then

[151] If this is the correct interpretation, we could conclude that the Anglo-Saxons had somewhat of a different conception of a hero than we do. Or perhaps not, since nothing suggests that Beowulf ever kills human women and children, only trolls (or whatever the Grendelkin are).

building temporary models. If these seem to account for the situation, we build further upon them. If they lead to contradictions, we revise. In the specific case of trying to understand *Beowulf*, we see that the interpretation given above can help account for some features of the poem that might otherwise be difficult to understand.

One of these features is the pacing of the story at the end of the poem. At some of the most exciting points in Beowulf's battle against the dragon, the poet suddenly enters into long digressions about the historical background of the Geats and their wars with their neighbors the Swedes. My students are always frustrated that, while Beowulf lies dying from the dragon's venom, they have to translate many lines about obscure political conflicts before they can get back to the hero's death and his funeral. The structure of the narrative seems wrong if the poem is about the life of Beowulf.

It could be the case that the poet—an effective storyteller for more than 2,500 lines—just makes a gigantic error of pacing here, or it may be that we have a fundamentally different aesthetic sense than the audience of *Beowulf*: maybe they liked the tension brought about by this long digression. But we can avoid both of these awkward hypotheses and understand the logic behind the structure of the poem if we take Beowulf's deeds as being part of a larger historical narrative rather than being just a story about a guy who fights monsters.[152] If we synthesize the literary, historical, and archeological information we have available, we see that perhaps the only thing about Beowulf's people, the Geats, that the poet and the audience would have been sure about was that they no longer existed at the time the poem was written. The Geats had once been a mighty nation, but thanks to war and misfortune, by the eighth century (which is the most likely date for the composition of *Beowulf*), they were gone. This absence fits our interpretation that *Beowulf* dramatizes the idea that kingdoms can fall either because they have internal flaws *or* because

[152] The story of *Beowulf* devolves to just "a story about a guy who fights monsters" not only in pop-culture representations (which we might expect) but even in much academic work from the 2000s. You can find whole articles about the meaning of the monsters that never discuss the 70% of the poem in which no monster-fighting occurs.

some unmotivated external force destroys them. The only king of the Geats who appears in the poem who is not at least mentioned in some other literary or historical source is Beowulf himself. He is the creation of the poet's imagination, but he is set into the historical matrix, his rule being a last twilight period of Geatish success before the collapse that began with failures within the royal family (the disaster of Hygelac's failed raid on Frisia). The poet, therefore, sets his imaginative creation firmly within history and so must give the audience a summary of the historical situation before he can end the poem with Beowulf's funeral.

This interpretation does not contradict anything within the poem, but that does not necessarily mean that it is correct. As we have already seen, information from outside the poem can be very significant for understanding *Beowulf*. In particular, the date at which the poem was composed could call any interpretation into question. The poet seems to be assuming that his audience knew who the Danes and the Geats were and how they interacted with other peoples, including the Swedes, the Frisians, and the Franks. Such an audience would be unlikely to be found in England after the year 800, but the manuscript of *Beowulf* was copied around the year 1000. We must decide if it is reasonable that the poem could have been composed so many years before the manuscript was copied.

That this question is the most contentious problem in *Beowulf* studies shows us the importance of disciplines developing methods of weighing and evaluating evidence. Scholars disagree so fiercely about the date of *Beowulf* because they place radically different weights on the different kinds of evidence. Those who focus on manuscript studies want to emphasize the importance of the unique manuscript and are less interested in any hypothetical, now-lost manuscripts that antedate the one manuscript that we do possess, so they see the poem's being copied in 1000 far outweighing the linguistic and historical evidence supporting an earlier date. There is also always an aspect of the cliché about the drunk man looking for his keys under the streetlight not because he dropped them there, but because that's where he can see. Far more detailed historical information survives from the years 900-1000 than from all the earlier centuries of Anglo-Saxon history put together, and scholars who want to read *Beowulf* in relation to politics and culture would prefer for the poem to come from a time about which they know a lot. On the other hand, since *Beowulf* celebrates Danes in the very opening of the poem, it seems unlikely to have been composed in England after 800, when the Viking invaders, descendants of the Danes in the poem, spent a century laying waste to the English countryside, looting, burning, raping, and murdering and then eventually seizing territory in which they settled. Historian Dorothy Whitelock suggested that after the ravaging of the Danish armies, no English audience would tolerate a poem that began with the praise of the Danes, but this idea is based on some assumptions about the uniformity of attitudes across long periods of time that are not necessarily correct. A historian a thousand years in the future might think it was safe to conclude that since America and Germany fought two brutal wars in the twentieth century, any American poem that included a positive depiction of Germans must come from some other time period. From our vantage point, we know this would be an oversimplification, since there were decades in the twentieth century in which America and Germany were close allies. Similarly, we cannot necessarily conclude that there were absolutely no years after 800 in which an English poet could depict Danes positively.[153]

The linguistic evidence for *Beowulf* being composed around 750 is extremely technical, and much of the key scholarship is written in German. There are today only a few dozen scholars of English literature who have mastered this material, which, sadly, may be a reason that other scholars date the poem to a later period—it is the path of least resistance to say "I'm dating the poem to the manuscript" so you do not have to spend immense time and effort learning enough about this particular subdiscipline of philology to have an informed opinion.[154] However, some of the arguments

[153] As long as *Beowulf* is (3018 lines), the poem could easily have been composed in a few weeks or a month, so the composition most likely occurred within a single year, not a decade or longer. Our not knowing which year that was is not a good reason for assuming that the poem was composed over the course of a decade, or even longer.

[154] Scholars are, sadly, human and therefore, like all humans, are subject to the same temptations to believe what is most convenient. Time spent reading long, complex,

for an earlier date are also vague or impressionistic. J.R.R. Tolkien thought that he detected in *Beowulf* the sadness that a Christian would feel when thinking about his noble but pagan ancestors who would never reach heaven even though they accomplished great deeds. For this (and many much more secure technical reasons), he thought that the poem must have been written within one or two generations of the time when the Anglo-Saxons converted to Christianity (597-660). There is also historical and literary evidence that suggests the poem is quite a bit older than the manuscript. One line of the manuscript that is incomprehensible as it stands makes sense if some of the nonsense words are emended to the phrase "the favor of the Merovingian has been denied to us," so it seems that although the poet knew that "the Merovingian" was the ruler of the Franks, one or more scribes had no idea what the poem was talking about. This mismatch would be explained if the poet was *composing* while the Merovingian dynasty still ruled (before 751), but at least someone in the chain of copyists did not recognize the name because for his whole lifetime the Franks had been ruled by the Carolingians (who had made every effort to erase the memory of their predecessors). Some scholars, however, disagree with this interpretation, noting that if an initial copying error—which could be caused by any number of reasons, including a damaged exemplar—was particularly bad, subsequent copyists might not be able to recover the "Merovingian" from a garbled mess even if they knew who the Merovingians were.[155]

Unfortunately, we have no objective and agreed-upon standard for sorting out the likelihood of all of these claims, so scholars always have to argue not only for the significance of a particular piece of evidence, but also

---

scholarly articles in German is time not spent on other tasks, so it is easy to self-justify avoiding that labor by somewhat uncritically accepting the idea that all that old scholarship is outdated or disproven.

[155] However, as Tom Shippey notes, although the spelling of Merovingian (with a <w> instead of a <v> is unique to *Beowulf*, this spelling is almost certainly a better representation of the original form of the word, *Merowech, than any of the other documented forms (writers of Latin had trouble with the /w/ sound, which did not have a good single-letter representation in the Roman alphabet. They would often indicate the sound using two letters, <vv>, from whence we get our letter's name "double u").

for how much weight to give it in the final synthesis. This is frustrating, both to scholars of *Beowulf* and to students who want to know the right answers, but that very messiness and lack of resolution teaches important lessons in how to think. This process of groping our way towards the truth, which, in all its chaos and conflict, is so visible in *Beowulf* studies, is actually occurring in very similar ways in all disciplines, and it is important to be aware of this.[156] Scholars—and those who use the results of their work—must try to synthesize contested facts into accurate explanations, and how to create such syntheses is never as simple and straightforward as it seems after the fact: most scientific fields look a lot like *Beowulf* studies before someone has the insight to fit all the pieces together. When this happens about a big enough problem or a complex enough field, we celebrate the synthesis as a work of genius.

Beowulf studies seems to be an esoteric field, far removed from what many call "real world" problems, but the intellectual skills it develops have intensely practical applications. A substantial number of my former students who did advanced work on *Beowulf* and other medieval texts have ended up as successful lawyers. One of them told me that, while the other people she worked with feared the task of synthesizing a mass of confusing and contradictory documents into a coherent story, she found it easy after translating all 3,182 lines of *Beowulf* into Modern English and intensively studying all of the material I have sketched out in the above discussion. The kinds of thinking that are taught by detailed study of *Beowulf* are powerful intellectual tools that can be used for many other purposes.

Deep study in any given field teaches us not only about the field itself, but also the more general skills required to extract useful information from biased sources. An approach that is sometimes labeled "Critical Thinking,"[157] which is often taught as a potential replacement for the study of specific Liberal Arts disciplines in the undergraduate curriculum,

[156] Whenever you read something like "97% of all scientists believe X," you are not hearing about settled science; you are hearing about the politics (internal, external, or both) of a scientific field. When something really is settled, there are no percentages at all—can you imagine reading "94% of physicists believe that a positron is in all ways the same as an electron except for having a positive charge"? High percentages just tell us which side of a debate is currently ascendant.

focuses on detecting the presence of prejudice or "implicit bias" and teaching students to be wary of its effects. But that approach is not particularly effective at finding ways of using the information contained in sources that have particular agendas. Such sources, however, are often all we possess. Our "meta-study" of *Beowulf* studies does a reasonably good job of teaching us how to handle this kind of material, in part because the political agenda of the poem's author, whatever that was, is now so obsolete that it is free of the emotional baggage that is attached to less-esoteric subjects (the very abstruseness of a topic helps it escape from being a political or cultural football). Similarly, although the Roman historian Tacitus was more focused on criticizing his contemporaries in Rome for their softness and lack of vigor than he was in presenting an accurate picture of the Germanic tribes, we can make good use of his work (once we account for that bias), especially because we are not particularly angered by it. Likewise, we no longer care whether or not the people of southern Denmark in the sixth century were really proto-German or proto-Danish, so we can more fairly and rationally decide how to weigh the arguments of older scholars whose judgment could not entirely be trusted since they were so emotionally excited about the topic. We can then recognize similar patterns in the tendentious presentation of information by biased sources in the present day, even when we are dealing with subjects in which we are now emotionally engaged.

Every Liberal Arts discipline is the combination of a body of information and a set of procedures for evaluating it. Knowing the ways in which any single field creates and judges knowledge allows you to recognize that every field accomplishes the same goals in its own way. You are therefore better prepared to evaluate the quality of information and to synthesize it. The case of *Beowulf* shows how the disciplines of the Liberal

[157] The capital letters are often the distinguishing mark of the very socially centered approach that focuses on phenomena like bias and prejudice. The word "skills" appended to "critical thinking" is often the marker of an approach similar to what I have been trying to model throughout this chapter (and throughout the book). I have great sympathy for that approach, but I myself have found it impossible to teach "critical thinking skills" in the abstract without some specific content that those skills can be applied to understanding. "Critical Theory" (discussed briefly below) is an altogether different beast.

Arts teach the kinds of thinking that are necessary for solving complex problems. It also demonstrates how the study of a particular artwork can preserve and transmit culture across the generations. Between the years 1200 and 1815, the number of people who even knew that *Beowulf* existed could be counted on two hands, and the number who had read the poem was even smaller (for the first five of those centuries, this number was probably zero). *Beowulf* survived so long primarily by luck: if there had been another fire at the library, not only the edges of the manuscript, but the poem itself and all the information associated with it would be lost forever. But because British antiquaries wanted to collect old things, and Danish and German scholars were interested in using *Beowulf* to argue about questions of Germanic identity and politics, the poem was edited, published, distributed, and discussed. Then, because British scholars were proud to have the oldest poem in a Germanic language as part of their own cultural heritage, *Beowulf* was put on school syllabi, taught to students, and spread throughout the English-speaking world. After World Wars I and II, when "Germanic" things were unpopular, *Beowulf* fell somewhat out of favor, but its study gained new life when people learned that the poem was one of the inspirations of J.R.R. Tolkien's popular fantasy works *The Hobbit* and *The Lord of the Rings*. In 2000, translation by Seamus Heaney, a poet who had recently won the Nobel Prize in Literature, brought the poem back to more syllabi and into the minds of additional readers. The *Beowulf* manuscript was photographed and digitized, and the poem was translated, adapted, dramatized, and filmed, spreading its ideas throughout the world. Information that at one point only barely survived in a single charred, crumbling manuscript in the British Library is now disseminated around the globe in many languages and forms. None of this would ever have happened without the disciplines of the Liberal Arts, but because these disciplines did exist, and because *Beowulf* was studied and interpreted and taught, more culture can now be built on top of and around the poem, enriching our understanding of humanity and its works and enabling the creation of new art and knowledge.

Student Success Stories:
"At least it's all in English."

Many of my students go on to become lawyers. English majors tend to excel on the LSAT and subsequently in law school. When you can think rigorously, write effectively, and read and synthesize vast quantities of written material in short periods of time, you are well on your way to success at law school or lawyering.

I personally know very little about the law, but I hear stories from my former students. There is, apparently, something called a "Friday afternoon document dump." These occur when one side of a dispute is required to turn over documents to the other side but wants to make life as difficult as possible for their opponents. Document dumps, at least in the pre-email days, could be box after box of unlabeled papers deliberately mixed together and scrambled: a judge had ordered all the relevant documents to be turned over, not to be organized.

No one enjoys dealing with document dumps, and the obnoxious trick of sending the material over on a Friday afternoon so that it ruins someone's weekend, combined with the amount of time it takes to sort everything out, makes cleaning up the mess the job of interns or newly hired, young lawyers.

One of my students told me about this phenomenon, adding, "I have to say that compared to what you had us do for the Lexomics project, document dumps are a piece of cake. For one thing, everything is Modern English, and for the other, they're pretty standard in formatting and printing so you don't have to deal with not being able to read them."

All of sudden, I didn't feel so bad about having students work to organize hundreds of dendrograms, tree-diagrams that indicate the distribution of vocabulary in Old English poems. We were drowning in printouts, and the students had come into the lab one morning, gotten frustrated at not being able to find something, and worked out a set of naming conventions, abbreviations, and color-codings that brought order to the chaos.

The connection to the Liberal Arts was this: the students had studied Old English, Chaucer, and other medieval texts, so they had come across multiple examples of the ways scholars had labeled, classified, and arranged large collections of texts. Their general Liberal Arts training led them not just to apply a single scheme (developed for some other problem) into which they would force all the material, but instead to develop their own system—one that synthesized the best features of the other approaches, customizing them to the specific characteristics of our problem. Their hybrid scheme worked for Lexomics (eight years later, we are still using that organizational system), and the more general approach of devising an organizational system worked when transmuting the chaos of a document dump into the order of a collection of useful documents.

Chapter 8
The Power of the Liberal Arts Tradition: *The Dream of the Red Chamber* and Re-learning How to Learn

Our investigation of *Beowulf* shows how the study of the Liberal Arts can help us evaluate and synthesize immense bodies of complex and conflicting knowledge, blending together fuzzy and seemingly contradictory ideas from multiple sub-disciplines into a coherent picture of a literary and cultural masterpiece. In this chapter, we will see a different—though related—set of benefits that derive from the study of the Liberal Arts: the ability to learn in new and unfamiliar situations. I have been studying *Beowulf* for thirty years, but I have absolutely no formal training in the study of the work that is the focus of this chapter: Cao Xueqin's eighteenth-century novel *The Dream of the Red Chamber* (*Hong lou meng*). Indeed, although Cao's masterpiece is one of the four classic Chinese novels, it was not until 2016 that I read the book for the first time, and not until the following year that I began trying to understand the remarkable scholarly tradition that surrounds it. Fortunately, my general training in the Liberal Arts was (just barely) sufficient preparation for this task, as it turned out that in learning about medieval literature and culture, I had learned *how to learn*, and could apply that ability to classical Chinese literature and culture.

In 2016, my student Wenzhuo Shi asked me to be the advisor for her Honors thesis. The first part of her project—how the earliest scribes, readers, and editors of *The Canterbury Tales* dealt with the unfinished nature of that text—was both very promising and well within my area of expertise. But the second half of her thesis proposal brought me up short. Wenzhuo wanted to compare the creation and reception of *The Canterbury Tales* to those of another masterpiece whose author had also died before putting his work into its final form: *The Dream of the Red*

Chamber. Wenzhuo's request created a significant problem, because even though Cao's work is universally acclaimed as China's greatest novel, it had not been a part of my own literary education. *Dream of the Red Chamber* is also extremely long (the best English translation, by David Hawkes, takes up five volumes—about 2,500 pages), and unlike myths or epics, which might be set in some generic fairyland, the book assumes that its reader has deep knowledge of a specific and very complex and sophisticated culture—that of China during the reign of the Qianlong Emperor in the Qing Dynasty—which I had never studied. A sensible professor would have politely declined to supervise a project so far outside his or her area.

But I found it hard to give a flat "No" to a student who, despite English not being her first language, had mastered Old English well enough to translate *The Battle of Maldon, The Dream of the Rood,* and *The Wanderer* from Anglo-Saxon and had then read the entire *Canterbury Tales* in Middle English. So I agreed to consider the project over the summer and took the first two volumes of *The Dream of the Red Chamber* along with me on a tour I was leading in England.

The very patient and indulgent people on that tour ended up hearing a lot more about *The Dream of the Red Chamber* and eighteenth-century China than they must have been expecting on a tour of Anglo-Saxon sites in Britain. That I was completely captivated by Cao's novel is a massive understatement. The first two volumes went by so quickly that I had to re-start volume I before returning home, where I raced through the remaining 1,400 pages and then lamented that there was no more left to read. Even in translation, *The Dream of the Red Chamber* turned out to be one of the most beautiful, profound, and fascinating books I have ever read.

The novel is the story of the Jias, an aristocratic family in eighteenth-century China that appears (at least from the outside) to be at the peak of wealth and prestige—a daughter is one of the Emperor's concubines—but internally is weakening from years of mismanagement and lack of personal discipline. The plot focuses on the oldest son, Bao-yu, a sensitive and insightful but also extremely spoiled thirteen-year old. Grandmother Jia, the family matriarch, indulges Bao-yu by allowing him to live in the family's enormous formal garden (which contains multiple dwellings) with his young female cousins. These happy, golden days are rendered with a heart-aching, nostalgic beauty that comes through even in translation.

At the emotional heart of the story is a triangular relationship between Bao-yu and two of his cousins: the graceful, self-disciplined Xue Bao-chai and the sensitive, emotional Lin Dai-yu. Each young woman lacks some of the qualities found in the other, and while both love Bao-yu and he loves them, in the end none of them have any choice in the matter of who will become his wife. These characters—and nearly a dozen others—are unforgettable. Their plight becomes tragic when accumulated moral and financial failures lead to the collapse of the family's wealth, power, and prestige. The "happy golden years" of Bao-yu and his cousins in the garden become nothing more than bittersweet memory.

I love this novel, which combines beauty and tragedy like few others. But enthusiasm for a text is not enough to allow a teacher to guide an advanced student trying to produce original research. Fortunately, in addition to my enthusiasm, I had a remarkably gifted student who did not need very much guidance from me, and I had the Liberal Arts. At the beginning of the previous chapter I argued that it does not matter *which* Liberal Arts major you choose as long as you devote yourself to learning its particular ways of creating and evaluating knowledge. Once you have mastered a specific discipline, the knowledge gained and the skills developed become generalizable throughout the Liberal Arts. Most of my students who specialize in medieval literature do not pursue careers as professors of that subject but instead go on to success in law, finance, management, art, politics, and other fields not obviously related to their undergraduate studies. Directing Wenzhuo's thesis, I realized, would be a real test of my belief that skills and knowledge developed in one sub-specialization were generalizable.

But it is one thing to tell your students to do something and quite another thing to have to try it yourself: there are good reasons that the first words people use to describe aged professors like me are not usually *flexible* and *adaptable*. But I found trying to understand *The Dream of the Red*

Chamber and its associated scholarship far less daunting than the prospect of having to tell a deserving student that she could not write an Honors thesis because it would be too much work for her professor. So I did some reading. A *lot* of reading. And it was so worth it. The Liberal Arts really did help me navigate a completely unfamiliar sub-discipline, and eventually I began to understand the work of art itself, the culture in which it arose, and the critical tradition surrounding it. Here is what I learned and, perhaps more importantly, how I learned it.

Entering an unfamiliar discipline often feels like walking into the middle of a long ongoing conversation in which you know very few of the speakers and almost nothing about the topic. This metaphor is a particularly helpful intuition pump: you try to follow the conversation, but it jumps around with such rapidity that you keep losing your place. Everybody nods at fast-moving chains of reasoning with many steps left out or unexplained; people drop references that everyone else seems to get; and sometimes people laugh out loud at an elliptical statement that, you infer, must be an inside joke. You may be fascinated, because these people obviously think what they are talking about is important, and they seem to be enjoying themselves, but you also become frustrated, and the longer that frustration goes on, the more likely it is that a daunting feeling of exclusion —and a concomitant sense of self-inferiority—will take over, eventually causing you to withdraw, both ashamed that you are too stupid or uneducated to participate, and angry that the insiders in the conversation are hostile elitists (and it is a very short step to believing that you are being excluded because of your demographic characteristics—your race, gender, social class, age, or nationality).

That I experienced this exact dynamic upon trying to enter the scholarly sub-discipline of the study of *The Dream of the Red Chamber* was one of the more important lessons I learned from the entire process. I absolutely felt the way I have just described, but I was incorrect in the motives I attributed to the people in the field. It turned out that no one (not even the editor who rejected the first version of our paper) had any intention of being exclusionary. A chance meeting with a friend of that editor allowed me to find out that she had been genuinely excited that an

English professor was interested enough to have taken a dive into the scholarship.

When I taught a class on *The Dream of the Red Chamber* in 2022, multiple scholars sent me resources, teaching tips, links to videos, and encouragement. They were all happy to help me and my students better appreciate this great work of art—and the edifice of scholarship surrounding it—that they love so much. I only *felt* excluded because they were talking the way they always did about their topic, which is the way all specialists talk about their own topics. The experience gave me insight into how both students and outsiders may sometimes feel about my own discipline. Because we Anglo-Saxonists are similarly genuinely thrilled on the rare occasions that other people care about the same esoteric things that we do, we believe that we are extremely welcoming to new entrants to the field, and as individuals we are. Nevertheless, the communication dynamics of our—and of any well-developed discipline—can cause visitors to feel that they are being excluded even when the intention is entirely the opposite. There may be no easy fix for this situation, but being aware of it not only as an abstraction but as an experience has been extremely useful in helping me to reshape the ways I talk with other specialists in discipline-specific conversations when newcomers or visitors are present.

The fundamental problem is that a new person joining a conversation is ignorant of almost all that has gone on before, but no conversation could persist if each time someone joined it had to start over again at the beginning.[158] We know intuitively that in order to join a conversation, we must make an effort to catch ourselves up, to understand what everyone else is talking about. Probably all of us have cringe-worthy memories of jumping into a conversation prematurely and making some kind of social mistake, which is why we have learned to spend time listening without speaking, perhaps even laughing when everyone else does, even if we do not understand the joke. Eventually we catch on and can contribute.

[158] If such a dynamic were required, I think scholarly conversations (and personal ones, for that matter) *would* become actively exclusionary, because under those rules the only way to keep the conversation going would be to prevent new people from joining.

These characteristics of ordinary conversation apply also to academic discourse. We have the great benefit of there being a written archive of the previous stages of the conversation, and there is no particular social awkwardness associated with taking plenty of time to read scholarly articles and books before commenting, but entering such a conversation is still a nerve-wracking experience because of how unpleasant our memories of awkwardness are. It perhaps helps a little to remember that we are not the only ones joining an academic conversation in the middle of things: every single current participant in the conversation had the same experience. Absolutely nobody started at the beginning, and the current comfortable-seeming insiders were themselves once the awkward newcomers trying to figure out what the people in the field were talking about.

Entering into the conversation in an unfamiliar field is both essential and difficult, but there are some ways to orient yourself that can speed up the journey and smooth the way. The most obvious of these is to seek out formal instruction from an expert in the field. But for a variety of reasons, that approach is not always possible; we often have to find ways to teach ourselves. Perhaps the next best thing to an expert is a guide to a discipline that has been put together by experienced scholars. These sorts of books have titles like *Current Topics in* [*Field of Interest*] or *An Introduction to* [*Field of Interest*] and are often collections of essays by mostly senior scholars with a few "up-and-coming" junior researchers thrown into the mix. Haun Saussy's *Approaches to Teaching The Story of the Stone* (an alternate title for *The Dream of the Red Chamber*) is a good example of this sort of book, which provides a wealth of information for someone teaching the work for the first time (I drew freely upon it) and sets out the major questions and problems recognized by contemporary scholarship.

However, entering a new field through such a work does entail some risks, the most serious of which is that contemporary views are often presented as far more definitive than they actually might be. Questions that have recently arisen are often represented as the truly important ones, and issues that a scholar does not feel like discussing are sometimes prematurely treated as settled. The illusion of an "arc of progress" is particularly pernicious when a newcomer lacks background and context and so cannot differentiate between partisan claims, for which contradicting evidence is downplayed, and a true scholarly consensus (although this can, in the long run, turn out to be wrong). In other words, the scholarship in "Introduction to..." collections has a tendency to present the field as the current people in power in that field want it to be perceived.

In my experience, the discipline of history is particularly good about preventing junior scholars from accepting a snapshot of current opinions as eternal disciplinary truths. Unfortunately, most students—even history students—dislike the necessary method, which is to insist upon *historiography*, that is the study not of history itself but of what has been said about history. A member of my dissertation committee was a historian, and I remember being utterly frustrated with her insistence that I read what a bunch of nineteenth-century (and even some eighteenth-century) historians had written about the tenth-century Benedictine Reform in England. Why did I need to read what these tiresome books said about my topic when I could read more contemporary works to find out the truth—as opposed to what some moldy old scholar thought had happened? But historiography, when done properly, allows you to see exactly how our contemporary understanding of historical events has developed. We can therefore see the biases and the blindspots, and we can recognize where the cliches come from and what they originally meant. We are thus skeptical in the best way about contemporary scholarship because we can see the parts of the ongoing conversation that scholars are reacting against or trying to recover. The problem with historiography, and the reason graduate students hate doing it, is that it is massively time-consuming with the only obvious payoff for all that work being inside the student's mind. A big reason that even the best dissertations are not usually publishable is that they are filled with enormous explanatory footnotes that do nothing but tell the dissertation committee "Yes, I *did* read all the historiography on this issue as a dutiful grad student should."

I did not have the time or the language skills to do a full historiographic analysis of the scholarship on *The Dream of the Red*

Chamber, but thanks to my experience studying other Liberal Arts, I knew that I would be making a mistake if I just took the most current introductory essays at face value. So I used one weird trick that I have developed over the years for crossing into a new field. Locating the section in the library stacks where scholarship on *The Dream of the Red Chamber* is shelved (around PL 2727), I searched for a reasonably thick volume, with a somewhat generic title, published between 1950 and 1970, with a preference for a book in the later '50s or earlier '60s. This seems oddly specific, but my experience with Anglo-Saxon studies suggests that a work published in this time period would be well-written, engaged in explicit debates about long-standing questions in the scholarship, and not extremely partisan or political. Research from before WWII is often more difficult to read because scholarly communities were much smaller and so much could go without saying or with only an oblique reference or explanation. Pre-war books also rarely provide translations of any passage not in English. Scholarship in the 1970s, on the other hand, is often so devoted to the notion of "debunking" that it regularly throws the genuine-insight baby out with the conjecture-disguised-as-fact bathwater, and scholarship from the '80s and '90s is more focused on applying various theoretical templates to the material being studied. Nothing is inherently wrong with any of those approaches, but books doing that sort of intellectual work are much less helpful for orienting yourself in the ongoing scholarly conversation in an unfamiliar field.

Based on its physical size, publication date (1961), publisher (Oxford University Press), and very generic title, I chose Wu Shih-Ch'ang's *On the Red Chamber Dream: A Critical Study of Two Annotated Manuscripts of the XVIIIth Century*, which I then read through from beginning to end.[159] Fortunately, I was extremely lucky in my semi-random

[159] Wu Shih-Ch'Ang, *On the Red Chamber Dream: A Critical Study of Two Annotated Manuscripts of the XVIIIth Century* (Oxford: Clarendon Press, 1961). The book is so beautifully written and argued that I highly recommend it even though the text can at times be confusing to the novice (in part because Wu uses the older Wade-Giles system of Chinese spelling whereas all the more recent works, and Hawkes' translation, use modern Pinyin spelling). Because Hawkes' translation and all contemporary scholarship use the Pinyin system, a non-reader of Chinese must make up a table of equivalent names in order

choice. Wu is a wonderful prose stylist in English, and his writing is full of energy as he strongly makes the case for his interpretations. I took extensive notes as I worked through the book, always having an eye out for the issues that were particularly relevant to my student's thesis about the masterpiece being unfinished, but also trying to assemble as many essential facts about the novel and its history as I could. One great advantage of entering into a field this way, instead of through a more formal introduction, is that you learn those essential facts not as a student who is given a list to memorize, but as a detective who has to piece together a coherent picture from a bunch of fragmentary clues. It is exciting, and you remember the facts much more easily when you have ferreted them out of asides, unexplained references, and footnotes. It was my generalist and wide-ranging work in the Liberal Arts that allowed me to learn in this way (which was so enjoyable that I neglected work in my home discipline) about Cao Xueqin's brilliant novel and the multi-century scholarly conversation that accompanies it. Knowing how to learn was more valuable than anything other than the most specific training would have been.

The pleasure of doing literary detective work continued when I started following up on references in Wu's book—anyone he praised or criticized strongly was worth a look—putting together a pretty clear picture of the scholarly conversation up through 1961. I then began looking for Wu's name in the indexes of books published after 1970 and flipped to the pages in which he was mentioned. This effort helped give me a general idea of how his arguments had been received over the past half-century. It was easy to see that Wu's deductions about the manuscripts and the original commentaries had become widely accepted, but his literary

---

to match up the names in Wu's book with those in the other texts (for example, in Wade-Giles, Xi-feng is Hsi-Fêng, Cao Xueqin is Ts'sao Hsüeh-ch'in). English speakers generally find it easier to *pronounce* Chinese words that have been romanized in the Wade-Giles system, but Pinyin is more compact and easier to read, and, more importantly, it is the system contemporary Chinese speakers use for writing their own language in the Roman alphabet. My only quibble with Wu's book is that he insists on translating 麒麟 (Qilin) as "unicorn." (207-213). Although a qilin is a mythical beast that brings good luck, the creature in Chinese mythology most definitely has *two* horns, so "*uni*corn" is, to me, a singularly inappropriate translation.

interpretations were basically ignored, mostly because the conversation about literary value had taken a different turn. At this point I was ready to read Saussy's Introduction, which, while focused on teaching, has a great deal to say about literary interpretation, and then follow up on the issues raised in that book that seemed relevant or interesting. Eventually I came to understand reasonably well (I hope) not only the novel itself, but the edifice of scholarship it had spawned.

The Dream of the Red Chamber,[160] (紅樓夢; Pinyin *Honglou meng*) by Cao Xueqin (曹雪芹) has a very different reception-history than *Beowulf*. The book became widely known relatively soon after Cao's death in 1763 and has long been recognized as China's greatest novel. Unlike *Beowulf*, whose visibility over the past two centuries has waxed and waned in response to larger political and social trends, *The Dream of the Red Chamber* has been continuously popular despite the massive political, cultural, economic, and technological changes in China since it was written. Cao's book has inspired art, music, drama, opera, and literary imitations in every subsequent period of Chinese history.[161] Even during the Cultural Revolution of the 1970s, when so much traditional Chinese culture was destroyed, *The Dream of the Red Chamber* itself was not attacked, in large part because Mao himself asserted that study of the book, which he had read five times, was essential for understanding Chinese

---

[160] The author's preferred title for the novel is an unresolved problem. The most frequently used title in Mandarin, *Honglou meng,* can be translated several ways in addition to the most common *The Dream of the Red Chamber,* including *The Red Chamber Dream* and *A Dream of Red Mansions*. The general idea, which is difficult to express in a single English title, is that the novel is the kind of dream that would be dreamed inside a red (to indicate good luck) chamber in a mansion or in a chamber in a red mansion (the Mandarin is——almost certainly deliberately——ambiguous). The best English translation, *The Story of the Stone*, by David Hawkes and his son-in-law Bruce Miniford, does not use *Honglou meng* as the title.

[161] Schools of criticism have come and gone, falling in and out of official and popular favor, but never the novel itself. See Xiajue Wang, "*Stone* in Modern China: Literature, Politics, and Culture," in *Approaches to Teaching* The Story of the Stone (Dream of the Red Chamber), ed. Andrew Schonenbaum and Tina Lu (New York: Modern Language Association, 2012), 413-426.

culture.[162] The television mini-series of the novel was so popular that it is said that when it was first broadcast in 1987, the streets of Beijing emptied out as everyone went home to watch, and bookstores sold out of copies of the two-hundred-year-old novel. The twenty-seven-hour series has been rebroadcast close to seven hundred times, and each of the thirty-six individual episodes have been viewed millions of times on YouTube. In 2007, the death of the actress Chen Xiaoxu, who played the heroine Lin Dai-yu, generated several million comments on internet forums,[163] and even the garden created as a set for the television series remains a tourist attraction.

Beowulf and *The Dream of the Red Chamber* did not influence each other at all—they were written on literally opposite sides of the planet, and the cultural distance between them is possibly even greater than the physical. *Beowulf* was, for most of its history, obscure, and its study still is the province of academic specialists whose work is unknown to the public. *The Dream of the Red Chamber* has been enormously popular, and most of the novel's millions of readers have strong opinions not only about the work's overall meaning, but about some of the major scholarly problems associated with the text. There is, however, one deep similarity between the two works: not only are both masterpieces, but their respective critical traditions are themselves also monuments of human intellectual achievement.

This interdependence of a work of art and its scholarly tradition—which I think is itself also a work of art—was my entry into the study of *The Dream of the Red Chamber* because it turned out that the same sorts of problems, and similar ways of solving them, developed independently in separate traditions of writing, editing, reading, and scholarship. My knowledge of medieval literature and the editorial and scholarly work required to understand it gave me a template for organizing and evaluating knowledge about the text of *The Dream of the Red Chamber*, and my

---

[162] Li Zhisui, *The Private Life of Chairman Mao* (New York: Random House, 1994), 82.

[163] Xueping Zhong, "*The Story of the Stone* on Television," in *Approaches to Teaching* The Story of the Stone (Dream of the Red Chamber), ed. Andrew Schonenbaum and Tina Lu (New York: Modern Language Association, 2012), 427-29.

general education in the Liberal Arts helped me engage (and fall in love) with what was to me a completely unfamiliar culture: China in the Qing dynasty during the reigns of the Kangxi, Yongzhen, and Qianlong Emperors.

In order to help guide Wenzhuo's research, I knew I needed to identify the literary problems associated with Cao's work, understand why they are problems, and determine what scholarship was authoritative or at least widely accepted. The first step is to figure out exactly what we are studying and how we know what we know. With *Beowulf,* we begin with that single unique manuscript. The situation is a little more complicated for *The Dream of the Red Chamber*, as there are multiple early manuscripts of the text, but the principle is the same: first identify the physical artifacts from which we get our knowledge of the text and then see how scholars have organized and evaluated this information to produce the text we read.

Right away I learned that, as is the case with *Beowulf*, it is impossible to read *The Dream of the Red Chamber* as it was produced by its author because the text that has come down to us is in various ways incomplete. *Beowulf* is an imperfect copy and has suffered minor damage throughout, so we must rely on scholarship to clarify opaque passages. The situation for *The Dream of the Red Chamber* is far more dramatic: in every manuscript of Cao's work, the final forty chapters are missing.[164] This absence has led to an intense authorship controversy that has been the single biggest area of debate for two centuries in both popular and scholarly discussion of the novel; no piece of scholarship can fail to address

[164] Manuscripts of *The Dream of the Red Chamber*: A. Jiaxu (甲戌) copy, Shanghai, Shanghai Museum; B. Jimao (己卯), Beijing. National Library of China (Chapters 1-20, 31-40, 61-70); National Museum of China (the second half of Chapter 55 to the first half of 59); C. Gengchen (庚辰), Beijing, Peking University Library, NC/5753/5616.7; D. Qihu (戚沪), Shanghai, Shanghai Library (1-40); E. Qining (戚宁), Nanjing, Nanjing Library, GJ/I/622; F. Mengfu (蒙府), Beijing, National Library of China; G. Yangcang/Menggao (杨藏/梦稿), Beijing, The Literature Research Institute of the Chinese Academy of Social Science; H. Jiachen/Mengue (甲辰/梦觉), Beijing, National Library of China, 18352; I. Shuxu (舒序), Beijing, Capital Library of China; J. E'cang (俄藏), Saint Petersburg, The Institute of Oriental Manuscripts at Saint Petersburg; K. Zhengcang (郑藏), Beijing, National Library of China; L. Jingcang (靖藏), Lost; M. Biancang (卞藏), Private.

the problem, although some—like Wu's book that was my initial guide—make it more central than others.

Chapters 80 to 120 first appeared in the first printed edition of *The Dream of the Red Chamber*, which was published in 1791-92, about thirty years after Cao Xueqin's death.[165] The editors, Cheng Weiyuan (程 伟元) and Gao E (高 鹗), state in their preface that they tried to find as many manuscripts of the novel as possible and then compiled, sorted, and edited these fragments of the text. But they were unable to produce a complete version of the novel until, one day, Cheng unexpectedly found in the marketplace a manuscript containing the missing chapters, which Gao used to complete the edition. The final forty chapters in Cheng and Gao's edition, however, differ stylistically from the first eighty, and the plot that they reveal often conflicts with the foreshadowing in the first two thirds of the novel.[166] Readers suspected that the story of finding the manuscript in the marketplace was a convenient fabrication by two literary entrepreneurs who wanted to profit from their edition.[167] A massive debate about the "real" ending of the novel began almost immediately and continues today with unabated intensity. Every person who reads *The Dream of the Red Chamber*, regardless of how much he or she tries to avoid the topic, ends up having an opinion about how Cao intended the story to end.[168]

[165] Two editions of the book were published by Cheng and Gao. Both are named 新镌绣像红楼梦 *Xin Jian Quan Bu Xiu Xiang Hong Lou Meng (Newly printed complete illustrated edition of the Dream of the Red Chamber)* and contain 120 chapters. The first version was printed in 1791 (Chengjia 程甲) with a preface from Cheng explaining how and why he published the book and Gao's introduction describing how he emended the story. The second edition, Chengyi (程乙), was published several months later, in 1792. It maintains the format and illustrations of the first edition, but there is another preface added to explain the reason for reprinting. Although published only a few months later, more than 20,000 words in this volume differ from the first edition.

[166] For a brief critical history through the first half of the twentieth century, see Wu 2-11.

[167] Haun Saussy, "Authorship," in *Approaches to Teaching* The Story of the Stone (Dream of the Red Chamber), ed. Andrew Schonenbaum and Tina Lu (New York: Modern Language Association, 2012), 70-77 at 76.

[168] For the current state of authorship questions, see Saussy, "Authorship" and Shengli Zhang, Zhang, Shengli, "The Significance of Stating the Author of the Last 40 Chapters as 'Neither Gao nor Cao' in the Contemporary Era—A Focus on Wang Peizhang's Emendations of Chengjia and Chengyi Texts," Studies on "A Dream of Red Mansions,"

Based on what Cheng and Gao say in their preface and on the interlinear and marginal comments written in the surviving manuscripts, we can deduce that at least the first eighty chapters of *The Dream of the Red Chamber* circulated in manuscript form during the life of the author. A statement in Chapter 1 that Cao Xueqin worked on the novel for ten years and revised it five times indicates that Cao had completed the book, or at least drafted the ending, before he died in 1763, but we have no evidence that the final chapters were ever circulated.[169] Scholars have inferred that someone, perhaps a member of Cao's family, either kept Chapters 81-120 out of circulation or substantially changed the ending of the novel, probably to avoid running afoul of the literary inquisition. This was not an irrational fear. During the Qing dynasty, works could be placed on an *Index Expurgatorius* and their authors (and the authors' families) punished for seemingly trivial reasons.[170] From the foreshadowing in the first eighty chapters, it seems that in Cao's original version many of the characters suffered intensely from the Emperor's punishment of their family's corruption. The implication that the regime was cruel may have been seen as too politically dangerous in the 1790s.

Many early scholars called Gao E a forger, concluding that he simply invented the final forty chapters based on his own reading of the

4(2016): 224-244. 张胜利.后四十回作者"非高非曹"说的当代意义——以王佩璋程甲、程乙本校勘为中心[J].红楼梦学刊, 2016 (04): 224-244. The idea of "neither Cao nor Gao" was first raised by Wang Peizhang, the assistant of Yu Pingbo, in her article "The Issues about the Author of the Last 40 chapters of *The Dream of the Red Chamber*" in 1957. In the first edition published by People's Literature Publishing House in 1982, Feng Qiyong indicated that the authorship of the last forty chapters was still unclear; when the third edition was published in 2008, the authors of the book were changed to Cao Xueqin and Anonymous, while Gao E was listed as the editor.

[169] Hawkes 51.

[170] For instance, in the eighth year of Yongzheng (1730), a poet named Xu Jun (徐骏) was beheaded at the direct command of the Emperor: a line in one of the poet's works "the breeze did not learn to read, then why does it bother to turn the book's leaves?" was taken to imply that the Manchu aristocracy did not know how to read, since the word "breeze" in Chinese—qingfeng (清风)—maintains the same character and sound as the name of the Qing Dynasty. For this and many other insights throughout this section, I am grateful to Wenzhuo Shi and her infinite patience with her professor's slow pace of learning and his poor pronunciation of Chinese words.

first eighty. Others are not so sure. Perhaps Gao was telling the truth about a manuscript source, but that source was a censored version of Cao's text. Or perhaps Cao's original text was indeed lost, and one of his readers reconstructed it, as best he could, from memory, or various chapters circulated independently, and some of these were lost or damaged to different degrees. It is also possible that the creator of the final chapters based them on the 120-chapter table of contents mentioned in Cheng's preface. Contemporary scholars have become cautious about assigning the end of the novel to anyone; in Hawkes' translation, the final volume is attributed to Anonymous, *edited* by Gao E.

Even if the authorship question could be resolved, there are many other uncertainties about the text. Within the first eighty chapters, there are substantial variations among the surviving manuscripts. Dai-yu's eyes and eyebrows are described eight different ways in the third chapters of various manuscripts, and there are five different versions of the title of Chapter 8. Several manuscripts do not contain Chapters 65 and 67 (and others import these two chapters from the printed edition), and there are two different versions of the latter chapter. In some manuscripts, there are blank spaces left for poems that only appear in other manuscripts, and some chapters are undivided, suggesting that some manuscripts were copied from work in progress that circulated among the author's friends.

Further evidence for the early reading and reception of the novel comes in the form of interlinear or marginal comments in the early manuscripts. I learned that it was an important part of Chinese elite literary culture in the eighteenth century to write comments—often in different colored ink—in smaller characters between the columns of text or in the margins.[171] In their comments, readers analyzed, explained, complimented, and critiqued the work, engaging in dialogue with both the author and other readers. I was—and still am—thrilled by the existence of these comments (probably unreasonably so, since I have only read a small selection of them because no complete translation of the comments into English has been made).[172] The ways that scholars of *The Dream of the Red Chamber* use the comments to interpret the text and the text to understand

[171] I wish such commentary by early readers had been a tradition in Anglo-Saxon England.

the comments and then synthesize this material with historical data to build up a picture of Cao's life and literary intentions is intellectually awe-inspiring.

One of the earliest readers of *The Dream of the Red Chamber* was the prolific commenter known as "Zhiyan zhai" ("Red Inkstone"), who appears to have been one of Cao's family members. Red Inkstone's comments—which are found only in the first eighty chapters—often note that he remembers events Cao is fictionalizing: "Ah, yes, I remember her," or "Not many of us still left who know about this."[173] A comment on Chapter 20 indicates that Cao did not always receive back the chapters of his manuscript that he had circulated among his friends, thus forcing him to re-compose chapters: "I saw [this chapter] once, when I was making a fair copy. That and five or six other chapters, including 'A Sympathizer Consoles Bao-yu in the Temple of the Prison God,' were all lost by someone who borrowed the manuscript to read."[174]

There is also evidence that feedback from his circle of readers influenced Cao's revisions of the novel. I was again unreasonably pleased to learn this, because I would be willing to sacrifice a limb to see the *Beowulf*-poet adapting his text as a result of the criticism of his first readers. Also, as it turns out, it was in regard to Cao's revisions that I was able to make a small contribution to the great tradition of scholarship on *The Dream of the Red Chamber* (though only with Wenzhuo's knowledge and some software tools). At the end of Chapter 13 in the Jiaxu manuscript, there is the following comment:

> "Qin Keqing (秦可卿) dies at Tianxiang Pavilion with lustfulness" [is a chapter] where the author uses historians' writing style (with intimations and suggestions). I am moved by how her spirit

[172] I tried to convince Wenzhuo to undertake this project, but, as she pointed out, the comments would be almost impossible to read if they were not printed along with an English translation of the novel, and since David Hawkes' translation is widely acclaimed as a masterpiece, it is unlikely that anyone will soon make a new translation simply to provide a matrix for a translation of the comments. The solution would be for me to learn to read Chinese, but this has turned out to be easier said than done.

[173] Hawkes 22, 36.

[174] Hawkes 39.

> appears in Xifeng's dream and illustrates to Xifeng about the future of the family of Jia. People who are satisfied with their great properties, high ranks and enjoy the fruits of others could barely think of those two things.[175] Although her secret[176] is not explicitly stated, her words and her intention are mournful and impressive. Therefore, I remit her and ask Qinxi [芹溪, another name of Cao] to delete [the sub-plot].

Another comment on the same page states that "there were only 10 pages in this chapter, and about 4 to 5 pages were cut due to the amputation of the plot at Tianxiang Pavilion."[177] As Lin Guanfu (林 冠夫) points out, from these comments we learn the original title of Chapter 13, that it has been revised to the extent of pages being deleted, that these revisions were finished before the exemplar of the Jiaxu manuscript was produced, and that they were required by the commentator.[178] In the same place in the Gengchen manuscript appears the comment: "The whole chapter has put the reason of Keqing's death out of sight—it is the author's mercy. Alas."[179] That a commenter could get the author to change the plot of his novel illustrates the significance of the give-and-take between the writer and his early readers. Scholars believe that the commenter who got Cao to change the cause of the death of Qin-shi (the young wife of Jia Rong, who is Bao-yu's second cousin once removed) from suicide to illness was likely a close relative who did not want the book to expose the family's shameful secrets.

These comments explain a major discrepancy between foreshadowing in the novel and the actual plot. In Chapter 5, Bao-yu has a prophetic dream in which he pages through a large book that contains a

[175] The original sentence in Chinese is a rhetorical question with a suggested answer, but for reasons of clarity it is translated here as a statement. My thanks again to Wenzhuo Shi for all of her help.

[176] For Liu Xinwu (a scholar who believes that Qin-shi was intended to be the daughter of the former crown-prince), the secret here is her family background.

[177] 此回只十页，因删去天香楼一节，少却四五页也。

[178] Lin, Guanfu, "The Revision of Qin Keqing's Denouement," *The Orthodox Views of The Dream of the Red Chamber*, 2006, 262-264; 林冠夫. 秦可卿结局的修改[C], 2006, 262-264.

[179] 通回将可卿如何死故隐去，是大发慈悲也。叹叹！(Gengchen 282).

series of illustrations and poems that foretell the fates of the young women —the Twelve Beauties of Jinling, many of whom are his cousins—whose stories make up most of *The Dream of the Red Chamber*. The last of these paintings depicts a beautiful young girl hanging by her neck in the upper room of a tall building. The poem says:

> Love was her sea, her sky; in such excess
> Love, meeting with its like, breeds wantonness.
> Say not our troubles from all Rong's side came;
> For their beginning, Ning must take the blame.[180]

Both picture and poem seem to foreshadow the suicide of Qin-shi, but in all the surviving manuscripts and in the first printed version of the novel, the young woman does not hang herself but dies in bed after an illness. So it seems that Cao must have reacted to the criticisms of his commenters, but for some reason this revision was not quite complete: Cao did not change the poem and picture about Qin-shi in Chapter 5, and there are some additional subtle inconsistencies. Analyzing these in light of both the unchanged poem and the comments allows us both to reconstruct the original version of the plot and to see how Cao changed it.

From the foreshadowing, the comments, and the surviving text, we can infer that Qin-shi's suicide at Tianxiang Pavilion occurred after someone discovered that she was having an adulterous affair with her father-in-law, Jia Zhen. In Chapter 7, an old servant, Jiao Da (焦 大), drunkenly rants one night, lamenting that the family he has long served is now so corrupt that the father-in-law (焦 大) "pokes in the ashes" (爬灰) and "auntie has it off with nevvy."[181] Supporting the conclusion that there had been an improper relationship are the efforts of the father-in-law Jia Zhen's efforts to secure extravagantly expensive wood for Qin-shi's coffin and his reaction to his uncle Jia Zheng's advice to be cautious: Zhen was "even anxious to die for Qin and refused to listen."[182] The extreme shock and despair with which Qin-shi's two maids, Ruizhu (瑞珠) and Baozhu (宝珠), react to their mistress' death are inconsistent with Qin-shi's quietly

180 Hawkes 135.

181 Hawkes 183.

182 Gengchen MS, 273.

succumbing after an extended illness, but would be reasonable and expected in the context of the surprise suicide of the young woman.

If comments from readers could motivate the author to modify the plot even at a fairly late stage of composition, *The Dream of the Red Chamber* becomes a somewhat collaborative work, but only to a limited extent, because the revision was not thorough enough to remove all traces of the original plot. Careful close reading of the published version in light of the comments shows that changing the cause of Qin-shi's death from suicide to illness required many more modifications than simply excising four to five pages from a single chapter. Replacing the death scene was only a small portion of the cascade of changes Cao had to make. Reference to an illness had to be inserted earlier in the plot (Chapter 10). A subplot of escalating worry about the failure of Qin-shi's health to improve was followed by the insertion of a visit from a doctor and a detailed explanation of the illness and its treatment (Chapter 11). Throughout these chapters, the other characters discuss the steady decline in Qin-Shi's health, making her death sad but expected.

The ambiguities introduced by this kind of revision present a set of fascinating intellectual problems. If we try to read the novel in its published form, we find the foreshadowing poem in Chapter 5 contradicted by Qin-shi's death by illness, and both the specifics of the drunken retainer's accusations and the reaction at the young woman's death strangely unmotivated. But the text that Zhi had made Cao change is now lost, so we have no way of knowing the specific original subplots in Chapters 10 and 11 or the details of Qin-shi's shame and death. We also have no way of knowing which other details throughout the long and complex plot were connected to or resonant with the adulterous relationship and the tragic suicide. That it is Qin-shi who brings her young cousin Bao-yu to her bedroom to take the nap in which he dreamed the vision of the futures of the twelve ladies (and also had his first erotic experience) makes her seem more central to Cao's original plan than is the case in the published novel. But the missing text forces us to invent as much as we reconstruct, producing, for the thoughtful reader, a tangled multiplicity of interpretations. *The Dream of the Red Chamber* ends up being read as a combination of the text in the published edition, the plot that scholars have determined was once there, and what readers' imaginations construct to fill the gaps or resolve the contradictions.

When we combine these qualities of the text with the problem of the seemingly non-authorial final forty chapters, we can see that *The Dream of the Red Chamber* perfectly fulfills the post-modern cliché that a text is a creation of not only its author but also its readers. Without being able to be sure what Cao's plan was for the end of the novel, we are forced, whether we want to or not, to think that the entire conclusion of the plot might have been intended to be very different, so that when we encounter some feature that we do not understand or which seems contradictory to what has come before, we begin doubting whether or not it is genuine.

In an amazing and beautiful irony, the difficulty of distinguishing truth from fantasy is one of the most important themes of *The Dream of the Red Chamber*.

Truth becomes fiction when the fiction's true;
Real becomes not-real when the unreal's real.[183]

This couplet, inscribed on either side of an archway that leads into the "Land of Illusion" in Bao-yu's dream, could be the epigraph for the entire novel. The name of the Jia family can mean "false" or "imaginary," and the Jias of Beijing are somehow connected with a family in Nanking named Zhen, which means "real" (each family includes a young man named Bao-yu). An introductory passage claims that the entire story is merely a dream, but also explains that the book is actually the story of a stone that had temporarily transformed into a human (presumably Bao-yu), whose story is inscribed on it—this is why some translations of the novel, including Hawkes', are entitled *The Story of the Stone*. In Chapter 1, a monk named Vanitas is said to have found the stone and, after some contemplation, decided to change his name to Brother Amor and the title of the novel to *The Tale of Brother Amor* (or *The Passionate Monk's Tale*). Other names for the book are proposed, including *A Mirror for the Romantic* and *A Dream of Golden Days*. Then we read that

[183] Hawkes 130.

> Cao Xueqin in his Nostalgia Studio worked on [the novel] for ten years, in the course of which he rewrote it no less than five times, dividing it into chapter headings, renaming it the *Twelve Beauties of Jinling*, and adding an introductory quatrain. Red Inkstone restored the original title when he recopied the book and added his second set of annotations to it.[184]

Thus the passage in which the true name of the author is given—a name which appears to be confirmed by the comments and by references in other texts—begins by disavowing any truth in the book, thus confusing the real and the imaginary. And in a further irony, this particular passage, as Red Inkstone's commentary suggests, may not have been written by Cao Xueqin himself, but by his younger brother, Cao Tangcun. Some scholars, however, think that the passage is not by the author *or* his brother, but is instead a reader's comment that was at some point erroneously copied into the main text rather than remaining interlinear or marginal.[185]

The uncertainty generated by this interplay between real and imaginary is also seen within the plot. The great wealth, power, and prestige of the Jia family turn out to be built in great part on illusion, even deceit. But at the same time, their wealth and power are real enough that they can they bring into the world beautiful things, like the Grand View Garden (built for the visit of the Imperial Concubine, Bao-yu's older sister Yuan-cun); the artworks, artifacts, and poems described in such sensuous and loving detail; and even the memories of the happy, "golden days." Time and again, the novel shows both the real effects of illusion and the illusory aspects of the real.

The methods of the Liberal Arts are really the only approaches that have any chance of making some sense of the tangle of complex, interrelated, and ambiguous problems that arise when trying to understand *The Dream of the Red Chamber*. Not only must each small piece of evidence be evaluated on its own terms and in light of other small pieces, but also in relation to some larger whole—which can only be constructed out of all the separate pieces. But that whole must be provisional and temporary and

[184] Hawkes 51.

[185] Saussy 73.

subject to revision while each new piece of evidence is taken into consideration. The scholar is thus required to hold multiple views of the work in mind at the same time, juggling an immense number of variables to see how they might best hang together. Trying to tease apart the interactions of the author, his culture (both his present and his remembered past), his early readers, and then those of editors and publishers, later readers, adaptors, revisers, scholars, and artists may in the end prove impossible, but it is endlessly fascinating.

That the approaches of the Liberal Arts, which began in Greece and Rome and evolved for most of their history only in the West, can usefully be applied to a work from a completely distinct cultural tradition is a good indicator that these methods are built upon deep, human truths. My education about one of the great masterpieces of Chinese culture was woefully inadequate, but the Liberal Arts had taught me how to learn, so I was able to find my bearings in an unfamiliar field, in part because I understood that a scholarly tradition is not just a collection of facts or opinions from which to extract information but is instead a long-running conversation. Any given argument is almost always to some degree a reaction to something that has been written by a previous scholar. Even the most seemingly authoritative research has been shaped by what has come before, which makes understanding the tradition's evolution over time an essential aspect of scholarship. Although I did not have the linguistic skills to read for myself much of the most important scholarship on the novel, I knew that I must try to determine the place of each book and article I read in the larger conversation. By the end, I understood the novel and its scholarly tradition well enough not only to help guide Wenzhuo through the writing and defense of her truly superb Honors thesis, but also to co-author with her an article on *The Dream of the Red Chamber*.

In that research, Wenzhuo and I were able to demonstrate that "Lexomic" computer-assisted methods of pattern-recognition and statistical analysis (which I will discuss in detail in the next chapter of this book) could shed light on the problems of authorship in the novel, thus, we hope, contributing a brick or two to the tower of knowledge built by previous scholars. A method we call "Rolling Window Analysis" allows us to produce a graphical representation of the frequency of individual words (or characters or letters) in a text, letting us see where there are concentrations or absences and thus, perhaps, identify patterns that are not readily apparent to the unaided eye. In previous research on Western languages and cultural traditions, these patterns of word distribution have helped to identify changes in authorship, source-text, and editor. It took some effort to adapt the software and methods for Chinese-language texts, but eventually we were able to produce graphs showing the distribution of "function words" like conjunctions and prepositions in *The Dream of the Red Chamber*.

The plot in Figure 1 of the frequency of the character *ér* (儿) in a rolling window of 5,000 characters is representative of our results: the frequencies of many function words in the final forty chapters differ substantially from those in the initial eighty. Even more interesting were the patterns we identified inside these large sections of the novel. For example, the frequencies of multiple function words are very different in Chapters 10, 11, and 13 than in their neighboring chapters, a finding that is consistent with the idea that Cao had revised these chapters after he changed the cause of Qin-shi's death to an illness from a suicide.[186] Of potentially even greater interest were Chapters 97, 98, and 105 in which the frequencies of function words were unlike those in the other final forty chapters but very much like those in the first eighty. If we are correct in our interpretation, this is evidence that the words of Cao survive in these chapters.

[186] Our Lexomic analysis ends up being almost completely consistent with the arguments of Wu.

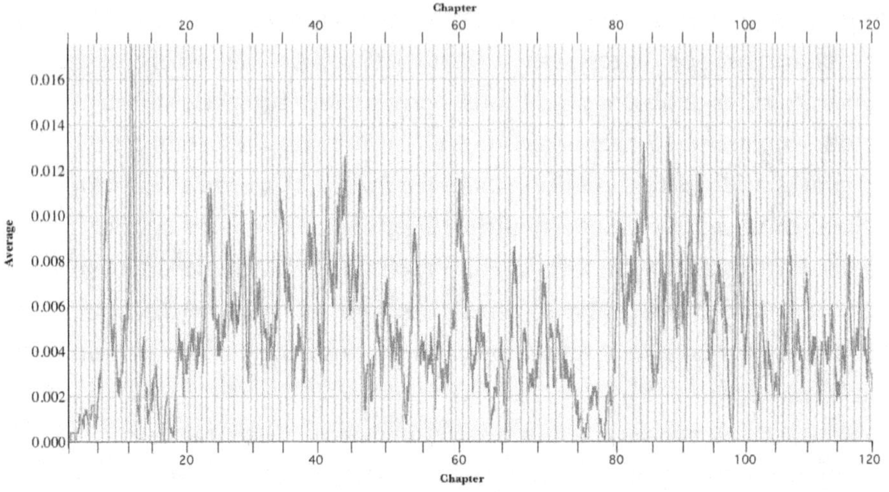

Chapter 105 is the moment that the Emperor's minions descend upon the Jia family mansion and confiscate nearly all of their goods. Readers have long praised the genuinely frightening tone of the chapter and, most of all, its realism. The depiction of the forced confiscation is so detailed and (based on what we know from other sources) accurate, that it seems as if the author of Chapter 105 must have suffered through such a trauma. Indeed, when Cao Xueqin was thirteen years old, his family's mansion and possessions in Nanking were seized by agents of the Emperor, and the Caos were forced to relocate to far more modest circumstances in Beijing (where they were under the watchful eye of the Imperial bureaucracy). Chapter 105, however, is not among those attributed to Cao, and Gao E never experienced a confiscation. The inference that Chapter 105 somehow preserves Cao's writing is not particularly shocking, as it is shared by many scholars of the novel. What is quite remarkable, however, is that our relatively simple computer-assisted techniques, which merely analyze the distribution of vocabulary, produce evidence that supports this deduction that is based on biographical information and aesthetic evaluation.

Attributing Chapters 97-98 to Cao is much more controversial than suggesting that he wrote Chapter 105. These two chapters are at the heart of one of the greatest controversies in the history of *The Dream of the*

Red Chamber: which of his two beloved cousins Bao-yu marries. In the published version of the novel, it is Bao-chai, whose high intelligence and refinement, coupled with an unfailing sense of duty, respect, and obedience, are thought to make her the ideal Confucian wife. However, in the first eighty chapters of the novel, Cao seems to be somewhat critical of such traditional social models—far more so than Gao, who seems to be a strong supporter of, among other things, the Emperor, the system of examinations, and traditional roles for women. For these reasons, among others, many readers have concluded that Cao originally intended to marry Bao-yu to the sensitive, free-thinking, and emotional Dai-yu, but that Gao changed the ending of the novel to be more socially conservative. Although this is perhaps wishful thinking on the part of the many readers who simply love Dai-yu and want to see her rewarded with the marriage she desired, the authorship question does leave open the possibility that Cao could have chosen the more romantic pairing over the more plausible one. But if the vocabulary distribution in Chapters 97-98 is, like that of Chapter 105, closer to Cao's than to Gao's, then we might conclude that the Bao-yu and Bao-chai pairing is what the author intended.

In this section of the book, Dai-yu, after learning of the decision of the family matriarchs to marry Bao-yu to Bao-chai, burns all of her poems and stops struggling against her illness. Bao-yu, who is tricked into believing that he will be marrying Dai-yu, suddenly falls sick when he realizes that his bride is Bao-chai, and then Dai-yu succumbs to her illness. If, as our evidence seems to indicate, the second half of Chapter 97 and Chapter 98 preserve some of Cao's original text, then the published version of the novel has at least gotten the pairing right. However, the misdirection that makes Bao-yu think he is marrying the other cousin and his surprise when he lifts his bride's veil and sees Bao-chai instead of Dai-yu is very clumsily done, showing little of the subtlety Cao displays in the first eighty chapters. On the other hand, Dai-yu's burning of her poems and her death are among the most beautiful and poignant scenes in the entire massive novel. Complicated, messy problems are that way for a reason, so although the new evidence is certainly welcome, it cannot definitively resolve the issues by itself.

Indeed, evidence by itself is never sufficient to resolve controversies: new evidence about *The Dream of the Red Chamber* needs to be weighed and considered in the context of all the other evidence relating to a given problem. For both parts of that process we need the kinds of thinking developed by the Liberal Arts. And as is also the case with *Beowulf*, the study of the combination of *The Dream of the Red Chamber* and the scholarship that has grown around it is both rewarding in and of itself and superb training for other sophisticated intellectual work.

These case studies in these past two chapters show how the disciplines of the Liberal Arts build new knowledge by successive approximation. Rarely does everything come together in a grand, beautiful, and unquestionably obvious synthesis. Instead, we sometimes inch steadily closer to understanding, sometimes take two steps forward and then one step back, and sometimes are forced to demolish and then rebuild whole edifices of learning. But eventually we make progress by building on the knowledge accumulated by our many predecessors, standing upon the shoulders of giants. Two hundred years ago, we understood very little about either *Beowulf* or *The Dream of the Red Chamber*. Now, thanks to the patient work of scholars—the missteps and the triumphs—we understand a bit more. If we are diligent in preserving and transmitting the traditions so that others may build upon them, our cultural heirs will possess even more knowledge—which they will access by their own study of the Liberal Arts.

Chapter 9

Tentative Steps on the Path to Becoming a Science: Lexomic Methods

For centuries the Liberal Arts, adapted to various cultural contexts, were not just the heart of the educational system but almost all of its body. Only in the middle of the twentieth century, as World War II progressed, did it become obvious even to the most slow-moving and oblivious leaders that a country's success—and even its very survival—would depend upon its technology. Soon after the war, when the Soviet Union surprised the West by successfully launching Sputnik, the first artificial satellite, a panic over a perceived lack of scientific education in America and a fear of falling behind adversaries led to a large shift in the allocation of resources.[187] Not only did new money for technological research and education pour into the rapidly expanding universities, but a substantial portion of the time, money, and energy that had previously been spent on the Liberal Arts was moved into scientific and engineering education. In the three quarters of a century since, Science, Technology, Engineering, and Mathematics (STEM is the endlessly repeated acronym)[188] have consistently been prioritized over the Liberal Arts.

But a society's decision to value science, technology, engineering, and mathematics does not *have* to lead to a concomitant loss of the Liberal

[187] Ironically, the launch of Sputnik proved very little about Soviet science and engineering in general, since most of the initial development of the Soviet space program was done by captured German scientists, and the Soviets got an additional leg up in their research through the espionage carried out by ideological sympathizers in the West.

[188] Even more annoying than the constant repetition of STEM (usually by people who do zero science, technology, engineering, or mathematics) is the new-and-improved STEAM acronym which adds "Arts." Adding the arts to just about anything is in itself good, but essentially STEAM says "Anything, absolutely anything, other than those icky Humanities." Un-ironic use of the STEAM acronym should therefore inspire skepticism if not contempt.

Arts. First of all, elimination of the disciplines of the Trivium is simply impossible, since every scientific field requires a foundation of education in grammar, logic, and rhetoric as well as in mathematics and basic science. Perhaps more importantly, the skills developed in the Liberal Arts disciplines lead to improvements in science itself, as the ability to solve complex and ill-defined problems meshes perfectly with training in science-specific methods. The two sides of the "two cultures"[189] complement each other, both as intellectual foundations (I think of switching between the sciences and the Liberal Arts as "mental cross-training") and in practical application.

For example, my students, colleagues, and I are currently working on a project to use computer-assisted statistical analysis to identify patterns in literary texts. This approach, which we call "Lexomics," has been remarkably successful, far more so than could have been predicted from the resources devoted to it.[190] Using software created by our team of programmers and literary researchers, we have made significant discoveries about texts in Old English, Old Norse, Latin, Middle English, and Modern English, and (as I mentioned in the previous chapter) we currently have very exciting preliminary results from our analysis of classical Chinese literature. The Lexomics software allows literary researchers to apply methods of "hierarchical agglomerative clustering" and "rolling window analysis"[191] to the distribution of words, spellings, or letters in texts, identifying patterns that are usually too subtle or distributed to be noticed by the unaided mind. To our surprise, we have been able to use the software to identify places in texts where authors are influenced by an external source, and we can also distinguish between the work of two different writers even when they were both contributing to the same work (i.e., we can tell where one author stopped writing and another took over). This research is a fully joint project between English and computer science,

---

[189] To use C. P. Snow's formulation in *The Two Cultures and the Scientific Revolution* (Oxford: Oxford University Press, 1959).

190 For more information, see http://lexomics.wheatoncollege.edu. To use the Lexos software we have developed, go to http://lexos.wheatoncollege.edu.

[191] Discussed below. The former is a standard term from statistics and data science; the latter is our own coinage.

as neither could have developed the software and the methods for using it without the other.

The success of Lexomics is thus a perfect example of the ways that the Liberal Arts can improve science-centric research (and vice versa), especially since the collaboration was unplanned. My colleague in computer science, Professor Mark LeBlanc, and I were simply trying to create some assignments that would help teach beginning computer science students to learn how to manipulate text files—they had to create programs that would count the number of words in the text, or put the words in alphabetical order, or delete all words beginning with the letter <k>, or tabulate all words ending in *-ing*. It was only by luck that we discovered that computer-assisted methods could be used to identify those segments of a text that had an author or source different from the main body of the text. That happy accident would never have occurred, and we would never have recognized the significance of the patterns we found, if I had not already possessed a lot of traditional knowledge about the texts we were investigating. Even the most powerful software and the most sophisticated statistical analysis could not replace the kinds of learning acquired through study of the Liberal Arts.

Mark wanted me to come up with an assignment that would let the students test the power of what is called "hierarchical agglomerative cluster analysis," in which the distribution of the vocabulary (i.e., the relative frequencies of every single word in a text) can be used to calculate which segments of a text are most similar and most different. When Mark explained the technique, I immediately thought of a minor puzzle in Anglo-Saxon studies. There is a short poem called *Azarias* in the manuscript known as the Exeter Book[192] that is similar to, but not precisely the same as, a section of a long poem, *Daniel*, which is found in the Junius manuscript.[193] I thought it might be a useful exercise to cut *Daniel* into segments and see if, using hierarchical clustering, students could match *Azarias* to the correct section of the much-longer poem.

---

[192] Shelfmark: MS Exeter, Cathedral Library, Dean and Chapter 3501.

[193] Shelfmark: Oxford, Bodleian Library, Junius 11.

It turned out that in order to compare the two texts, we had to do a great deal of pre-processing of the electronic files (which, fortunately, had been created by the University of Toronto *Dictionary of Old English*, so we did not have to type in the poems by hand). The initial challenges were not related to the software or the technological methods, but to very old-fashioned problems having to do with subjects within traditional Liberal Arts disciplines: writing systems, scripts, and manuscripts (similar to the information about fonts that we discussed in previous chapters).

As might be expected, the Roman alphabet is a very good fit for Latin, since it was developed to write that language. But every language uses its own inventory of sounds, and a writing system devised for one language may not include symbols to indicate all the sounds of a different language. Unfortunately for the Anglo-Saxons adopting the Roman alphabet, their language included sounds and sound-combinations that were not found in Latin. The Roman alphabet, therefore, needed some modifications. Some of those innovations are still familiar to us today: because the sound /h/ is not pronounced by itself after consonants in English, the letter <h> can be combined with consonants to represent entirely different sounds.[194] These *digraphs* include the familiar two-letter combinations that we all had to memorize when learning to read: <ch>, <ph>, <sh>, <th>. Both Modern English and Latin use <th> for both the sound at the beginning of the word *thin* and the slightly different sound in the middle of the word *feather*,[195] but Anglo-Saxon had words like *nathwylc* in which both the <t> and the <h> had to be pronounced as two separate sounds (nat-hwylc). The digraph <th>, therefore, would be

[194] When referring to a sound, the convention is to put the letter or letters representing the sound between slashes: /m/, therefore, indicates the sound at the beginning of the word *mumble*. When referring to a word in general, rather than any specific word in a text, we used italics (as in the previous sentence). When we are discussing the writing sign, or grapheme, itself, we put it within pointed brackets. For example, "Prof. Drout's handwritten <g> is perhaps the ugliest thing you have ever seen, but it nevertheless represents the /g/ sound at the beginning of the word *goblin*."

[195] The distinction between these two sounds, in that for the first you do not buzz your vocal chords the way you do when saying the second, is the difference between a sound being an *unvoiced* or a *voiced* consonant.

misleading, and so Anglo-Saxon scribes came up with alternative solutions. Some, borrowing from Irish orthography, put a cross through the ascender in the letter <d>, creating the letter <ð>, which is called *eth*. Others borrowed a Germanic runic letter <þ> called *thorn* from continental Europe. The two letters very soon became interchangeable, but, we learned, they appear in different ratios in different texts.

The existence of two different letters that represent the same sound created problems for our computer-assisted analysis, as the software in which we wanted to implement hierarchical agglomerative clustering did not know that <ð> and <þ> are the "same" letter. We therefore had to write programs to "scrub" our texts, replacing all <ð> with <þ> so that *ðis* would not be counted separately from *þis* (because both spellings indicate the same word, which means "this"). This *consolidation* of letter-forms allows us to compare the vocabulary distribution in text-segments by counting up all the different *words* used, not all the different alternate *spellings* of those words.

We also had to deal with other variations of spelling and the inconsistent use of abbreviation. The word in Anglo-Saxon that means "and" can be written as *ond* or *and*, or it can also be abbreviated with a symbol that looks like the number seven called Tironian note, *7*, which has the same meaning as our ampersand, &. Unfortunately, consolidation did not help us here, because although we wanted to make all forms of *and* have the same spelling, we could not just use search-and-replace, because that would also end up changing the <and> or <ond> spelling in words like *hand* or *sand*. We therefore wrote another program to *lemmatize* the three words, making them all take the same form (*ond* was most convenient, but we could have used any one of the three forms). Lemmatization only applies to whole words rather than to letters or groups of letters the way consolidation does. Fortunately, for languages that use the Roman alphabet, "word" is easy to define: it is a letter or group of letters with a blank space on either side.[196]

[196] That the typographic representation of words in Chinese is fundamentally different from the representation of words in Western languages is one of the largest problems we have faced in adapting Lexomic methods to Chinese. White space is not used in Chinese

Even if none of the Lexomic experiments had borne fruit, this work would still have been fundamentally valuable because it forced us to think very carefully about the types of differences among words, and how these distinctions sometimes get missed when using computer-assisted methods. There are differences between variations in letter-forms, variations in spelling, and variations in abbreviation, and each of these sets of differences needs to be handled in specific ways depending on what we are trying to do with the text. Even if we had never gone on to make any Lexomic discoveries, we still gained a much deeper understanding of textual and editorial conventions.

Once we had produced electronic versions of *Daniel* and *Azarias* from which all scribal variation (spelling, orthography, abbreviation) had been removed, we could cut these texts into segments and compare the vocabularies. We divided *Daniel* into ten segments of approximately 450-words, kept *Azarias* as a single segment of 1,064 words, and used hierarchical clustering to see which of these segments were most similar to each other.

Hierarchical clustering works by first compiling a list of every word in the entire collection of segments and then tabulating the number of each of those words in each segment (there will be some words on the main list that may not occur in every segment). We then calculate the relative frequency of each word in each list by dividing the number of times the word appears by the total number of words, so that for each segment we have a list of words and frequencies (see Table 1).

---

to separate words within a sentence, and a given "word" can be one, two, or more characters. Chinese thus requires fundamentally different text-processing strategies.

Rank/ Segement		Average	Dan1	Dan2	Dan3	Dan4	Dan5	Az
1	and	0.0324	0.0167	0.02	0.06	0.03	0.014	0.0574
2	þa	0.0271	0.0389	0.0256	0.0289	0.0178	0.0343	0.0153
3	þæt	0.0211	0.0222	0.0189	0.0167	0.0267	0.0254	0.0163
4	on	0.0179	0.0156	0.0222	0.0244	0.0233	0.0114	0.0086
5	him	0.0156	0.0256	0.0178	0.0122	0.0167	0.014	0.0057
6	to	0.0142	0.0156	0.02	0.0122	0.01	0.0114	0.0163
7	þe	0.0136	0.0122	0.0211	0.0111	0.0144	0.0127	0.0096
8	þam	0.013	0.0144	0.02	0.0111	0.0133	0.0089	0.0096
9	in	0.0126	0.0089	0.0111	0.0089	0.0067	0.028	0.0124
10	he	0.0122	0.0122	0.01	0.0044	0.0211	0.0203	0.0038
11	se	0.011	0.0067	0.01	0.0189	0.0144	0.0064	0.0096
12	wæs	0.01	0.0144	0.0122	0.0089	0.0089	0.0102	0.0048
13	hic	0.0098	0.0133	0.0222	0.0133	0.0033	0.0051	0
14	ne	0.009	0.0122	0.0167	0.0044	0.0044	0.0102	0.0057
15	swa	0.0088	0.0078	0.01	0.0056	0.0122	0.0089	0.0086

Table 1

We then move through the list, comparing the frequencies of each word in each segment to calculate what is called a *distance metric*. For example, if *and* makes up 4% of the words in Segment A, 2% of the words in Segment B, and 1% of the words in Segment C, there is a 2% difference between A and B, a 3% difference between A and C, and a 1% difference between B and C. Segments B and C are therefore more similar, with Segment A being an outlier. We represent this relationship in a branching diagram called a *dendrogram* (see Figure 1). The vertical distance to the branching point is based on the size of the distance, so in this case B and C are separated by 1% and then the two of them averaged together (1.5%) are 2.5% different from A. We repeat this calculation for every single word in the entire text, a process which would be incredibly tedious to do by hand but which a computer can do in milliseconds.

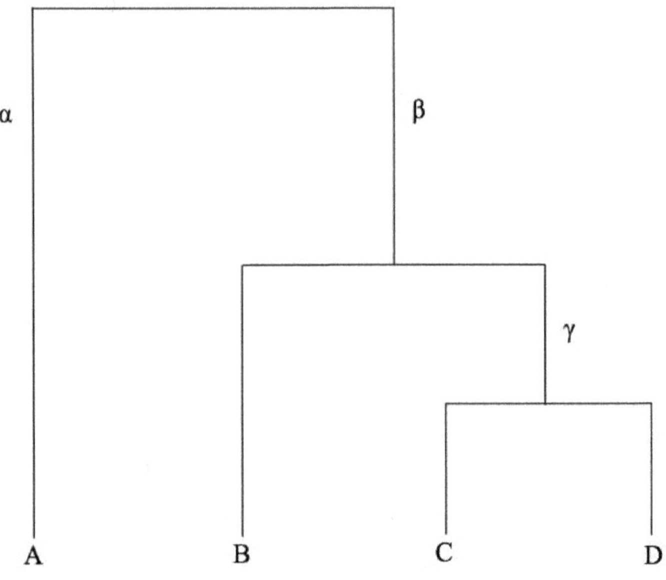

Figure 1: Sample Dendrogram

Just for fun, I refused to tell my research partners which segment of *Daniel* was parallel to *Azarias*—I wanted to see if they could figure it out from the cluster analysis alone, and to my pleasant surprise, they could! The resulting dendrogram (Figure 2) perfectly matched *Azarias* to the right part of *Daniel*. As you can see from the excerpts below, *Azarias* and the parallel lines of *Daniel* are not exactly the same, so it was exciting to see that hierarchical clustering could nevertheless match the correct segments to each other. We wondered if we might be able to detect more obscure relationships in and among other texts.

Dendrogram of ten chunks of *Daniel* and *Azarias*

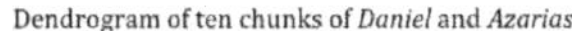

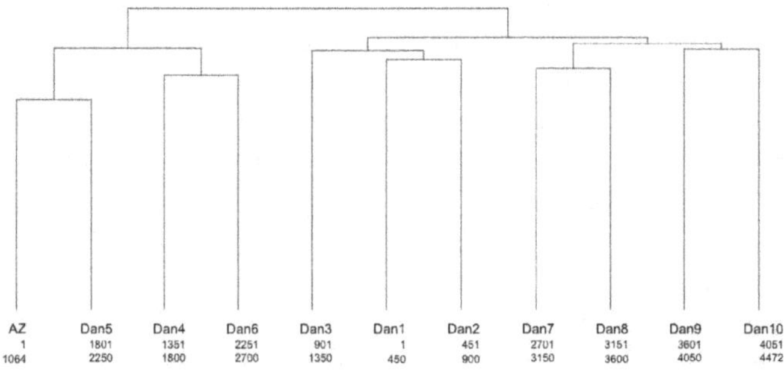

Figure 3. Dendrogram showing the results of a cluster analysis using nine 450-word chunks of *Daniel* and one (ending) chunk of 422 words, and the entire 1064-word poem *Azarias* (AZ). The consecutive, non-overlapping 450-word chunks of *Daniel* are labeled from 1 to 10 where the initial chunk is labeled Dan1. The exact word boundaries of each chunk are labeled under each leaf on the dendrogram; for example the fourth chunk of *Daniel* (Dan4) comprises the 450 words of *Daniel* from word 1351 to word 1800, inclusive.

Figure 2: Daniel in 450-word segments and Azarias (all)

Daniel, lines 279-295a	*Azarias*, lines 1-16a
ða Azarias ingeþancum hleoðrade halig þurh hatne lig, dreag dæda georn, drihten herede, wer womma leas, and þa word acwæð: "Metod alwihta, hwæt! þu eart mihtum swið niðas to nergenne. Is þin nama mære, wlitig and wuldorfæst ofer werðeode. Siendon þine domas in daga gehwam soðe and geswiðde and gesigefæste, swa þu eac sylfa eart. Syndon þine willan on woruldspedum rihte and gerume, rodora waldend. Geoca user georne nu, gasta scyppend, and þurh hyldo help, halig drihten, nu we þec for þreaum and for ðeonydum and for eaðmedum arna biddað, lige belegde.	Him þa Azarias ingeþoncum hleoþrede halig þurh hatne lig, dreag dædum georn, dryhten herede, wis in weorcum, ond þas word acwæð: "Meotud allwihta, þu eart meahtum swið niþas to nerganne. Is þin noma mære, wlitig ond wuldorfæst ofer werþeode. Sindon þine domas on dæda gehwam soðe geswiðde ond gesigefæste, eac þine willan in woruldspedum ryhte mid ræde. Rodera waldend, geoca us georne, gæsta scyppend, ond þurh hyldo help, halig dryhten, nu we þec for þrearfum ond for þreanydum ond for eaðmedum arena biddaþ, lege bilegde.

Parallel Passages of Daniel and Azarias

Then we had a very happy accident. At this stage in the development of the Lexomics software, we did not have the user-friendly, intuitive user interface that we use today. Instead, the programs were controlled from the command line, and various parameters had to be typed in by hand. It was easy to make mistakes, and I made a big one: re-running the cluster analysis with 900-word segments, I forgot to include *Azarias*! Yet the result, as you can see from Figure 3, was very similar to the results when *Azarias* was included. That is, the single branch of the dendrogram that contained the parallel lines was separate from all the rest of the poem. But without *Azarias* being in the analysis, there was no reason—as far as we knew—for those particular lines of *Daniel* to be in any way different from the rest of the poem. Now, instead of a simple exercise for Professor LeBlanc's "Computing for Poets" class, we had a research project: why were lines 362-408 of *Daniel* different from the rest of the poem in their vocabulary distribution?

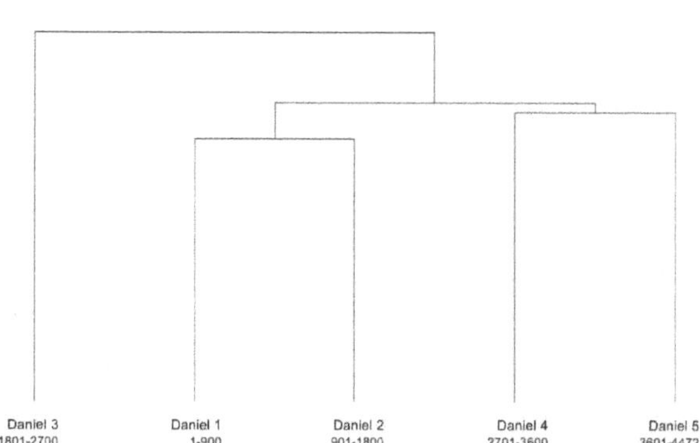

Figure 12. Dendrogram showing the results of cluster analysis using 5 approximately 900-word chunks of *Daniel*.

Figure 3: Dendrogram of 900-word segments of Daniel

Eventually, and thanks to an investigation using traditional Liberal Arts methods, we came to the conclusion that these lines had a different source than the rest of the text. *Daniel*, as the name suggests, is a poetic, Old English re-telling of the Book of Daniel in the Latin Bible. The story of Daniel in the Lion's Den may now be the most well-known story in that book, but in the Middle Ages the tale of the Three Youths in the Fiery Furnace was equally or more famous, and the lines of *Daniel* with a different vocabulary distribution were those that matched this section of the story.

A scholar named Paul Remley had noticed that the order of the events in the Old English *Daniel* is not precisely the same as in the Bible. Instead, the Anglo-Saxon poem follows the slightly different order found in two Latin canticles—hymns or chants, adapting a biblical text, that are used in church services. These particular canticles, the *Oratio Azariae* (*Prayer of Azarias*) and the *Canticum trium puerorum* (*Song of the Three*

Youths), were regularly sung by monks as part of the Divine Office.[197] If the poet who wrote *Daniel* was a monk (as most scholars have assumed), he would have been more familiar with these canticles, which he heard regularly, than he would have been with the text of this part of *Daniel* in the Bible. We inferred that when the poet reached the relevant part of *Daniel*, he perhaps stopped reading the Latin text sentence by sentence and instead relied on his memory of the canticles, and so his style in Old English changed slightly. It was this slight change, we thought, that our Lexomic analysis was detecting.[198]

This was an exciting development, because the differences in style were so subtle that the unaided eye and brain could not detect them, but they were utterly obvious to the software. The same techniques, then, might be useful in detecting similar variations in texts whose sources were not known as well as those of *Daniel* and *Azarias*. And indeed, we were able to identify a similar passage in the poem *Guthlac A*, in which the poet actually says "as books tell us" right before the passage we thought was being quoted.[199]

Then we had another happy accident. We were trying to see if our Lexomic methods could determine which Old English poems were written by Cynewulf. One of the only Anglo-Saxon poets whose name has survived, Cynewulf wrote at least four poems, and we know this because he worked his name, in runes, into the poem, in effect "signing" them. There are also a number of additional poems that seem stylistically similar to the ones that include the runic signatures. For about 100 years, scholars have been arguing about which of these are actually by Cynewulf and which are not, but no one can agree as to how to weigh the different pieces of evidence.

---

[197] Paul G. Remley, "*Daniel*, the Three Youths Fragment and the Transmission of Old English Verse," *Anglo-Saxon England* 31 (2002): 81–140.

[198] Michael D.C. Drout, Michael J. Kahn, Mark D. LeBlanc, and Christina Nelson, "Of Dendrogrammatology: Lexomic Methods for Analyzing Relationships among Old English poems," *Journal of English and Germanic Philology* 110.3 (2011): 301-336.

[199] Sarah Downey, Michael D. C. Drout, Michael J. Kahn and Mark D. LeBlanc, "'Books Tell Us': Lexomic and Traditional Evidence for the Sources of *Guthlac A*," *Modern Philology* 110 (2012): 1–29.

We decided that we would jump into this critical briar patch and see if Lexomic techniques could settle the question once and for all. We cut all the possible poems into segments and then did a cluster analysis, producing one huge dendrogram to try to see which parts were most similar in vocabulary. By this time, our software was more sophisticated. The student programmers had set things up so that it was possible to *consolidate* <þ> and <ð> with the click of a single button, and that's what we had been doing in a series of investigations, when I forgot to click that button. Suddenly dendrograms were appearing on the screen that were differently shaped than those we had created only a few hours before.

At the beginning of the summer I had written Isaac Asimov's famous adage on the whiteboard in the Lexomics Lab: "The most exciting thing to hear in scientific research is not 'Eureka!' but 'That's odd.'" This was certainly a "that's odd" moment, but as we were under some time pressure, once I figured out what had happened, I was tempted to ignore the weird result, but I remembered the Asimov quote, and we decided that figuring out the cause of these anomalous dendrograms was important. Eventually my student Elie Chauvet noticed that in the segments whose locations in the dendrogram had changed, there was a much higher frequency of <ð> rather than <þ> than elsewhere in the texts. Consolidating, then, changed these segments more substantially than others. We thus had a simple explanation for the experimental results themselves, but that only raised a new question: Why on earth would a poet or scribe prefer <ð> to <þ> in some places but not others? We therefore started counting *thorns* and *eths*, trying to see where there might be clusters of one or the other.

It turned out, however, that finding clusters of features is not as straightforward as it might seem. The size and boundaries of a segment can substantially affect whether or not we detect a cluster of features in it. Make a segment too large, and you obscure small clusters or gaps without being able to see them. Place a boundary in one place, and you split a cluster in half. Put it in another, and you swallow up two smaller clusters in one segment. We produced hundreds of different segmentations, but none of them seemed definitive, and we were well aware of how easy it would be to produce artifacts. Another adage I had written on the whiteboard was Richard Feynman's "The most important thing is not to fool yourself, and you are the easiest one to fool." After having had Asimov's quote proven true, it seemed unwise to ignore Feynman's.

By this point in the book, it should be utterly clear that I think the approaches of the Liberal Arts are immensely powerful and valuable, but that does not mean that they are the only approaches that work. In this particular case, it was habits of thought developed by working with mathematicians that provided the insight that led to our big break.

In trying to identify the locations in texts that had the highest or lowest frequencies of *eth*, we kept dividing the texts into smaller and smaller segments. I joked to my students that we might as well go all the way and use one-word segments, and we tried to, but the resulting diagram was, as you might expect, nearly impossible to read. Then I realized that what we needed was the *continuous* frequency of *eth* rather than *discrete* counts of *eth* (hanging out with mathematicians makes you start to think this way).

To facilitate this, Elie wrote a program that calculated the *continuous rolling average* of <ð> throughout the text. The program allows us to select a "window" of a certain number of words or letters (for this explanation, let us choose 100 words) and then count every <ð> in that *window*—so, from the first word to the hundredth. Dividing this number (p) by the total number of words in the window (w) gives us a data-point in the form of (1, p/w). Plot this point, move the window one word to the right (so, from word 2 to word 101), and repeat the process. Keep repeating until the leading edge of the window reaches the end of the text.[200]

The plots that resulted from rolling window analysis were obviously not random fibrillation. Instead, there were sometimes very abrupt changes in the frequencies of the graphemes that then persisted for some distance. In some poems we found what we started calling *w-* or *m-*

[200] At first we produced plots of both <ð> and <þ> and compared them to each other, but then we realized that because the two graphemes are interchangeable (i.e., if you are using a *thorn*, then you are not using an *eth*, and vice versa), the ratio of one to the other made it easier to read the resulting graphs.

formations, in which the frequency of a feature which to that point in the text had varied only slightly within a visibly distinct range around a central value abruptly shifted to a different median, remained there for some distance, and then returned to the original median frequency (see Figure 4).

Unfortunately, we had no idea what this might mean.

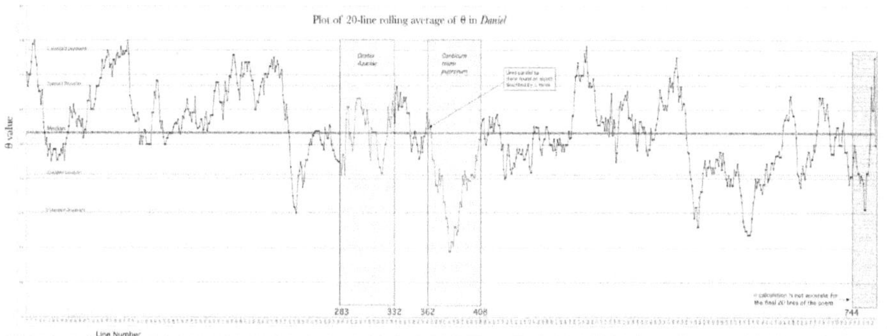

Figure 4. Rolling Window Plot

In summer 2013, our research group went to the International Society of Anglo-Saxonists' biennial conference in Dublin, where we ran a workshop on Lexomics for scholars who were interested in doing "digital humanities" research on Old English texts. While my students (undergraduates all) were teaching some of the world's leading scholars of Anglo-Saxon how to perform hierarchical cluster analysis, I was sneaking surreptitious glimpses at rolling window plots and trying to figure out what they possibly could mean.

And then came the third happy accident. Professor John Hines of Cardiff University gave a presentation on a newly discovered metal object on which there was a runic inscription in Old English. The "Honington Clip," which looks like a pair of tweezers, may have been used to snuff out candles. I had been listening to Professor Hines' presentation with general but not intense interest and staring at my <þ> /<ð> plots when I heard him say "the runic inscription matches lines 362-64 of the Old English poem *Daniel*," and inadvertently blurted out, to my embarrassment "Holy [fewmets]!" because I had in front of me a rolling window plot of the ratio of *thorn* to *eth* in *Daniel* in which there was a dramatic and abrupt change in frequency precisely at line 362.[201]

What followed was an extremely intense period of research into the history of writing systems in the British Isles, the distribution of *thorn* and *eth* throughout the entire Old English poetic corpus, and medieval traditions relating to the Book of Daniel, the Prayer of Azarias, the Song of the Three Youths, and the image of an angel protecting the three youths from the fire of Nebuchadnezzar's fiery furnace. Elie and I knew we potentially had discovered something important, so we had to be absolutely certain that we were not fooling ourselves.

We were eventually able to demonstrate that if there are interchangeable graphemes in a writing system (such as *thorn* and *eth* in Old English, or open- and closed-*a* in the handwriting of many contemporary Americans), each scribe will reproduce an individualized distribution of the forms. For example, the A-scribe of *Beowulf* preferred *thorn* instead of *eth* for the beginnings and middles of words, reserving *eth* for the last letter. In contrast, the B-scribe used *eth* both medially and terminally, which makes *eth* much more common in lines 1939-3182 than it is in the first two-thirds of the poem. We also discovered that the distribution of alternative letter-forms in the text from which a scribe was copying influences the scribe's performance. For example, if a *thorn*-favoring scribe copied an *eth*-heavy text, the resulting copy will have more *eths* than the same scribe would produce if copying a more evenly distributed text. These dynamics of scribal performance can allow us to use a rolling window plot to determine when a scribe switched from one exemplar to another, or from using an exemplar to composing from scratch.

By combining the results of our rolling window analysis of <þ> and <ð> with the runes on the Honington Clip, our previous cluster analysis of *Daniel* and *Azarias,* art-historical work on the popularity of images of the three youths in the fiery furnace being protected by an angel, and knowledge of the liturgy of the Anglo-Saxon church, we were able to

---

[201] John Hines, "The Benedicite Canticle in Old English Verse: An Early Runic Witness from Southern Lincolnshire," *Anglia* 133 (2015): 257–277.

reconstruct lost cultural history and finally understand, in detail, why the texts of *Daniel*, *Azarias*, and the Honington Clip have the forms that they do.

The cluster analysis of *Daniel* strongly suggested that two parts of the text (the Prayer of Azarias and the Song of the Three Youths) had a somewhat different composition history than the rest of the poem. Remley had observed that the events in these two sections do not precisely follow the order of the biblical text but instead match up with two Latin canticles. We therefore had hypothesized that, although the poet was in general following the Latin prose of the Bible closely, when he got to these two places, he relied more on his memory (since the canticles were so familiar, being sung so frequently), and that this changed slightly the distribution of vocabulary that he used. This was a strong theory: simple, elegant, and now that we have additional information, most likely wrong.

The rolling window analysis gave us additional information, and the traditional Liberal Arts discipline of logic helped us work through its implications for our understanding of the composition- and transmission-history of the poem. First, although the sections of both the Prayer of Azarias and the Song of the Three Youths differ in overall vocabulary distribution from the rest of the poem, it is only the Song of the Three Youths that has a strikingly different frequency of <ð>. Since *thorn* and *eth* are only used in Old English writing and do not appear in Latin texts, differences in their frequencies indicate the influence of a written Old English text, not a different Latin text. It was not yet possible to determine whether that influence was on the Song of the Three Youths lines and not the rest of the poem, or was on all of the poem except the Song of the Three Youths lines, but either way, we were forced to conclude that there was a written Old English text involved. *Daniel* is usually thought to be one of the very oldest Old English poems, so evidence for a written Old English source pre-dating it was a big surprise and has the potential to overturn the received view of Anglo-Saxon literary history.

That the runes on the Honington Clip are precisely the first lines in which we see variation in the frequency of *thorn* and *eth* implies (though it does not prove) that behind the Song lines there was a written Old

English source: a short poem **The Song of the Three Youths in the Fiery Furnace*.[202] Further support for this hypothesis comes from the actual content of the lines:

> Ðe gebletsige, bylywit fæder
> Woruldcræfta wlite and weorce gehwilc!
> Heofenas and englas.
>
> [Merciful father, let the beauty of the world's creations
> and every work bless you! Heaven and angels.]

This is fairly generic praise of God for creating the world and does not seem particularly connected to the hypothesized function of the Honington Clip as a candle-extinguisher. However, if these were the opening lines of a poem about how God protected Shadrach, Meshach, and Abednego from the flames of Nebuchadnezzar's furnace, then they invoke a highly appropriate inscription for a device used to put out candle flames by pinching the wicks.

From literary scholarship we know that Christians in the early medieval period were particularly interested in the Three Youths episode because it was seen as a rare prefiguration of Judgment Day events in an Old Testament book. Just as God had sent an angel to save the youths from the fire, so too was Jesus sent to save mankind from the fires of Hell on Judgment Day. The *Benedicte* canticle was derived from the biblical text to thank God for this miracle and praise him in anticipation of his saving the faithful from eternal fire. From art history, we know that images of the angel protecting the three youths were very popular in stone sculpture on the continent at the approximate time (in the eighth century) that the **Three Youths* poem would have needed to be written in order to be incorporated into *Daniel*. Singling out this particular episode from the

---

[202] The asterisk in front of the title is a convention used to indicate that this poem does not actually survive but that its existence has been inferred by scholars based on various pieces of evidence.

(long) Book of Daniel for poetic adaptation, therefore, seems consistent with what we know of religious culture at the time.

We concluded that sometime in the early Anglo-Saxon period a poet translated the Latin *Benedicte* canticle into an Old English poem, the **Song of the Three Youths*. This now-lost text then became the core of the long biblical "paraphrase" poem *Daniel*. Furthermore, since we know that the vocabulary of both the Prayer of Azarias and the Song of the Three Youths segments differs from the rest of *Daniel*, it seems likely that the existence of the Old English **Song of the Three Youths* poem inspired a later poet to similarly translate the *Oratio Azariae* canticle into an Old English poem. Then some poet (perhaps the same one) decided that if translations of the *Prayer of Azarias* and the *Song of the Three Youths* were good, a poetic translation of the entire book of *Daniel* was even better and set to work producing the 764-line poem that survives in the Junius Manuscript.

That we can deduce the existence of a lost Old English **Song of the Three Youths* from variations in vocabulary distribution and changes in the frequencies of two letters is more than enough to demonstrate the potential of Lexomic methods. But further application of the techniques uncovered a completely unexpected pattern in other Anglo-Saxon poems. *Daniel*, it turns out, is not the only poem that retains subtle signs of an Old English poetic antecedent. The shifting frequencies of *thorn* and *eth* in the famous and much-loved *Dream of the Rood* are consistent with there having been a core short poem narrating the crucifixion that was then put into a matrix of a dream-vision in which a narrator hears a jeweled cross speak and tell the story of how a tree in the forest was transformed into the cross on which Jesus was hung. To this combination poem, someone then added a poetic sermon, telling the reader the religious significance of the story. Indeed, not only are the variations in the ratio of *thorn* to *eth* consistent with this interpretation, but so are the different frequencies of three orthographic variants of <s>,[203] which we were able to investigate because a new electronic edition of the poem differentiated between them —usually the three forms of <s> and the two forms of <y> found in

[203] See Michael D.C. Drout and Kevin ElKhoury, "The tripartite composite nature of *The Dream of the Rood*: Evidence from Lexomic analysis," forthcoming.

Anglo-Saxon manuscripts are all printed as just *s* and *y* in published editions because no one ever suspected that orthographic variations could be at all significant.

Similarly, a famous scene in the poem *Guthlac A,* in which demons drag St. Guthlac to the Mouth of Hell and threaten to throw him in, appears to have an Old English source, which we hypothesize was a standalone Old English poem that served as the core of the longer epic.[204] There is also evidence that *Genesis A* (like *Daniel*, a biblical-paraphrase poem in the Junius Manuscript) was built around or swallowed up a short poem on Cain and Abel and a generic Anglo-Saxon battle-poem scene, which was repurposed to dramatize the War of the Nine Kings.[205] The poem *Andreas* seems to have been created by splitting a short poem into pieces and then expanding each of those fragments.[206]

Discovering evidence that many of the long Old English poems have at their cores short Old English poems—usually about the most famous scene in the larger story—changes our view of Anglo-Saxon literary history. For a variety of reasons, primarily relating to the metrical and linguistic features of the poems, most contemporary scholars of Old English think that there are essentially four eras into which the poetry can be located. The very earliest poem (if we believe the Venerable Bede), *Cædmon's Hymn*, dates from the middle of the seventh century; *Beowulf, Genesis A, Daniel*, and *Guthlac A,* are usually dated to the eighth century; Cynewulf's four signed works and some poems that seem similar to them are thought to have been written sometime in the 800s; and we know that the *The Battle of Maldon* and the poems of the *Anglo-Saxon Chronicle* (including *The Battle of Brunanburh*) date from the tenth and early

---

[204] It is even possible that this *Hellmouth poem (or an Old English prose text telling the same story—the methods in this case cannot easily differentiate between poetry and prose) antedates all the Old English prose Lives of St Guthlac. Research is ongoing on this question.

[205] See Michael D.C. Drout and Audrey Dubois, "Lexomic evidence for the incorporation of short Old English poems into *Genesis A*: Cain and Abel and the War of the Nine Kings," forthcoming.

[206] See David Maddock, "The Composite Nature of *Andreas*," *Humanities* 8.2 (2019), https://www.mdpi.com/2076-0787/8/3/130 [accessed 6 December 2022].

eleventh centuries, so we infer that poems stylistically and linguistically similar to them are also come from that period.[207]

But although such a literary history doesn't contradict the evidence, it does not make much intuitive sense. If we accept the consensus view, we are forced to believe that in a couple of decades Anglo-Saxon poetry evolved from 11-lines of somewhat repetitive praise for God creating the world into sophisticated, multi-thousand-line epics. Somehow, the longest, most complex, and most formally beautiful poems the culture ever produced were among the earliest. No wonder early scholars often interpreted Anglo-Saxon poetry as demonstrating "decay" or "decline." But, as Tolkien said of a similarly strained but widely held interpretation of *Beowulf*, "there is something irritatingly odd about all this."[208] However, if we take the Lexomically recovered evidence seriously and accept the idea of there being short, written Old English poems that eventually became the kernels of much longer and more elaborate epics, Anglo-Saxon literary history starts to make a lot more sense.

The Anglo-Saxons first became literate via the teaching of Christian monks, but before their conversion they, like all Germanic peoples, had a well-developed traditional oral poetry. This poetry was metrically regular, and it possessed a rich "word-hoard" of formulas and type-scenes that were appropriate for the subjects of warfare and heroism (for example, there were ways to say "king + name" that could be adapted for any king's name and any metrical or alliterative requirements). We can see traces of this "heroic" poetry preserved in *Beowulf, Widsith, Waldere, Deor* (maybe), and the now-lost Finnsburg Fragment. But because the oral heroic poetry had evolved before the Conversion, it did not include poems

---

[207] *The Battle of Brunanburh* and the *Battle of Maldon* must be tenth-century poems because they had to be written after those battles (926 and 991, respectively). For a discussion of the dates of the poems, see R.D. Fulk, *A History of Old English Meter* (Philadelphia: University of Pennsylvania Press), 1992, 2-3 and 393-418, and R.D. Fulk and Christopher M. Cain, *A History of Old English Literature* (Oxford: Blackwells, 2005), 37-47.

[208] J.R.R. Tolkien, "*Beowulf*: The Monsters and the Critics," in *The Monsters and the Critics and Other Essays*, ed. Christopher Tolkien (London: HarperCollins, 1997), 5-48 at 13.

on Christian subjects, so there were no formulaic phrases or established metaphors for the things that were important in Christian poetry: God, Jesus, the Holy Spirit, Mary, the Crucifixion, Resurrection, the Saints, miracles, and other Christian tropes, rites, and beliefs.

A newly literate Anglo-Saxon who cared for poetry therefore had two options: (1) write down the traditional, non-Christian, oral poetry that he had grown up hearing, either by taking dictation from a source or by writing or composing from memory; or (2) compose entirely new Christian poems. Option 1 presented the problem that the stories might include things offensive to Christians, but it also potentially allowed the literate Christian to do something useful for the secular aristocracy from whom he was descended and among whom he probably lived: record the heroic stories that they enjoyed hearing so that they could hear them again whenever in the presence of a literate person with access to the manuscript rather than having to wait for the appearances of a *scop* (an Anglo-Saxon oral poet). The challenge presented by Option 2 was that there were no traditional tropes, themes, type-scenes, formulaic expressions, or generative formulas for Christian subjects, and so writing poems with Christian content required either repurposing material about pre-Christian topics (i.e., taking formulaic expressions for secular kings and adapting them for the King of Heaven) or inventing new formulaic expressions—not always easy when working in a traditional idiom, and certainly time-consuming and cognitively demanding work.

My hypothesis is that both options were pursued: some poets wrote down the traditional poetry they had grown up hearing, while others tried to compose new Christian poems with the material of the old tradition. The Venerable Bede tells the story of the cowherd Cædmon, who, after fleeing to hide in the stable when it was his turn to sing at Northumbrian karaoke night,[209] was given the miraculous gift of being able

[209] My characterization is anachronistic but not misleading. Bede's story describes Cædmon as running away to the stable when the harp was passed to him, indicating that it was his turn to sing. We surmise that an Anglo-Saxon harp was tuned to an open chord so that, even without musical training, people could support their singing just by strumming across the strings. The practice of passing the harp to seemingly every member of the company suggests that most Anglo-Saxons knew songs they could recite in such

to compose orally poems on Christian subjects in the traditional Germanic form. After the wise Abbess Hild of Whitby[210] recognized his talent and had Cædmon brought into the monastery, other monks would tell the former cowherd Christian stories (which had originally been in Latin) and, after ruminating—like a clean animal chewing its cud—for a while, Cædmon would produce Old English poems about them. Bede tells us that Cædmon composed poems about the stories of Genesis, Exodus, and many other events from scriptural history, as well as the Incarnation, Passion, and Resurrection of Jesus. He also sang about the Last Judgment, the pains of Hell, and the joys of Heaven.[211] Bede's catalog of Cædmon's poetry was the cause of the Junius Manuscript's being, for many years, called the "Cædmon Manuscript" and *Genesis A* the "Cædmonian Genesis."

However, only one poem can definitely be attributed to Cædmon: his eponymous hymn,[212] which is an extremely short, simple poem that seems to be an effort to employ pre-existing formulae from heroic poetry to describe the creation of the world. There is a formula in almost every line of the poem, most of which are used to describe God. The majority of the formulas, including *heofonrices weard* [guardian of the realm of heaven], *ece dryhten* [eternal lord], *frea ælmihty* [almighty lord], look like slightly repurposed traditional formulas for a heroic king or the leader of a troop of

circumstances.

[210] My patron Saint, but my characterization of her as "wise" is entirely evidence-based.

[211] Bede, *A History of the English Church and People*, trans. Leo Shirley Price (New York: Penguin, 1955), 248-51.

[212] Bede wrote in Latin, so he paraphrases *Cædmon's Hymn* from Old English, noting with a hint of chagrin that it is impossible to convey the poetic qualities of the *Hymn* in a language different than the one in which it was composed. In some manuscripts of Bede's *Ecclesiastical History,* the Latin paraphrase has been glossed with an Old English version of Cædmon's first poetic composition. What we do not know is whether the Old English text is a back-translation of the Latin or if the scribe was transcribing the original poem from his memory. To me, the latter seems somewhat more likely, as there are substantial commonalities among each poem, perhaps more than would be expected if they were each unique translations of the Latin. For discussion, see Michael D.C. Drout, "'Variation within Limits': An Evolutionary Approach to the Structure and Dynamics of the Multiform," *Oral Tradition* 26.2 (2011): 447-474.

warriors.[213] *Cædmon's Hymn* shows us the first stages of adapting traditional heroic poetry to Christian topics.

But the process of poetry-writing that Bede describes for Cædmon —learned men translating or paraphrasing Latin text in Old English and the poet, after contemplating what he had been told, producing a poem in Anglo-Saxon that the learned men wrote down from dictation—was hardly an effective process for a 1000-line epic. But it would work for short poems about the most famous and dramatic short episodes in Christian history; "Sunday School's Greatest Hits" is how I characterize them for my students. The stories of the new religion were still fresh and exciting, and new converts to Christianity would not see these episodes as clichés or old chestnuts, so an Anglo-Saxon poet would likely focus on these sturdy highlights, not the esoterica favored by some later medieval writers.

The kernel poems that we have detected via Lexomic methods fit this characterization: Cain and Abel, the Three Youths in the Fiery Furnace, the Crucifixion, and St. Guthlac at the Hellmouth are short, formula-dense depictions of "greatest hits" moments. These short, dramatic pieces, not sprawling epics, are what we would expect the first generation of literate Old English Christian poets to produce. It makes more intuitive sense, therefore, to see the long poems as the products of a subsequent generation of poets, who inherited a more Christian-adapted Old English poetic tradition and could find examples and inspiration in those first-generation short poems. Reading an Old English **Song of the Three Youths*, a second-generation poet perhaps thought, "This is good, but you know what would be better? The entire book of Daniel!" and then set out to produce it by paraphrasing the Latin text of the Bible into Old English verse, often sentence by sentence.

The combination of familiarity with the pre-Christian poetic tradition and sufficient Latin literacy to poetically paraphrase *Genesis A, Guthlac A*, or *Daniel* probably did not exist in England until there was a generation of people, like the Venerable Bede, who were brought into the

213 Substituting the name of the kingdom or people for "heofonrices" [of the realm of heaven], another positive adjective for "ece" [eternal], or a different positive adjective for "ælmihty" [almighty] would produce phrases appropriate for secular contexts.

monastery as children and grew up reading and writing both Old English and Latin. The previous generation, who joined monasteries as adults, although they might come to read well, just would not have the necessary fluency in writing both languages. That Bede attributes a large number of poems to Cædmon does not prove that an actual person at Whitby composed them at the end of the seventh century, but it does indicate that Bede believed that Old English poems about those subjects existed by the time he wrote his account of the cowherd's miraculous gift. This in turn suggests that by 731 the Christian poetic tradition was primed to develop —if it had not already—beyond short poems. The epic Christian poems, then, would come from Bede's generation or perhaps the next.

But that "Golden Age" of Anglo-Saxon culture came to an abrupt end when the Viking assaults began at the very end of the eighth century. Within a few decades, the attacks had almost completely destroyed monastic life in England, massively reducing the production of all texts, poetic and otherwise, for a century. The cultural revival started by King Alfred and culminating in the tenth-century Benedictine Reform is responsible both for the copying of the manuscripts that preserve older Anglo-Saxon culture and for the creation of new poetry that was more fully Christian and less connected to the now-ancient heroic poetry.

We thus can reconceptualize Anglo-Saxon literary history as being composed of three or four phases or waves. First was the initial development of literacy in England that began with the Conversion in the seventh century. This new literacy resulted both in the recording of traditional, Germanic, non-Christian heroic poetry (*Beowulf*, *Waldere*, the *Finnsburg Fragment, Widsith*) and the creation of short poems using the traditional poetics but treating Christian subjects like lost **The Song of the Three Youths*. We can tentatively date this phase to the years 600-700, with an emphasis on the last two decades (Bede dates Cædmon's compositions to the 680s). The second phase was the expansion of the kernel poems into the long, quasi-epic, biblical "paraphrase" poems like *Genesis A* and *Daniel*. These poems were written by people who had high-level Latin literacy as well as an understanding of the traditional poetic system, so we hypothesize that they entered the monastery as children (which would explain their mastery of Latin) just as Bede apparently did. This "Golden Age" comes to an end around 800 with the Viking attacks. Not much Anglo-Saxon culture is produced in or survives from most of the ninth century.

Phase three, King Alfred's rebuilding of the culture, increased the amount of writing in the vernacular because almost all those who could read Latin had been killed by Viking raids on monasteries and nunneries. Some new works may have been created, but, more importantly, the Alfredian cultural program was initially focused on preserving or recovering material that would otherwise have been lost. Finally, the Benedictine Reform of the tenth century gave a new impetus to both the copying and the production of Christian Old English poetry.[214] We owe all our manuscripts to the Reform, and we are in debt to the zealous followers of Archbishop Dunstan and Bishops Æthelwold and Oswald for the further expansion and explication of traditional poems (even those on Christian subjects). If the author of *Daniel* had thought "You know what's better than a short poem on the three youths? A long poem on Daniel!" then the authors of the poetry of the tenth century seemed to have thought, "...and you know what would make it better still? A sermon!" because that is indeed what tenth-century poets did. For example, someone attached a sermon about the Virgin Mary to the *Dream of the Rood*'s dream-vision—which was built around a kernel-poem depicting the crucifixion—hanging the connection on the very flimsy hook that just as God chose the Virgin out of all the possible women on earth, so too did the "enemies" pick, out of all the trees in the forest, the tree that was made into the cross.

Cynewulf, whether he wrote in the ninth or the tenth-century, and the poets of the Reform era (who may have been inspired by Cynewulf) seem to have wanted to ensure that their readers understood the religious significance of the core stories, and so they incorporated substantial

[214] It is not immediately obvious when precisely Cynewulf's poems were composed. They are usually thought to be substantially later than the biblical paraphrase poems but earlier than the mid-to-late tenth-century poems like the *Battle of Brunanburh* and the *Battle of Maldon*.

quantities of hortatory and homiletic material into their poems. It may be that having pagans living down the street spurred these writers to emphasize Christian morals and doctrine so intensively: they were worried that some of their readers might stray and adopt Viking cultural practices (Archbishop Wulfstan's *Sermo Lupi* complains that many did).

The picture of Anglo-Saxon literary history that emerges from this combined Lexomic- and traditional-research program is both intuitively plausible and consistent with the specific details of the evidence. It also suggests a path towards better literary analysis: instead of treating the cultural context of a poem as just "Anglo-Saxon" or, only slightly better, "early Anglo-Saxon" or "late Anglo-Saxon," we can see poems in the context of the ways their literary period adapted the traditional poetic system to Christianity, or expanded kernel poems to epic length, or integrated sermon-like material. This improved specificity helps us better understand the culture of the past, even when we have to find traces of literary history in the distribution of vocabulary or the frequencies of letter-forms.

This long excursus on the Lexomic contribution to the literary history of Anglo-Saxon England highlights the many ways in which traditional Liberal Arts are essential for even a science- or technology-assisted literary investigation. Every "happy accident" in the development of the Lexomic methods only occurred because we were able to apply knowledge of the history, culture, and literary traditions behind the texts to explain the apparent anomalies found with the computer-assisted methods. The only way to know that *Azarias* is very similar to a section of *Daniel* is to have read them both. That this section is parallel to the Prayer of Azarias and the Song of the Three Youths episodes, that there were Latin canticles based on those parts of the biblical text, and that the Three Youths in in the Fiery Furnace was a common artistic trope in the stone sculpture of the relevant time period can only be determined by study in the Liberal Arts disciplines of history, literature, religion, and art history. There is no way to automate this kind of connection-making and synthesis—it requires study of the traditional Liberal Arts.

Could Lexomic and other computer-assisted methods lead to the study of literature evolving into a science? Could English be the next field to get its intellectual house in order and become a science rather than a Liberal Art? It is unlikely, because, as just noted, a wide-ranging study of the traditional Liberal Arts is essential for the successful pursuit of research on literary texts (for which Lexomics is just a powerful new tool). It may be that some elements of English or literary study eventually do become sufficiently formalized for them to be considered a science, but if this occurs, that particular smaller portion of the discipline will likely split off to develop its own methodologies, as linguistics did in the 1970s. And if that happens, I predict, the relict English scholars will say, "Well, that stuff was never really a part of English, anyway. It's really kind of straightforward and boring, isn't it?" and soon enough, no one in the discipline will even remember that various Lexomic questions, like linguistic questions before them, were critically important to many scholars of English.

What might be the questions that get pulled from literary studies into Lexomics? In addition to the discovery of evidence for lost kernel-poems in the longer Old English poetic texts, we have also been able to identify as composite some texts that were only suspected to be (and to rule out multiple authors for others). Lexomic methods have also succeeded in settling an issue of textual priority in Old Norse literature that had been disputed for over 200 years. *Víga-Glúms Saga* and *Reykdæla Saga* each contain a well-developed sub-plot of the conflict between the protagonist Víga-Glúm and another man with the "Víga" (Killer) nickname, Víga-Skúta. The question of which account was the original (or derived from an original) and which was an adaptation had been hotly debated for many years until my student Rosetta Berger and I performed some clarifying experiments in cluster analysis. We divided both texts into chapters and then performed hierarchical agglomerative clustering. The resulting dendrogram (Figure 5) shows that almost all of the chapters cluster together with the others from their own texts, with one exception: the Víga-Skúta episode in *Reykdæla Saga* clusters with its counterpart, and the pair of episodes attaches to the rest of *Víga-Glúms Saga.* We then ran the same clustering experiment, but with the Víga-Skúta episode removed from *Reykdæla*. The dendrogram now separated the two sagas perfectly (Figure 6). But when we repeated that experiment, but with the *Víga-Glúms Saga* episode removed, the segment from *Reykdæla Saga* left its home text and attached itself to *Víga-Glúms Saga*, elegantly demonstrating that its distribution of vocabulary was closer to that text than even to its home saga (Figure 7). The inescapable conclusion is that the Víga-Skúta episode belonged originally to *Víga-Glúms Saga* and was borrowed by *Reykdæla Saga*, which must therefore have been composed later.

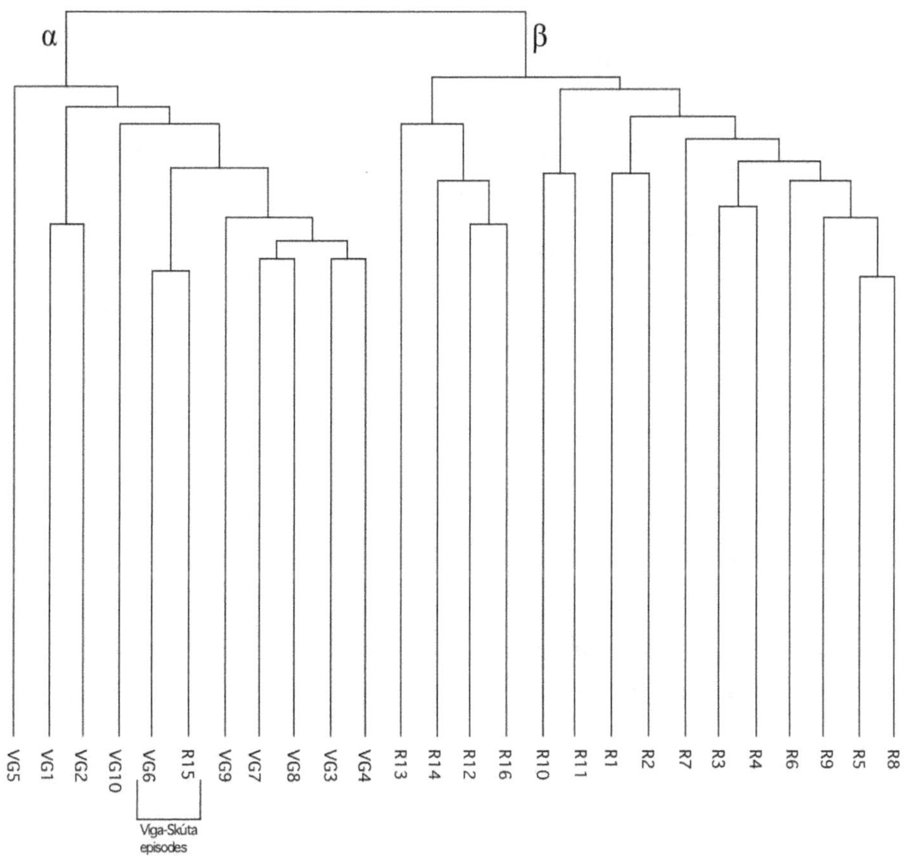

Figure 5: Dendrogram of all segments of Reykdæla Saga and Víga-Glúms Saga

Cluster Analysis of Two Icelandic Sagas,
Víga-Skúta episode from *Víga-Glúms saga* removed

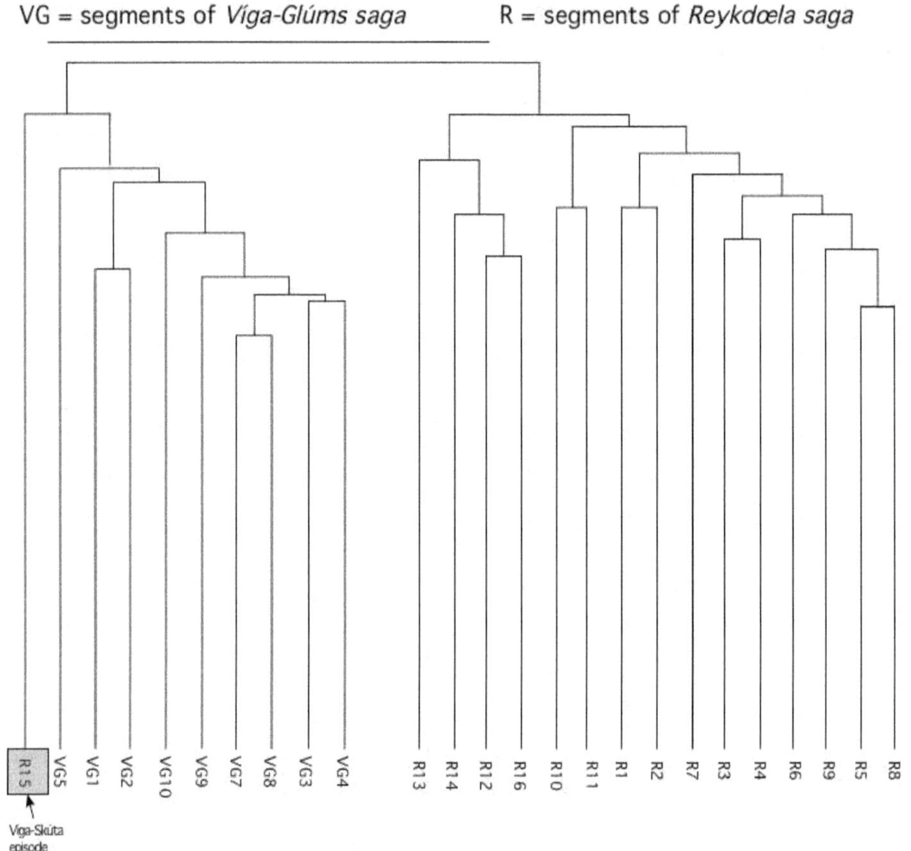

Figure 6: Dendrogram of Reykdæla Saga and Víga-Glúms Saga with the Víga-Skúta episode segment from Víga-Glúms saga removed

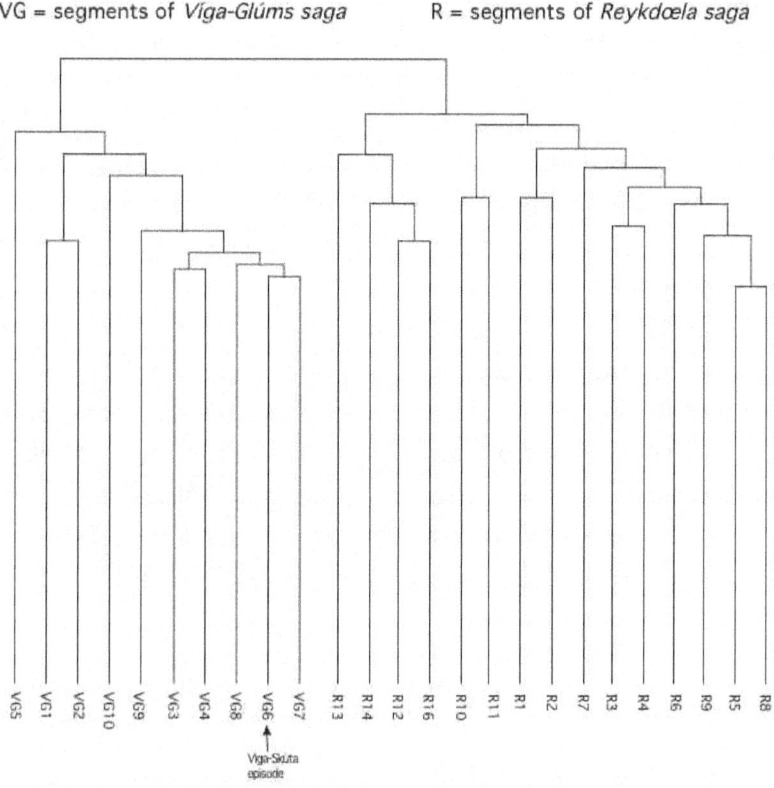

Figure 7: Dendrogram of "Dendrogram of Reykdæla Saga and Víga-Glúms Saga with the Víga-Skúta episode segment from Reykdæa Saga removed

Moving beyond technical questions of composition history and authorship, some of our recent work has suggested that rolling window analysis can be used to investigate the writing process of a single author, even when he or she is not using any external sources. For example, we found that the frequency of *and* in Ernest Hemingway's *The Sun Also Rises* follows a quite regular pattern of abrupt peaks followed by slow declines. These patterns, however, were not perfectly correlated with the book's chapters or with any other features that we could detect while reading. However, when we compared our rolling window plots to the original manuscripts in Boston's John F. Kennedy Library, we discovered that the oscillating pattern was closely correlated with Hemingway's writing stints. When he began to write each day, Hemingway tended to use *and* much more frequently than he did as he went on. In part this was because he tended to start with descriptions and only after getting "warmed up" (as we interpreted it) did he switch to dialogue and action, both of which used *and* much less frequently. This pattern repeated itself through every day's writing whether or not Hemingway had completed a chapter or was picking up in the middle of one when he began to write the next morning.

The ability to identify patterns like these, which are simply invisible to the unaided eye and brain, is what makes Lexomics such a promising field and gives it a small chance of becoming a quasi-science. But even if in the future there is a new "science" of Lexomics, it will remain dependent upon the Liberal Arts, for only minds educated in this tradition will be capable of synthesizing the new information and explaining how it fits into the enormous matrix of existing human knowledge.

Student Success Stories:
"If you can deal with English professors as clients, you can deal with anybody."

As you no doubt have realized, I think very highly of my students at Wheaton and am very proud of their successes. You may have also noticed that all of the students I have thus far highlighted have been English or philosophy or art history or other traditional Liberal Arts majors. But we have science majors at Wheaton, too, and they are also extremely good students and have been very successful in their post-Wheaton careers. I am lucky to know many of them not only through the Lexomics Research Group, but because Wheaton's science faculty have been so welcoming of my crazy ideas and so collaborative in trying to disprove (and maybe sometimes even prove) them.

For instance, from 1999-2003, I collaborated with colleagues in biology to test Old English medical remedies to see if they might actually have real-world efficacy. We mixed up various salves and creams and tested them on bacteria on agar plates, seeing if any of the remedies might inhibit the growth of the organisms that cause the specific diseases that the remedies were intended to heal. Our results were ambiguous (at least statistically) so that when we published them, we said that it was possible that one particular salve would have worked, but we could not say so definitively.

Several years later, a research group at the University of Nottingham followed up on our research, testing the remedy not against bacterial colonies in a petri dish, but on mouse skin that had been infected with *Staphylococcus aureus*. They found that it worked surprisingly well, so well, that they tested it against *Methicillin-resistant Staphylococcus aureus*, a dreaded "superbug" that plagues hospitals and other health-care settings. Shockingly, the 1,000-year-old remedy killed the *MRSA* bacteria that are immune to modern antibiotics! The research group suddenly had offers of support from pharmaceutical companies and worldwide publicity. And now I will write a sentence that no one has ever previously written and which I certainly never expected to write: If only we'd had some infected mouse skin!

That project, and an effort to sequence the sheep-DNA from medieval parchments,[215] plus the Lexomic research, has given me the chance to get to know many science students. As you might expect, science students at a Liberal Arts college tend to have more knowledge and experience beyond the science disciplines than students at other kinds of institutions, and, as you also might expect at this point in the book, this versatility turns out to contribute to their successes.

Many of the computer science majors who have worked to create the Lexomic software have had career success far beyond what you might expect from graduates of a Liberal Arts college. After all, they are competing directly with graduates from MIT, Carnegie Mellon, and other engineering schools whose computer science departments are much larger and more famous than Wheaton's. Yet currently there are Wheaton graduates who are veterans of the Lexomics Research Group working at Apple, Google, Microsoft, Facebook, Cisco, Raytheon, and the National Security Agency, and others of our students are enrolled in some of the elite computer science graduate programs in the world.

The reason for this success—in addition to the excellence of our faculty and the incredible work-ethic of these students—is that in their job interviews for these elite companies, our students talked about their experience creating the Lexomics software (all of which is student-written) and being part of the Research Group. Since we insist that all the computer science and English students and faculty work in the same large room so that it is easier to exchange ideas and share information, our "Code

[215] We were able to sequence some DNA from manuscript fragments, but librarians were unwilling to allow us to cut off sufficiently large samples of their precious manuscripts in order to try to figure out which sheep's hides made up which manuscripts; we're still hopeful that improvements in the sensitivity of sequencing technology will reinvigorate the project.

Wrangler" students come to know their "Word Meister" counterparts[216] very well, and therefore they understand the needs of the users of their software far more deeply than programmers usually do. It turns out that technology companies get hundreds and hundreds of applicants who know how to write good code, but they struggle to find people with that skill who can *also* communicate clearly with non-engineers and scientists and who understand how to work collaboratively on large projects in mixed-specialty teams. One recruiter told our student that she was already "expert" in the things that the company spends the most time and money attempting to teach their new hires: how to work with people who are not software engineers. Another student reported that the team that hired him said that the hardest part of their jobs was dealing with the clients for whom they wrote custom software, because the clients often could not clearly express what they needed, and the software engineers often were just as bad at communicating to the clients how to use the software to its greatest effect. This difficulty of dealing with clients was substantial even when the clients were also technically sophisticated and well-educated about software. "But if you can deal with *English professors* as clients," he said, shaking his head, "you can deal with anybody."

Happy to have been of service.

[216] I cannot (and would not want to) take credit for this nomenclature.

Chapter 10
Problems with the Liberal Arts

My personal opinion surely became obvious long before this part of the book, but let me state here once again that I believe that the study of the Liberal Arts is extremely valuable both for individuals and for society as a whole. I reiterate this point because in this chapter I am going to criticize the Liberal Arts, and I want to be certain readers understand that this criticism is not intended to undermine support for the Liberal Arts by providing intellectual ammunition for their opponents, but to reform and improve these disciplines by pointing out some flaws and weaknesses in their current institutional forms in academia.

There are, as I see it, four major problems. First, the contemporary Liberal Arts sometimes practice a poor imitation of the sciences by building upon bad or obsolete science and failing to recognize how much continual change there is in almost every scientific field. Second, there is an over-reliance in the contemporary Liberal Arts upon theorizing, and theories are too often given preference over evidence and thus treated as if they are more definitive than they are or ever could be. Third, in the contemporary Liberal Arts there is an over-emphasis on political analysis, which crowds out other types of investigation, restricts possible viewpoints, and can lead to political desires being mistaken for established facts. Finally, it sometimes seems that the Liberal Arts are hopelessly "fuzzy," that there are no objective ways of evaluating truth-claims in the disciplines of the Liberal Arts so that a reasonably clever person can argue any claim, unconstrained by logic or data. As we will see, all four of these problems can be attributed to an over-reliance on rhetoric at the expense of logic, and all could be mitigated by a shift in emphasis from abstraction to concrete data.

The first problem, the poor imitation of science, arises directly from the very multidisciplinarity that is required to make any progress towards solving the complex problems that we study in the Liberal Arts. As we saw in our case-study of *Beowulf*, there comes a time in any analysis of complex phenomena when we must synthesize information from multiple disciplines. But, as we noted, each discipline has its own ways of producing and evaluating knowledge, and no scholar trying to integrate information from multiple disciplines can be equally well trained in all of them. When working outside of your own field of specialization, it is particularly easy to make the mistake of confirmation bias, paying attention only to the research that seems to support the ideas you already hold. Information from a discipline that a scholar knows will often be subjected to rigorous analysis, while information from unfamiliar disciplines will be accepted or rejected too uncritically. In my study of *The Dream of the Red Chamber*, I was forcefully reminded of how hard it is to recognize that arguments are tendentious when you are a novice in a field. Several times I read scholarship that seemed not just utterly confident about particular interpretations, but treated them as if there were no other possibilities. Only later did I realize that much contrary or equivocal evidence was being left out. It is to avoid this problem that we generally require PhD students to work through the entire critical history of a discipline, usually as a series of enormous footnotes in the early chapters of their dissertations. Students hate writing these footnotes—I remember spending an entire eight-hour day writing a single footnote that was nearly a page long in single-spaced, 9-point type, while alternately cursing myself, my dissertation director, and my discipline—and professors hate reading them, but doing this *historiography* is essential because it ensures that you know where each scholarly argument fits into the long-running discussions in your discipline.

Unfortunately, interdisciplinary research would be impossible if we had to do this kind of full historical analysis of scholarship for every project, and no one would read what was produced: one of the first things new PhDs have to do when they convert their dissertations into books is to cut out all the material whose purpose was to say "See, I did *so* read all the background" (this is painful, because you remember exactly how much tedious work went into writing the things that you are deleting). Scholars trying to enter into a new sub-field without writing a new dissertation try to find extra-disciplinary methods of evaluating information, relying upon the evaluations of the most famous scholars or assuming the correctness of the most recent articles published in prestigious journals. Such forms of evaluation, however, are at best imperfect and at worst actively misleading. The most famous scholars at the most prestigious universities are often in the twilight of their careers and sometimes no longer knowledgeable about contemporary research, and their minds are often closed to new ideas. Prestigious journals tend to be biased against newer scholars, particularly if these researchers are challenging long-standing dogmas promulgated by the senior scholars on the editorial board. Although researchers within a subfield will probably know whether or not to trust the judgment of some particular colleague, scholars from other fields will not have all the relevant information and therefore must rely on inadequate proxies such as fame, prestige, or reputations earned for work done decades previously.

For example, for over a century, scholars in literary studies have recognized that they could improve their own analyses by augmenting their research with knowledge drawn from the discipline of psychology. Having some understanding of the mental processes of authors and readers, or even the imagined psychologies of literary characters, would be extremely useful for understanding many different features of literature. Unfortunately, at the time when scholars of literature first looked to psychology for insight, this discipline was utterly dominated by the theories of Sigmund Freud, and literary scholars (more than actual psychologists) became obsessed with concepts like the supposed stages of psycho-sexual development, the Oedipus Complex, and the Death Instinct. A huge intellectual edifice was built upon these theories, which literary scholars elaborated and extended, producing an entire subfield of "literary psychology." Literary scholars returned regularly to Freud's writings and read other literary scholars' interpretations of Freud, but they did not keep up with the evolution of the discipline of psychology, which came to recognize the major flaws in many of Freud's most dramatic claims—

exactly the ideas that had most captivated the literary scholars.[217] The result was a literary psychology that was out of date, unscientific, and logically circular, not only because it referred back to itself and not to the evolving discipline of psychology, but because much of Freud's theorizing, it turns out, was based more on his reading of literature than on unbiased observations of normal patients. Freud's literary erudition primed him to interpret the data he took from his case-studies of patients in ways that supported his literary-based theories (confirmation bias). A theory based on literature was adapted to examine literature and then used to justify conclusions about that literature, all under the aegis of a supposedly scientific psychology. It took many years, but eventually a new generation of scholars accepted that Freudian literary analysis was built on a theory of psychology no longer believed by any researchers in psychology. The subdiscipline rapidly collapsed and only survives today among a few elderly professors.

This is not to say that Freud should now be completely abandoned. In fact, understanding Freudian psychology is very useful for the study of twentieth-century literature because even though Freud was wrong in many of his claims, most twentieth-century writers *thought* he was correct and so based their own depictions of psychological behavior on Freudian theories. Studying Freud, then, lets us see what the authors of literary texts believed to be true in that same way that studying pre-scientific medicine informs us that people once believed that malaria came from the foul air of swamps (hence the name of the disease, which means "from the bad air") rather than from a protozoan infection transmitted by the mosquitoes that

[217] In graduate school, I was assigned to read many defenses of Freudian psychological interpretation. They were all unconvincing. It was only recently that I discovered Eric Kandel's *In Search of Memory*, in which the Nobel Prize-winning neuroscientist argues that, rather than being seen as a pseudo-scientific charlatan, Freud should be viewed as a proto-neuroscientist whose reasoning was simply too advanced for the limited biological research methods of his time. I am not entirely convinced, and I think Kandel is too generous to Freud (perhaps because of the connection to the city of Vienna that they share), but it is worth noting that the best defense of Freud comes not from a Freudian psychologist or a literary scholar, but from a neurobiologist. Eric R. Kandel, *In Search of Memory: The Emergence of a New Science of the Mind* (New York: W.W. Norton, 2006).

breed in the swamps. Knowing what people believed in the past is valuable, but assuming that those beliefs are objectively correct and trying to use them to explain phenomena outside of a particular historical era is unlikely to yield useful knowledge. Freudian theory may lead to insights about the works of T.S. Eliot, Jean Rhys, Philip Roth, Gayl Jones, or Alice Walker because these writers believed that the theory was more or less correct and so interpreted the world accordingly, but Freudianism is highly unlikely to be illuminating when applied to literature from previous centuries or other cultures, since—despite Freud's claims to the contrary—the theory does not describe universal features of human psychology.

Other disciplines have similar problems with the theories promulgated by their founders that turned out to be incomplete or flawed. Margaret Meade's conclusions about the dominance of nurture over nature, gender roles, and the lack of sexual inhibition in some cultures likely went beyond what could be supported by her data. Similarly, Marx's labor theory of value and his immiseration thesis have failed to find support in many empirical studies, which is why scholars in psychology, anthropology, and economics have thoroughly revised the theoretical frameworks of their respective fields. The disciplines still revere their founders, but—for the most part—they set those scholars' accomplishments in an appropriate historical context, as foundations built upon by later researchers. I have never met a scholar in the physical or social sciences who thought that the foundational work in his or her field was the last word, or that the early giants were correct in every detail (if they had been, there would be little point to continuing to work in the disciplines). Unfortunately, scholars in the Liberal Arts fields act as if Freud is the last word in psychology or Marx in economics, which is why it is often said by social scientists that the Liberal Arts are where bad theories crawl off to die. The general problem is that scholars in the Liberal Arts are not trained to evaluate scientific and social-science research, so they often end up using obsolete or discredited concepts, perhaps because these were the concepts used by their own teachers. Human nature being what it is, the ideas most likely to be selected are those that conform to the biases of the researchers.

A closely related problem is the use of scientific theories not in the rigorous and strictly limited sense that they are used in their home disciplines, but as metaphors that can be applied to almost any situation. Einstein's relativity is possibly the most abused of these theories, but the Heisenberg Uncertainty Principle is very much in the race. The Uncertainty Principle says that *at the subatomic scale*, the position and momentum of a particle can only be measured to a degree of precision such that the product of the two errors is greater than or equal to the reduced Planck's Constant. In physics itself, the Uncertainty Principle is not used in calculations of the position and momentum of macro-scale objects like planets, spinning tops, or pendulums, much less the behavior of people or social phenomena. But a pedagogical technique of trying to teach the Uncertainty Principle has been taken by non-physicists as true rather than as an intuition pump. Physics teachers often explain that you cannot discover a particle's position without bouncing another particle off of it, which changes the momentum.[218] This explanation, which is fine as far as it goes but is very oversimplified, has unfortunately been interpreted as demonstrating a physical basis and universality of the "observer effect," in which the presence of an observer can change the results of certain experiments—usually those that have a social component. But that is not accurate, nor are the many invocations of the Uncertainty Principle in Liberal Arts scholarship, which assert that we cannot have perfect knowledge of certain events or that the presence of an observer alters the physical universe. Neither of those assertions has anything to do with the Uncertainty Principle, which, again, only functions at the subatomic scale. The same over-application of scientific ideas can be seen in the use of relativity, the "deep structure" of language, the "butterfly effect" in chaos theory, "survival of the fittest," and other popularized scientific concepts that have become metaphors.

[218] The best explanation of the Uncertainty Principle in physics terms that I have read is that by Robert Serber, found in Robert P. Crease and Charles C. Mann, *The Second Creation: Makers of the Revolution in Twentieth-Century Physics* (New York: Macmillan, 1986), 68-71.

An obvious solution to both variations of the problem is for researchers, teachers, and students of the Liberal Arts to become more knowledgeable about contemporary research in the sciences and social sciences. Unfortunately, this is more easily said than done. Although a good Liberal Arts education must include basic instruction in mathematics and the sciences, such foundational learning cannot teach what is happening in the sciences right now. In fact, the basic science taught in survey courses designed for Liberal Arts students often has very little to do with what scientists are doing in their own research. The basics are essential, but they are only the basics. In order to know what is happening in contemporary science, scholars need to read research papers, not textbooks, but scholars in the Liberal Arts are busy reading research papers in their own fields and have not learned the discourse conventions of scientific writing. We are seemingly back where we started, faced with the difficulty of evaluating information outside of our own home disciplines.

All is not lost, however. There are a number of sources that can help a specialist in the Liberal Arts better understand relevant work in the sciences. The most important of these actually surround professors and students of the Liberal Arts every day: our colleagues in the natural and social sciences. Like scholars in all disciplines, scientists generally like to discuss their work, and they are usually willing to explain the details if you are willing to *listen* to them without feeling the need to *tell* them what their science means inside your own non-scientific disciplinary framework. When we try to learn about science in its own terms, without immediately critiquing it in relation to politics or culture, scientists are very willing to help us. I have found that personal relationships with colleagues in the scientific and social-scientific disciplines have been tremendously helpful in my own research, even in the most technical, discipline-specific work I have published. For example, in my book *Tradition and Influence in Anglo-Saxon Literature*, I needed knowledge from psychology in order to understand how human minds categorize and classify things. A colleague who specializes in cognitive psychology made a reading list for me, and I spent a number of months studying the relevant literature. I am sure that I did not grasp the subtleties of the first few papers I read, and I was probably initially too credulous and subject to confirmation bias, but after a while it was possible to recognize the conventions used in psychology research papers, and I was able to understand the arguments well enough to identify where there was disagreement among researchers and where there was broad consensus. This research significantly improved my book because I understood the ways humans classify and categorize information in a much more detailed and sophisticated way than I would have if I had relied upon my intuition or had only used a literary approach to the phenomena.[219]

Even if you do not have a working relationship with a professor or student in the sciences, there are opportunities to become sufficiently educated in these fields to at least have a sense of how they produce and evaluate knowledge. I am somewhat skeptical about what I learn from publications that are written for popular audiences by journalists (*Scientific American* has in recent years given up all pretense of publishing actual science), but magazines and websites aimed at the general public but written *by scientists* (like *American Scientist*) are often quite useful. The key is to try to understand the science in its own terms *before* using Liberal Arts techniques to criticize its rhetoric, style, or politics. If you save those types of analysis until after you understand the scientific content, you will find yourself better able to evaluate knowledge in scientific fields.

Gaining a better understanding of science is also a partial solution to the second great problem of the contemporary Liberal Arts: the misuse of both theory and Theory. I have capitalized the *T* in this last word to try to distinguish two different kinds of theorizing. The first, "theory" with a lower-case *t*, is an articulated set of principles that are used to evaluate information within a discipline. Everyone needs this kind of theory, since otherwise we have no way of fitting facts together to create a meaningful synthesis. You cannot know if you are comparing apples to apples or apples to oranges unless you have a background "theory of fruit" that explains what apples are and how they relate to oranges: we need to know if we are

[219] Michael D.C. Drout, *Tradition and Influence in Anglo-Saxon Literature* (New York: Palgrave, 2013).

investigating actual fruits or pictures of fruits, the color of fruits, or their nutritional values. Simple theory provides the matrix in which we evaluate data.

The potential problem with simple theory is that the abstractions it requires can overwhelm the specifics of the data the theory is being used to explain. The minds of most Liberal Arts academics seem to be prone to abstraction and theorization,[220] and the rewards for creating theories are, unfortunately, often greater than for collecting facts. An overemphasis on the abstract and theoretical can result in the theory overwhelming the evidence of the data, leading, in the end, to incorrect conclusions.

These problems are more acute with regard to Theory written with a capital *T*, which is what most current scholars, students, and critics of the Liberal Arts think of when they hear the word. "Theory" is often an abbreviation for "Post-Modern Theory" or "Critical Theory," which became intellectually dominant in Liberal Arts departments in the 1980s and remains, at the very least, strongly influential in most humanities disciplines, even if only as a set of background assumptions.[221]

The origin of Critical Theory lies in early twentieth-century Marxist approaches to culture, many of which were pioneered by a group of exiles from Weimar Germany who are sometimes called the "Frankfurt School."[222] Their intellectual roots explain, in part, the ways that Theory developed within academia. Marxist analysis has never been simple, as even its foundational texts require a great deal of interpretation (in this way they are similar to religious texts that require trained clergy to explain them).[223]

[220] Perhaps people whose minds tend to empiricism and the collection of data are drawn preferentially to fields like engineering and medicine rather than to the Liberal Arts.

[221] There are many books that introduce readers to Theory. I take as representative Roger Webster, *Studying Literary Theory: An Introduction*, 2nd ed. (London: Bloomsbury, 1995) and Frank Lentricchia and Thomas McLaughlin, eds., *Critical Terms for Literary Study* (Chicago: University of Chicago Press, 1990).

[222] Among the most notable of these theorists were Max Horkheimer, Theodor W. Adorno, Herbert Marcuse, Walter Benjamin, and Jürgen Habermas.

[223] And for some of the same reasons: both religious and Marxist texts possess great authority for their believers but at the same time include many statements that are ambiguous or appear to contradict each other. The job of both theologians and Marxist intellectuals has been to explain that, while on the surface the statements may seem to be

A tradition soon arose within political Marxism that every group of activists should include a "theoretician," a person whose job it was to interpret Marxist doctrine in order to be certain that the group was following it correctly. When the Frankfurt School developed their "cultural Marxism" approach, this intellectual tradition was carried along from political activism to academic institutions. Starting in the 1980s, each department in the humanities disciplines began to see the need to include a theoretician (often identified as "the Theory person"), whose publications were focused not as much on the traditional subjects of the Liberal Arts as on the theories that should be used for interpretations. All of those theoreticians needed to publish, and they did, producing an immense proliferation of theoretical discourse. Theory was built upon previous theory, leading eventually to an intellectual construction of such complexity that scholars had to devote their entire careers to trying to understand it.

As we might expect, when theories are based primarily on other theories, they have a tendency to become self-referential and therefore are so afflicted with confirmation bias that they run a serious risk of becoming disconnected from reality. Without the regular comparison to history, data, or experiment, small errors in logic can be massively compounded or obscured (or both), making it very difficult for the sorts of course-corrections that are necessary even in fields as mathematical and logical as physics. The problem is significantly worse in the Liberal Arts disciplines because we often cannot perform experiments to determine if our theories are consistent with reality, and so it becomes easy for theories that explain Liberal Arts phenomena to fall into traps of circular reasoning.

"Post-modern" or "Post-structural" Theory[224] is particularly prone to this kind of error because the Frankfurt School theoreticians who

---

contradictions, at a deeper level of understanding they are actually consistent and are therefore (believers assume) true.

[224] My rule of thumb—which to this point has never failed me—is that anything with "post-" or "late" in its name is neither correct nor useful, perhaps because methodologies or classifications that use the former prefix merely define themselves against something else rather than establishing their own identity, and those that use the latter imply impossible foreknowledge of future events.

founded the approach and their disciples abandoned the *materialism* that characterized economic Marxism. What had been so revolutionary about Marx's approach to philosophy and politics, and what had made it so effective in contrast to its intellectual competitors, was its relentless focus on the material world, on economic and physical relationships. Marx believed that *idealist* philosophers such as Immanuel Kant and Friedrich Hegel mistook ideas for real things and were thus both susceptible to errors in reasoning and utterly ineffective at improving the world.[225] The *historical materialism* of Marx and Engels was an attempt to escape the problems of philosophical idealism.

The Frankfurt School intellectuals who laid the foundations for contemporary literary and cultural theory wanted to understand the ways that ideology and culture influenced each other. At the beginning, they followed more traditional Marxist approaches in interpreting that ideology (and hence culture) as arising from economic relationships. But when you study ideas, it is very difficult to resist the pull of idealism, especially because scholars are generally much more facile with ideas than with actions in the physical world. It is an ever-present temptation to believe that if you can get the ideas or the culture right, the rest will follow, as such a belief makes the work of the scholar equivalent to that of people doing the hard (and often dangerous) work required to improve the material conditions of humanity.

If the first wave of cultural theorists resisted the initial pull of idealism, subsequent intellectual generations—for a variety of reasons[226]—fully embraced the abstract, ideological approach to culture. In the 1980s and 1990s, "high theory" as practiced in English departments was focused almost entirely on abstract ideas rather than on material things. Such abstract analysis can be extremely useful for investigating the ways that beliefs and ideas interact with art, literature, music, and other cultural phenomena. For example, theoreticians identified a fundamental flaw in

[225] Karl Marx with Friedrich Engels, *The German Ideology* (New York: Prometheus Books, 1998).

[226] Many intellectuals became disillusioned with Marxism after the violent repression by the Soviet Union of mass revolutionary movements, particularly the crushing of "Prague Spring" in 1968.

systems of thought founded upon paired opposed terms such as man and woman, light and dark, black and white. Although such terms are only truly opposites in very limited logical domains, cultural systems tend to treat them as opposed in other ways as well and to link the disfavored term in any pair to other disfavored terms. These subtle networks of ideas appear to influence ideology and hence culture.

But purely abstract analysis is as intellectually risky as it is powerful. Because abstraction removes the check of empirical confirmation from reasoning (which is one of the major criticisms that Marx and Engels had of Kant, Hegel, and the idealist philosophers), it is very easy when reasoning purely abstractly to miss flaws in logic or even simple errors of fact and thus to succumb to confirmation bias. That is exactly what happened within many Liberal Arts fields: Theory took over the intellectual discipline so thoroughly that contradictory data was explained away, then ignored, then rejected as irrelevant or politically prejudicial, and finally forgotten, all because the purpose of the approach was not to explain the world, but to change it by changing people's ideas about it.

For example, the French theorist Michel Foucault asserted that forms of technology and social control actually produce identities in people (i.e., instead of social control repressing people's "real" selves, "technologies of power" actually *created* people's particular identities).[227] Foucault stated that these technologies and forms of social organization arose in the beginning of the modern period in France and were associated with industrialization and the needs of capitalism. But the specific things about identities that Foucault claimed—that they were created in part by getting people essentially to spy upon themselves internally and then confess their thoughts, beliefs, and actions to powerful institutions—can be shown to have existed hundreds of years before, in the medieval period, when there was no industrialization or elaborate technological systems of

[227] Michel Foucault, *The Foucault Reader*, ed. and trans. Peter Rabinow (New York: Pantheon, 1984). See especially the essays "Truth and Power," "Complete and Austere Institutions," "The Birth of the Asylum," "We 'Other Victorians,'" and most especially "The Repressive Hypothesis." See also Michel Foucault, *The History of Sexuality Vol I: An Introduction* and *The History of Sexuality Vol II: The Use of Pleasure*, ed. and trans. Robert Hurley (New York: Vintage Books, 1990).

social control.[228] Thus although Foucault does seem to provide insight or at least an interesting new approach to understanding how people's identities are formed, his specific historical claims are utterly false. The material foundations of his theory, and thus the theory itself, are therefore wrong, but Foucault has remained influential because many scholars believed his ideas were helpful for bringing about the social changes that they desired.[229]

This attitude, which until very recently has been widespread within Liberal Arts academia, is a genuine problem. We usually do not have the capability of performing experiments in the Liberal Arts disciplines; we only have data. This data may be messy, but it is rich and complex, and we should not feel free to ignore it. In the scientific fields, if the data contradicts the theory, then the theory is wrong,[230] but in a Theory-dominated discipline, if the data contradicts the theory, then the data are often assumed to be wrong, and so discarded, in part because it is assumed that (at least contemporary) Theory is part of an intellectual movement that will lead to revolutionary social change and is therefore too socially good to be rejected. It is obvious how the replacement of other kinds of judgment by purely Theoretical criteria can lead to circularity in reasoning and, eventually, to the replacement of complex and nuanced analysis with the enforcement of a rigid orthodoxy founded on abstraction. Analyzing complicated phenomena in light of the question "Does my interpretation support the abstract Theory?" is comparatively easy, especially if the focus of analysis has become idealist rather than materialist (materialism eventually has to deal with the data; idealism does not). Over time, the easy approach will generally drive out the more difficult one, since there will be more of the former than of the latter.

Idealist approaches have a critical inherent weakness. Every form of analysis must strike a balance between the ideal and the real, between the map and the territory that the map describes. Without some abstraction, it is impossible to identify patterns. But too much abstraction leads first to

[228] See Allen J. Frantzen, *Before the Closet: Same-Sex Love from Beowulf to Angels in America* (Chicago: University of Chicago Press, 1991).

[229] See, for example, David Halperin, *Saint Foucault: Towards a Gay Hagiography* (Oxford: Oxford University Press, 1997).

[230] Richard Feynman, *The Character of Physical Law* (Cambridge, MIT Press, 2017), 156.

oversimplification and eventually to disregarding data. Idealist approaches tend always towards over-abstraction because the analysis of ideas in terms of other ideas ends up excluding phenomena in the physical world. And without the corrections that come from comparing theory to actuality, the self-referential theory tends to become both more extreme in its claims—as a means of gaining attention in a noisy and disorganized conversation—and less tangible in its effects.

Whatever literary and cultural Theory's original revolutionary intentions may have been, it has now evolved to the point where the background assumptions of scholars in multiple disciplines are a set of relatively extreme claims that no practicing scholar actually believes. For example, the assertions that all knowledge is contingent, situated, and political, or that language constructs rather than describes reality, or that there are no intrinsic limits on what a literary text or work of art might mean, have all been staples of literary theory classes for close to three decades. I have yet to meet a professor of literature who acts as if these statements are true in all situations.

It would be impossible to function in human society if you truly believed that *all* knowledge you and everyone else has about the world is not linked to physical reality or that arithmetic and geometry are politically determined. Replace the word "all" with the word "some" (or "much" or even, if you want to be extreme, "most"), and you get a defensible statement, but no one needed literary theory to realize that some fraction of our knowledge is belief rather than objective reality, that these beliefs are often self-serving, and that it is extremely difficult to determine if we really know what we think we know. But professors—like all humans—act as if what *they* know is less contingent, situated, and political than what other people know. That is, within their own specific domains of knowledge, they treat some information as absolute facts and other information as beliefs. Good scholars know to question their background assumptions, to make sure that what they think are facts are actually facts and not merely beliefs, and within their specializations most are very good about knowing why they know what they know.

If there were no possibility of there being objective knowledge, there would be little reason for scholars to strive to correct factual errors or to struggle against bias and cultural prejudice. But teasing apart the facts from the non-facts is one of the most important and valued practices of scholarship—in all fields. It is one reason why most Liberal Arts disciplines insist that the historiography of the field is an important part of a dissertation. No one outside the dissertation committee may ever read the interminable footnotes that do not much more than show that a student has read all the previous scholarship, but all the effort is worthwhile because it allows the student to learn *why* the field takes some things as facts and others as opinions.[231] No post-modernist literary theorist would publish a paper that said that Virginia Woolf wrote *Mrs. Dalloway* in 1976 in San Diego, or that Zora Neale Hurston was Belgian, or that Ken Kesey spent the Civil War living in a treehouse. Theorists might preach the contingency and the situatedness of knowledge, but they act as if they believe in pretty much the same facts as everyone else.

The notion that language constructs or creates rather than describes reality is likewise ridiculous when taken in absolute terms. You can call a tail a leg and therefore conclude that a dog has five legs, but the poor animal still can't walk with its tail if it gets a thorn in its foot. No matter what language we use, the brute laws of physics, chemistry, and biology are non-negotiable—and I have never met a literature professor who *behaves* as if they are not. Again, if we qualify the extreme and unsupportable assertion by changing "constructs" or "creates" to "influences," we get a statement that is very likely true but is also obvious. Everyone knows that the specific language used to describe something influences in some small way how we think about it. That is why people employ euphemisms or deliberately select words with negative connotations in order to influence their audiences.

---

[231] An eternal problem in Liberal Arts disciplines is the generational evolution of overt speculations into assumed facts. The initial scholar is very careful to label a speculation as such. The next scholar builds upon the first's ideas and spends less time on the caveats. After several scholarly generations, an initial speculation can evolve into a received truth. This provides an opportunity for the next scholarly generation to sweep away accumulated error.

It is true that in some very specific circumstances, language *can* directly and immediately change the world. If the umpire says "You're out!" then the batter is out. If the judge says "guilty," the accused is guilty. If I say "I bet you five dollars," you will expect me to pay if my prediction is wrong (which is why I don't bet). These "speech-acts" change the world because the belief is wide-spread among individuals that they do so and because there are powerful human institutions that enforce social reality. In truth the pitch might have been outside the strike zone, but the championship banner will be raised, the gambling winnings paid, and the record-book written once the speech-act has been performed by the socially authorized person.

The social power of speech-acts is so dramatic that it is easy to understand how theorists, always under pressure to one-up each other's claims, could over-expand the specific, context-dependent power of language from social reality to physical reality. But once we recognize the very restricted nature of most speech-acts, we understand that language "constructs" reality only in extremely specific circumstances. The rest of the time, language only *influences* how we perceive reality, and even this claim is debatable, since we do not have a good way of measuring the influence of language because there is no easy way of separating the content from the words used to communicate it.

The idea that there is no intrinsic limitation on what a work of art or literature might mean is probably the most widely held of the three claims I am critiquing, to the point where I think it is fair to describe it as dogma in contemporary literary studies. Yet again, the strong version of the claim—that the language of a text does not at all limit the possible meanings of that text—is nonsensical. If meaning does not arise from the language of a text, then there is no point to studying texts, since the same exact words could mean an infinite number of things and there is no relationship between the actual words of the text and the meaning. Absolutely no one believes this. But the weak version of the claim—that it is impossible for the text by itself to completely control its own meaning—is banal. It is obviously quite possible for any given text to have multiple meanings, since this is exactly what literary scholars argue about.

What the assertion that there is no intrinsic meaning in a text is getting at is the phenomenon that, if we take a text in isolation, there is no objective way to determine absolutely if it is more like one paraphrase or explanation than another very similar one. For example, if we see the sentence "Beware of Doug," we cannot, from the words themselves, be certain if this is simply a sincere warning to be careful of a man named Douglas, a typo for "Beware of Dog," or a joke based on the similarities between the name and the word for the animal.[232] Without additional context, the problem is irresolvable, and even with context, there could be room for dispute. In many cases, even after detailed and logically rigorous arguments, reasonable people can still disagree about the meaning, and, in cases where that meaning must be resolved (for example, if the text being interpreted is a law), the accepted meaning is that which convinces the most—or most powerful—people. The critic Stanley Fish extends this observation to its extreme form by asserting that a text means whatever a sufficient number of people can be convinced that it means.[233]

But in actuality, the vast, vast majority of possible meanings of any text are immediately excluded from consideration. People may argue about whether *Beowulf* is about heroism or death or old age or power, but absolutely no one thinks the poem is about lemurs, bratwurst, or the irrationality of the square root of two. You might be able, through brute social power, to force some group of people to *say* that *Beowulf* is about one of these ridiculous things, but they would not believe it. The idea that there is no intrinsic meaning in a text or that the meaning is produced solely from social power is another example of overgeneralizing rare, special cases and artificially constructed situations. People agree upon the general meanings of nearly all the sentences that have ever been spoken or written; otherwise we could never communicate with each other. And even in the cases of complex or ambiguous statements or texts, there is usually a fairly narrow set of meanings about which the critics are arguing. In other words, there is *some* intrinsic meaning in the language of a text, just not *all* of the

[232] Gary Larson, *The PreHistory of the Far Side* (Kansas City: Andrews McMeel, 1989), 75.
[233] Stanley Fish, *Is There a Text in this Class? The Authority of Interpretive Communities* (Cambridge: Harvard University Press, 1982).

meaning. In my view, the most interesting feature of the relationship between language and meaning, that there is a "variation within limits" of possible meanings rather than either a one-to-one mapping between language and meaning or an absolute free play of interpretation, is not fully explained by any current theory of interpretation.

In the three cases of Theory over-reach we have just discussed, and in many more besides, the problems arise from the failure of extreme claims. That those claims were even made is the almost inevitable result of too much abstraction. When abstract reasoning is built only upon other abstract reasoning, it is very easy for an argument to escape from the constraints of the real world and thus end up contradicting the actual evidence. Abstraction is always appealing, not only because it is very powerful, but also because it can be a shortcut. More than one graduate student in literary studies has realized that if you knew enough Theory, you could avoid the difficult work of reading all those literary texts: the Theory could tell you what they were going to say, anyway.

Even for the majority of scholars who never went that far, the abstractions required for (and allowed by) Theory ended up diminishing the value that disciplines put on their own specific knowledge, since theoretical claims were always larger. Without the constraints of discipline-specific data, theoretical claims turned out to be extremely susceptible to social pressure. Ironically, both Theory itself and Theory-centric analysis turned out to be rare special cases in which Fish's "interpretive community" assertion of the social construction of truth actually held.[234] And when truth is socially constructed without constraint, that "truth" will always be pressured to conform to the opinions of the social community doing the interpreting.

Since the most widely shared opinions in contemporary Liberal Arts academia happen to be political (150 years ago they might have been religious), Theory has also contributed to the third great problem of the contemporary Liberal Arts: politicization. Additional reasons why the Theory-focused approach devolved into the enforcement of a low-grade

---

[234] Stanley Fish, *Is There a Text in this Class? The Authority of Interpretive Communities* (Cambridge: Harvard University Press, 1982).

political orthodoxy (one that has been remarkably stable for nearly half a century) can probably be found in the interaction of American academia's social organization and class structure—features of the higher education system that scholars are often uncomfortable discussing—with the difficulties of evaluating research outside of one's own area of specialization. Ideally, in all scholarly disciplines, ideas would rise or fall on their own merits, on how well they accounted for the observed data. It should not matter who says something, only the content of what is said. But this ideal fails in practice for all the reasons discussed above: once we are outside an area of specialization, we need other methods of evaluating arguments, and a speaker or writer's prestige is a very tempting proxy for quality of argument or data. We tend to assume that the more prestigious an institution, the better the quality of the work done by the scholars who work there.

This is not, on its face, an entirely unreasonable assumption, since the most prestigious institutions tend to have the most resources and so, theoretically, can employ the best scholars. But in actuality the correlation between institutional prestige and individual scholarly quality is relatively loose. In any given field in any given year, it is probably true that, on average, the better the work done by a PhD student, the more prestigious institution at which he or she ends up teaching. However, this is only an average across entire disciplines. There is in fact so much subspecialization that it is common for a hiring committee—or even a whole department—to have no other individual in the same subfield as the one in which they are hiring, and so the committee ends up relying on proxies like institutional prestige or advisor's reputation. This arbitrary initial sorting is the single most important factor in determining in which institution a scholar settles into for the next thirty years or his or her career. Most institutions prefer to replace retiring senior professors with young assistant professors (whom they can pay less), so if you did not happen to receive your PhD in the year that Prestigious University was hiring a specialist in your area, it is unlikely that you will ever be a professor there. Movement within the hierarchy is sometimes possible for scholars more advanced in their careers, but job openings higher in the prestige hierarchy are both rare and highly coveted, and the processes by which individuals are chosen for them are often even more chaotic than the initial sorting of new PhDs. Although there is still a weak linkage between the quality of research and institutional prestige, the quirks of each institution, department, or hiring committee also play a large role in who ends up where.

It is a lamentable quality of human behavior that indications of group membership are among the more effective social signals, since people tend to discriminate in favor of members of their own group. It is thus in the best interest of scholars who want to move up to signal their membership in the same classes as those above them in the hierarchy.[235] The most powerful determinants of class identity in contemporary America—race, gender, sexuality, social class—are *in theory* out of bounds in hiring decisions, but other group identities are not, so there is enormous selection pressure for scholars at every level of the hierarchy to signal that they belong to the same social groups as those higher up in the pecking order. The most effective way to do this is to adopt the customs of that group: the jargon, style, mannerisms, and outwardly expressed beliefs that indicate membership. The resulting dynamic makes it very risky for any individual to dissent from whatever the current orthodoxy in either style or substance might be, because to do so could signal membership in an out-group. The balance between standing out and fitting in becomes strongly shifted towards the latter. The combination of this dynamic with the strong tendency of humans to imitate the behaviors of those higher in a hierarchy creates and maintains a vicious cycle of conformity, not to some objective standard, but to whatever those lower down intuit to be the key behaviors of those higher up.

That in-group membership in contemporary academia is marked by a general political stance as well as by the use of certain terminology and catch-phrases[236] is not the result of some grand ideological conspiracy, but

[235] Some grad students have called this phenomenon "the Great Chain of Up-Sucking."

[236] For example, in my academic lifetime, "imbricated," "liminal," and "fraught" went from rare words, to appearing in seemingly every paper in a given issue of a journal, to being now a marker that a scholar is middle-aged and running out of ideas. A viral outbreak of "lens" has somewhat abated among professors but is, unfortunately, still infecting many students.

merely another result of the difficulty of evaluating information across the specialized disciplines. Because there is so much variation in the ways the different disciplines of the Liberal Arts create and evaluate knowledge, any commonalities need to be very abstract, and there is nothing more abstract then general political ideology (which at its worst reduces to "us vs. them"). Once a particular ideological stance becomes sufficiently widespread, it becomes foolish for any lower-ranking individual to risk dissenting, but at the same time, the value gained from signaling group membership declines (if every applicant signals membership in the group, there is no way to stand out). This dynamic leads to a spiral of increased virtue-signaling and inflation of extremism that is almost certain to move the apparent ideological center of gravity far beyond what is likely to be useful for understanding the complexities of the cultural world (and usually beyond what the people in the field actually believe). Thus approaches that were originally revolutionary become first commonplace, then orthodox, and then dogmatic.

We associate orthodoxies with religion because that is the intellectual milieu in which they most commonly arise. Religious truths are so complex and contentious that it is very easy for believers to follow lines of reasoning to conclusions that could remove them from one sect and place them in another. Religious authorities, therefore, codified sets of opinions on these topics and created institutions that both spread the faith and policed the intellectual boundaries of each sect. Many of the great universities, including Oxford, Cambridge, Harvard, and Princeton, were originally created to enforce intellectual orthodoxy in religious matters. The extreme version of orthodoxy is dogma, a set of positions or opinions that a person must hold in order to be a member of a group. Although dogmas may have their roots in reasoned arguments about complex problems, they manifest themselves as a set of statements that may not be debated.

At its most basic level, "orthodox" means "correct," which is surely what most people who hold orthodox positions (on any subject) believe. It can also mean "widely held," which is also true for a whole range of positions on many topics in contemporary academia. However, when the "widely held" rather than the "correct" quality of the positions causes their adoption, an orthodoxy is well on its way to becoming a dogma. The dynamics of competitive virtue-signaling to indicate in-group membership and extreme social hierarchy in contemporary academia accelerate the process, which is unfortunate, since dogma is antithetical to the open investigation and questioning that is essential to the Liberal Arts.

Although the orthodoxies and dogmas in the current era are primarily political rather than religious and the enforcement mechanisms are, for the most part, informal and social rather than official and institutional, things work essentially the same way that they did throughout the history of academia. There are positions on controversial topics from which it is both socially and professionally risky to deviate because openly espousing conflicting opinions signals out-group membership. Most faculty, however, at work in their own specialized fields, do not spend the majority of their time thinking about the orthodoxy, especially because most of us agree with most of the orthodox opinions and so do not notice them any more than fish notice that they are all swimming in water. Outsiders may be surprised by the uniformity and the seeming power of the social enforcement mechanisms, but insiders rarely interact with outsiders and so rarely hear other points of view. The dynamics of the system have thus led to an orthodoxy maintained without any real central authority, secret police, tribunals for adjudicating deviance, or openly stated creed that every academic must recite in order to be allowed to teach or do research.[237] But even without these institutional mechanisms, contemporary academia ends up enforcing a high degree of conformity (especially with regard to national political opinions that do not significantly affect the day-to-day work of most scholars).

In some sense, it was ever thus. Historically the Liberal Arts have always been linked to politics of one kind or another. The very name of the

[237] Sadly, this sentence became less true during the Covid years (2020-22). Although academia never sunk quite so low as to have a central authority or a secret police—as far as I know—to our shame we did experiment with loyalty oaths (having to write "diversity statements"), mandatory public confessions of faith (standing at meetings for "land acknowledgments"), and show-trials for heretics. Fortunately that hysteria has (mostly) passed—for now.

Liberal Arts, the disciplines appropriate for "free" people, has political implications, since the category of free people implies the existence of those who are not free, and hence a hierarchical political order in which study of the Liberal Arts can help move a person towards the top. The link between the Liberal Arts and politics is thus inevitable, especially because, as we discussed in Chapter 3, the Liberal Arts, as the "tools to rule," give the people who are educated in these disciplines power over others, and there are obvious political implications in the uneven distribution of such social tools throughout the population.

The connection of the Liberal Arts to politics is further deepened by their not having *intrinsic* moral components. Although, as we discussed in Chapter 4, the study of the Liberal Arts may make people be better human beings, there is no guarantee that this will happen, so it is not surprising that there are regular efforts to blend the study of the Liberal Arts with political or moral teachings that seem to their proponents more likely to lead students to be good. The easiest way to do this is through the imposition of orthodoxy—political or religious—throughout Liberal Arts academia.

The study of intellectual history, however, shows that imposed orthodoxy, although often effective in the short run, usually fails in the longer term because orthodoxies become self-referential systems that steadily lose the ability to describe the real world. Eventually the difference between what the orthodox theory asserts and what the actual phenomena are becomes so great that the orthodoxy must be rejected if the value of logical reasoning is to be preserved. My sense is that we are just reaching such a turning point and that the intensity and ruthlessness of ideological enforcement within the contemporary Liberal Arts is a sign that the orthodoxies of the past half-century are eroding. If the past is any guide, what will follow will be a period of intense intellectual ferment and conflict that will eventually turn into a different orthodoxy, which will harden, drift away from reality, and itself then be overturned.

The eternal conflict between orthodoxy enforced through political power and systems of analysis built upon logic brings us to the fourth major problem facing the contemporary Liberal Arts, the one my colleagues in the sciences find most objectionable. There is no denying that, compared to the sciences and even some of the social sciences, many of the disciplines of the Liberal Arts are "fuzzy" or "fluffy," relying upon individual perceptions, emotions, and opinions (as well as politics and self-interest). When scientists are at their most annoyed, they assert that a clever person can make any claim at all in the disciplines of the Liberal Arts, and, as long as that claim is congenial to other scholars in the discipline, it will be accepted. In this view, truth in the Liberal Arts is whatever people can be talked into believing.

This is a variation of Plato's critique of the Sophists, whom he claimed cared only about victory in debate rather than in the discovery and promulgation of the truth. Both criticisms have at their heart a distrust of rhetoric unconstrained by the non-negotiable facts of the physical world. Plato trusted the intellectual discipline of philosophy to prevent convenient "social truths" from usurping logical truths. Scientists rely upon experiment and mathematical analysis to discipline their reasoning. As Richard Feynman once said, in science, "it does not make any difference how beautiful your guess is. It does not make any difference how smart you are, who made the guess, or what his name is—if it disagrees with experiment it is wrong. That is all there is to it."[238] Although this kind of logical rigor may be more an unreachable ideal than the actual practice of institutional science (particularly during the Covid years), it is at least a widely shared goal. Scientists worry—sometimes reasonably—that the disciplines of the Liberal Arts lack equally effective error-correction mechanisms.

I cannot deny that there is a lot of truth in this implied critique, but only when you match up the best of science with the worst of the Liberal Arts. At its best, science is based primarily on logic and is validated by rigorous experimentation. At their worst, the Liberal Arts are based primarily on rhetoric, politics, and self-interest—remember, the subjects that best lend themselves to experimental and rigorously logical approaches have already become sciences. However, science is not always at its best,

[238] Feynman, "The Character of Physical Law," 156.

and, luckily, the Liberal Arts are not always at their worst. There is, unfortunately, a long, sad history of fallacious scientific conclusions that, through the power of rhetoric, were the consensus beliefs among practicing scientists for long periods of time even though these ideas were not strongly supported by logical or experimental evidence. For example, from 1912 through the 1960s, despite continuously accumulating evidence that Alfred Wegener's ideas about continental drift were correct, geologists aggressively rejected his theory. This rejection is particularly damning not in itself,[239] but in the ways that the scientific establishment used its full range of social and political powers, often quite viciously, to attack not only the theory itself, but Wegener personally, calling him a crank and impugning the motives and intelligence of both him and any young scientists who tried to give his ideas a fair hearing. This sad episode shows the power of effective rhetoric in supporting the self-interest of institutionally powerful scientists,[240] but it also shows how a theory that better accounts for the data can eventually overcome resistance that is primarily social or political. For half a century, social reality had trumped physical reality, but eventually the accumulation of physical evidence and the refinement of the theory convinced geologists to change their minds (or, more accurately, the scientists who refused to believe in continental drift died off and were replaced by a new generation who were familiar with the evidence and did not see the idea as threatening).[241] The field of

[239] Many of the objections to continental drift were reasonable given the state of geophysical knowledge in the first half of the twentieth century.

[240] Naomi Oreskes, *The Rejection of Continental Drift: Theory and Method in American Earth Science* (Oxford: Oxford University Press, 1999).

[241] "Eine neue wissenschaftliche Wahrheit pflegt sich nicht in der Weise durchzusetzen, daß ihre Gegner überzeugt werden und sich als belehrt erklären, sondern vielmehr dadurch, daß ihre Gegner allmählich aussterben und daß die heranwachsende Generation von vornherein mit der Wahrheit vertraut gemacht ist." [A new scientific truth does not triumph by convincing its opponents and making them see the light, but rather because its opponents eventually die, and a new generation grows up that is familiar with it.] Max Planck, *Wissenschaftliche Selbstbiographie. Mit einem Bildnis und der von Max von Laue gehaltenen Traueransprache.* Johann Ambrosius Barth Verlag (Leipzig 1948), 22. English translation from Max Planck, *Scientific Autobiography and Other Papers*, trans. F. Gaynor (New York: Philosophical Library, 1949), 33–34.

plate tectonics and all historical geology now stands upon the foundation of Wegener's ideas. The lost intellectual opportunities caused by fifty years of faulty reasoning, as well as the unfair treatment of the individual scientist, who did not live to see his vindication, are extremely regrettable, but in the long run the power of logic and experiment was greater than the power of rhetoric. The error-correction mechanisms of science worked.

Ideally, the error-correction mechanisms of the Liberal Arts disciplines are very similar to those of the sciences. No matter how appealing the theory, it should account for the data, whether that data be experimental, historical, or phenomenological (i.e., the personal experiences and perceptions of individual scholars). Just as in the sciences, a theory that does not account for data should eventually be replaced by one that does. However, the kinds of data produced in the Liberal Arts disciplines are less quantitative and more easily influenced by perception and bias than data in the sciences. Fuzzy data that can be interpreted in multiple ways is less likely to conflict with any given theory, so proportionally more of it will be required to convince the members of a given scholarly discipline, thus causing the pace of error-correction to be slower in the Liberal Arts disciplines than it is in the sciences. Also, an overemphasis on pure theorization (as discussed above) can prevent researchers from noticing conflicting data, thus slowing down the rate at which theories are revised and improved. Nevertheless, fast or slow, as long as scholars in the Liberal Arts require logical reasoning and the continued preservation and collection of data, the errors eventually should be corrected.

Fortunately, although scholars may pay lip-service to the idea that there are no truths, only expressions of power, they act very differently in their home disciplines, where they will rigorously enforce methodological rules and preserve the accumulated knowledge of the field—particularly if that accumulated knowledge includes their own work. Faulty conclusions based on flaws in logical reasoning or ignorance of contradictory data are less frequently found within subdisciplines than they are in work that is more general or abstract. Too much abstraction, interpretation, or theory can lead scholars to get so far ahead of their data that they no longer notice essential corrective information. The greater the distance between abstraction and data, the more likely this gap is to be filled by opinion, prejudice, or political orthodoxy. Indeed, it seems as if there is some conservation law that causes the intensity of political orthodoxy in an interpretation to be inversely proportional to the quantity of data a researcher is taking into account. Subdisciplines usually place a very high value upon their data, as it is this data that makes the subdiscipline itself significant and thus worthy of retaining a separate identity. Within the context of English departments, scholars of Renaissance literature are valuable not for what they do in general—interpreting any old text (which, by definition, could be done by any scholar of English)—but because they possess specific knowledge that someone outside the discipline of Renaissance literature does not have. It is in the best interests of the subdiscipline, then, to ensure that its data are unique, accurate, and extensive enough to require specialization: exactly the sort of data that can also be used to correct faulty interpretations or theories. An emphasis on research within subdisciplines, therefore, is a partial solution for the problem of fuzziness in the Liberal Arts.

Subdisciplines carefully curate their data, and they are also concerned to preserve and transmit their histories, since the intellectual history of a field is part of what distinguishes it within the larger, overarching disciplines—and part of what contributes to the reputations of individual scholars. The history of how data is acquired provides context for that data, so the intellectual history of a field is meta-data that makes information within the field more valuable. For example, if we study Anglo-Saxon literature, which was created in the years 600-1100, we soon discover that the reasons particular texts were preserved and studied have a lot to do with how those texts were used as historical support for political actions in the years 1536-1900. Learning the intellectual history of the discipline of Anglo-Saxon studies allows us not only to read the texts themselves, but to understand why some texts and not others were preserved and transmitted and to identify the many ways they were misinterpreted (deliberately or not) by later readers. This history thus can help us recognize different ways to misread the texts. Knowing the history of the field does not eliminate confirmation bias, but the meta-data about how the information was used previously does help us to counteract the influence of our own desires and therefore correct flaws in our interpretations and theories. The intellectual rigor of subdisciplines, therefore, helps counteract the fuzziness that is inherent in the Liberal Arts. The more we learn, the more we contextualize information within a discipline's intellectual history, the closer we can come to creating methods —like those of science—that consistently find truth (or at least find it more often than they obscure it).

All four problems—poor knowledge of science, over-reliance upon theory, politicization, and fuzziness—are serious and need to be addressed by scholars in the contemporary Liberal Arts. But, as we have seen, there are solutions, all four of which can be reduced to a single commandment: Learn More. To eliminate the influence of bad or obsolete science, learn more current science. To avoid over-theorizing, learn more about the specific details of the phenomena that the theory is attempting to describe so that you will not accept over-generalization. Combat politicization by learning the full intellectual history of the discipline so that both theories and data can be interpreted in their full contexts rather than merely in terms of present, ephemeral political concerns. Reduce fuzziness by learning the details of how subdisciplines evaluate and synthesize information. Learn more! The solution for the problems of the Liberal Arts is more and better work in the Liberal Arts.

Chapter 11

A Defense and a Celebration of the Liberal Arts

I have been teaching the Liberal Arts professionally for a quarter century, so the critique presented in the previous chapter comes from the point of view of an insider. I have tried to be honest in my presentation of the issues and not engage in tendentious presentation of data, but since I am almost certainly biased by my own self-interest, readers should be somewhat skeptical of both my selection of problems and my proposed solutions. Criticisms of the Liberal Arts made by outsiders are usually focused on somewhat different issues than my four big problems. It is unwise to discount these critiques. Outsiders may often see problems more clearly than insiders, especially when insiders have financial, political, and personal interests in maintaining current social arrangements. In this chapter, therefore, I will present four major criticisms of the Liberal Arts that are regularly made by outsiders, but where these claims diverge from the arguments presented in Chapter 10, I will attempt to refute them. This chapter, therefore, will be a defense of the Liberal Arts and, by implication, a celebration of their value.

In 2013, when I recorded the audio course from which this book eventually arose, I said that the cultural respect given to the Liberal Arts had never been lower in my lifetime. Unfortunately, I can say exactly the same words today and still be telling the truth, as the institutional Liberal Arts in America have declined even further in respect and esteem. It should not be a surprise to any reader that I find this to be an unfortunate development. The less valued the Liberal Arts are, the fewer people will reap the benefits of studying them. This is bad for the whole culture, which will be deprived of the good leadership that is promoted by the study of the Liberal Arts (and it is also bad for me personally, since less respect for a discipline results in fewer excellent students for me to teach).

It sometimes seems that every day brings a new critique of the institutional forms of the study of the Liberal Arts in contemporary American academia. The number of individual criticisms is very large, and the pace at which these arguments appear and the passion with which they are made only increased in the aftermath of the 2016 U.S. presidential election and then the general decline in respect for academia (and the larger teaching profession) engendered by responses to the pandemic in 2020. All come from slightly different points of view and emphasize somewhat different features of the contemporary Liberal Arts, but nevertheless I think it is possible to group them into four fundamental critiques:

1. The financial rewards that students receive from studying the Liberal Arts are not large enough compared both to the cost of becoming educated in the Liberal Arts and to the economic benefits of studying the sciences.
2. The social and financial resources now spent on the Liberal Arts would provide a greater benefit for society if they were redirected to the support of the sciences.
3. The current scholars working in the Liberal Arts are almost entirely of the political "left." The institutions of academia not only exclude but are actively hostile to other points of view, so there is no reason for people who have those points of view to keep subsidizing their opponents by supporting the Liberal Arts.
4. The study of the Liberal Arts does not lead to valuable knowledge or skills but is merely a very expensive and time-consuming form of social signaling, the real purpose of which is to maintain a social hierarchy.

I must acknowledge that many of my colleagues, who are just as much insiders as I am, would probably reject out of hand all but the fourth critique, and those with whom I have discussed the issue do not entirely accept even that single argument. Like me, these colleagues lament the low value that many of our countrymen seem to place on the Liberal Arts, but they are inclined to place the blame for this decline outside of our own institutions. Some of them believe that the people who do not value the Liberal Arts are simply stupid or uneducated, or that they have been misled by political propaganda, or that they are consumed by hatred of anyone not exactly like them and therefore despise the Liberal Arts' power to humanize others. Some colleagues have also suggested that the Liberal Arts are not so widely supported because people's opinions have been manipulated by greedy corporate entities that prefer uneducated drones over individuals possessing the thinking abilities provided by the study of the Liberal Arts. Still others have said that the resources that by right belong to the Liberal Arts have been given to the sciences in part because those disciplines are supported by businesses that value technological development over culture. These statements may seem extreme, but I have heard every one of them expressed by fellow professors of Liberal Arts disciplines.

It is possible that there is some truth in each of the assertions in the previous paragraph, but over the past six or seven years I have had discussions with intelligent, educated people who, to the best of my knowledge, do not have corporate ties or extreme political views but who are nevertheless quite critical of contemporary Liberal Arts academia. All of those discussions boiled down to the four big criticisms I noted; no one seemed to resent the power of the Liberal Arts to humanize other people or to think that society would be better if it were peopled with obedient drones. So in what follows, I am going to take the outsiders' criticisms of the Liberal Arts at face value rather than assuming their ignorance or assigning nefarious motives to them.[242] I will therefore engage with what I think is the substance of those four major arguments against the current constitution of the Liberal Arts in American academia.

The first critique, that the study of the Liberal Arts is in various ways too expensive, is, of all the arguments, both the least contentious and the biggest threat to my colleagues' and my self-interest. For forty years, the

[242] Another reliable rule of thumb is that if, when faced with a critique, a person or institution attacks or questions the motives of the *critic* rather than demonstrating errors of fact or flaws in *reasoning*, the critique is usually right.

cost of attending U.S. colleges and universities has grown far more rapidly than family incomes—for example, tuition at Carnegie Mellon was $15,000 per year when I was a freshman in 1986; in 2025, it was over $65,000, an increase of 400% over 30 years.[243] Needless to say, the incomes of middle-class families have not increased that much in the same time frame. The financial crisis of 2008 and the decade of economic stagnation that followed further reduced parental resources and increased the uncertainty surrounding the financial returns on individual investments in higher education, and massive post-pandemic inflation only made things worse.

Although the Liberal Arts are the tools to rule, and although they are a foundation for individual and social success, it is undeniable that the immediate financial rewards for studying these disciplines are not as great as those that come from studying the sciences. The long-term payoff for studying the Liberal Arts may be larger than what students receive from other specialties—the ability to lead effectively is the single most valuable skill a person can possess, and it is rewarded accordingly—but not every student can afford to wait for that longer term when there are enormous student-loan debts that must be repaid right after graduation. This combination of factors—increased costs, economic uncertainty, longer path to rewards—has led many of the people who pay college tuition to be more reluctant to support their children's studies in fields that do not have rapid and definite payoffs, and students are more worried than ever before about how they can use their degrees to earn a living. Simply having gone to college is not the guarantee of career success that it once was.

This conclusion is not mere inference on my part. I often give talks on visiting weekend at Wheaton. Invariably, parents are worried about their children's career prospects if they chose to major in a solidly Liberal Arts discipline like English or Art History. One father, obviously proud of his daughter's superb academic record and her impressive accomplishments in a field as difficult and seemingly esoteric as Anglo-Saxon literature, spoke

[243] Inflation from 1986-2019 averaged approximately 3% per year, so an increase in tuition to $30,000 would be expected. However, the actual cost of tuition at Carnegie Mellon in 2019, before the extreme inflation of 2020-24, was $55,000.

for many when he said, “Professor, I don’t want to discourage my daughter —I am really proud of her accomplishments—but I worry that our family is not rich enough for her to major in English. She is going to need to pay off her student loans, and I don’t see what job she could get with an English degree—being a high school teacher or even a college professor doesn’t pay particularly well. What could she do with a degree in Medieval Literature that would let her have a decent standard of living when she’s got to make loan payments?”

I have been asked this same question, with only slight variations, every single semester since 2009, which is why I provided one answer earlier in this book: she will be the boss. A person with training in the Liberal Arts will eventually rise to be a leader in an organization and will therefore acquire the prestige and financial rewards (and responsibilities) that comes with such a leadership role. The ability to solve complex and messy problems, to communicate effectively, and to lead others is immensely valuable, and organizations reward those who possess these skills. Organizations also value the self-discipline and intellectual ability that are required to succeed in the Liberal Arts. Although it is undoubtedly true that merely having a degree in a Liberal Arts field does not guarantee that immediately upon graduation a student will step into a high-paying, prestigious career, if the experiences of my former students over the past twenty-eight years are any guide, those who succeed in their Liberal Arts studies do rise to the tops of their organizations.

Additional support for my contention that the study of the Liberal Arts is valuable for leadership, and thus for career success, comes from looking at what the elite do. Just like the Roman aristocrats, those “free people” after whom Liberal Arts were named, contemporary social, political, and financial elites educate their children in the traditional Liberal Arts disciplines. The most expensive and prestigious private high schools in America are essentially Liberal Arts colleges for children ages twelve to eighteen. The wealthy and powerful pay enormous sums, sometimes in excess of the extravagant tuition at elite universities, to educate their children in this way because members of the ruling class have every intention of having their children rule. It is not a coincidence that the curricula at the most elite private (and some public) high schools are heavily focused on the most traditional of the Liberal Arts (many, for example, include several years of Latin). If you watch what the elite *do* rather than what they *say*,[244] you can get a good idea of what approaches are most likely to be effective at teaching students how to rule.

These are both good arguments for studying the Liberal Arts, but neither of them is likely to be completely satisfying to the parents who worry that their family is not wealthy enough to afford the seeming luxury of a Liberal Arts education. The financial- and opportunity-costs that come from the delayed payoff of studying the Liberal Arts can be substantial, so this course of study may not be a good choice for all students in all circumstances. Faced with the need to make payments on large loans, an individual student might need the more immediate financial reward that can result from studying business or the sciences: a trade-off between long-term and short-term gains sometimes cannot be avoided, and all things being equal, the sciences and the economically focused disciplines on average do pay more initially.

But all things are never actually equal. It is a mistake to assume that any given person will *be equally good* at the sciences and the Liberal Arts, and it is not at all certain that a mediocre scientist or business-person will be more successful or well-compensated than an excellent teacher, writer, professor, or curator. In fact, as we have discussed in so much detail in previous chapters, it is very likely that the person who excels in English or history or philosophy will develop skills for solving complex problems and leading others and will therefore end up being rewarded. That same person may not excel in engineering, the sciences, or medicine. So although there is some truth in the criticism that the study of the Liberal Arts may not lead to sufficient financial rewards, this problem needs to be understood in the context of both the individual student's talents and enthusiasm and the potentially larger long-term rewards that accrue to the leaders of

[244] For example, the *Wall Street Journal* regularly publishes essays by CEOs and other business leaders arguing for increased vocational training or STEM instruction in high schools. But these people send their own children to preparatory schools, or elite public schools like Boston Latin, that follow a traditional Liberal Arts curriculum.

organizations. A good engineer who enjoys engineering may well make more money than a teacher or editor, but a bad engineer who is miserable doing engineering is unlikely to find more long-term financial success than an excellent Liberal Arts graduate. How to balance immediate reward with long-term gain, as well as many other factors, will determine if a formal education in the Liberal Arts is the right form of study for any given individual.

Fortunately, although it can be very expensive to go to college for the Liberal Arts, studying the Liberal Arts themselves does not need to be costly at all. No high-tech equipment or expensive laboratories or access to the latest editions of scientific journals is necessary. The materials for building a strong foundation in the Liberal Arts are available at almost every local library. The most important texts have long been out of copyright and so are widely available online, in used book stores, and in free libraries. It is certainly more difficult to study any subject without the support of a structured curriculum taught by gifted, committed teachers in an institutional setting, but, unlike those who want to be scientists or engineers, self-taught students of the Liberal Arts do not need to worry that their studies will be obsolete when they eventually reach their learning goals.

The second major criticism of the Liberal Arts is related to the first because both are at their core about comparing the rewards that come from studying the Liberal Arts with those that come from studying other fields. Many people believe that society as a whole would be better off if the resources devoted to the Liberal Arts were redirected towards the sciences. This idea can be quite appealing, since the benefits of scientific and technological progress are so obvious. Indeed, the educational policies of many successful countries have been focused on developing science and technology even if this means neglecting the Liberal Arts. Education, particularly specialized education, can be a zero-sum game. If you spend your hours studying literature, you are not spending them studying physics, so eliminating literature requirements and focusing on physics and other sciences theoretically will lead to students having greater knowledge of science.[245] Likewise, shifting resources from the Liberal Arts to science (for example, hiring more science professors or awarding more science scholarships), would, in theory, lead to greater scientific achievement and therefore concrete improvements in the lives of the people.

However, it is not certain that devoting ever more resources to science will actually produce better results over time. There is likely a point of diminishing returns, since it may be the case that all of the people who have sufficient aptitude for or interest in science are already working in the scientific and technological disciplines. If so, shifting resources in this way would only produce more mediocre (or even bad) scientists or engineers, and the presence of many such people within the disciplines could serve to retard rather than accelerate progress.

Indeed, the scientific and technical disciplines often need effective communication and leadership more than they need additional scientific workers. Many of the most significant problems faced by contemporary society require large teams of people to collaborate. Although there might be a few scientists and engineers who believe that it should be easy to reach consensus decisions on purely rational grounds, in reality a scientific or engineering organization is as human as any other group and therefore requires leadership. In fact, it is often harder to get very smart people to cooperate than it is to organize the less gifted. Leading a team of scientists or engineers is an exercise in herding cats: if you have twelve PhDs in a room, you often have thirteen opinions,[246] and in such circumstances, an effective leader is far, far more valuable than one additional scientist. Training in the disciplines of the Liberal Arts, therefore, can be valuable even when the advancement of science is a political, social, or cultural priority.

Several years ago I was part of a seminar at the Santa Fe Institute, where I met Murray Gell-Mann, who was awarded the 1969 Nobel Prize in Physics for his work on elementary particles (he also named the "quark,"

---

[245] This argument assumes that students are using their time with perfect efficiency. I can only speak for myself, but such an assumption is probably not warranted.

[246] I am not sure how this works mathematically, but I have personally observed the phenomenon.

using a word from James Joyce's *Finnegans Wake*). At this time, I was struggling to interpret the initial results of an investigation of *Beowulf* using Lexomic methods. Although I had the sense that there was some kind of pattern to the confusing and conflicting results of hierarchical cluster analysis of the distribution of vocabulary in the poem, I could not grasp the underlying logic. Then I heard Professor Gell-Mann discuss how he had brought order to the seemingly endless proliferation of elementary particles that were discovered in the 1950s and 1960s, the so-called "particle zoo," by identifying a pattern he called "the eightfold way," a reference to the Noble Eightfold Path of Buddhism.[247] I began studying Gell-Mann's research and eventually came to understand how he had recognized that the combinatorial possibilities of a relatively small and simple set of physical characteristics could explain the full range of particles that had been discovered. I saw that Gell-Mann's use of literary references like "quark" or "eightfold way" was not merely clever labeling but was actually a demonstration of how a deep knowledge of literature, philosophy, languages, religion, and history had contributed to two major scientific breakthroughs. Gell-Mann's vast erudition in traditional Liberal Arts disciplines—languages, literature, religion—combined with his scientific and mathematical knowledge to enable him to detect underlying symmetries in a mass of complex and incomplete data even when a key piece of evidence was missing—the detection of this omega-minus particle in 1964 was a thrilling vindication of Gell-Mann's theory.[248]

This is strong evidence of Liberal Arts thinking leading to better science. My own work is evidence for science improving the Liberal Arts, as, some weeks after I had studied Gell-Mann's work, I suddenly realized that the complicated and confusing initial results of the Lexomic analysis of *Beowulf* could be explained by the computer-assisted methods detecting the influence of a reasonably simple underlying structure. My book *Beowulf Unlocked* would not have been possible without cross-pollination

[247] G. D. Coughlan, J. E. Dodd, and B. M. Gripaios, *The Ideas of Particle Physics: An Introduction for Scientists* (Cambridge: Cambridge University Press, 2006).

[248] George Johnson, *Strange Beauty: Murray Gell-Mann and the Revolution in 20th-Century Physics* (New York: Alfred A. Knopf, 1999); Murray Gell-Mann, *The Quark and the Jaguar: Adventures in the Simple and the Complex* (New York: W.H. Freedman, 1994).

between the sciences and the Liberal Arts, a cross-pollination that occurred for me, as it did for Gell-Mann, as much in ways of thinking as it did with the particular technology used.[249]

The kind of qualitative, first-approximation approaches of many disciplines in the Liberal Arts—approaches that have evolved to try to draw conclusions from incomplete, confusing, or contradictory data—can be an essential first step for scientific or technological accomplishments. More than once in Lexomics research I have cobbled together an awkward, messy, one-time solution for a problem that has horrified my research partners, who are trained in computer science and therefore place a high value on elegance and simplicity. "That is such a hack!" was Professor Mark LeBlanc's comment when I showed him how we could use a simple script to count the numbers of certain letters in each line of a text, manually export that information into a spreadsheet program, calculate the ratio of relative frequencies as a moving average, and plot this on a graph, which could then be used to identify clusters or absences of the letters. It was indeed an inelegant "hack," but my collaborators and I were able to turn this improvisation into an effective technique of analysis. Later, once we had convinced ourselves that the approach was helpful, we built the customized software that allows users to perform this "rolling window analysis" on any electronic text—even if it is written in a non-Roman alphabet—without the awkward cutting, pasting, and shuffling between programs. This new technique, which, as far as we can tell, we invented and which has led to surprising new discoveries about the past, could not have been developed without the kind of thinking that is enabled by the disciplines of the Liberal Arts.[250]

Thus, although I highly value the achievements of science and technology, I cannot agree with the conclusion that the resources spent on the Liberal Arts would necessarily yield better results if instead they were

---

[249] Michael D.C. Drout, Yvette Kisor, Allison Dennett, Natasha Piirainen, and Leah Smith, *Beowulf Unlocked: New Evidence from Lexomic Analysis* (New York: Palgrave, 2016).

[250] Michael D.C. Drout and Elie Chauvet, "Tracking the Moving Ratio of þ to ð in Anglo-Saxon Texts: A New Method, and Evidence for a lost Old English version of the 'Song of the Three Youths,'" *Anglia* 133.2 (2015): 278-319.

used to provide additional support to the scientific disciplines. Not only do the Liberal Arts consume proportionally fewer resources—for most research we only need books and classrooms, which are far less expensive than laboratories and equipment—but they contribute substantially to all areas of human endeavor. Rather than sacrificing the Liberal Arts for science, societies that wish to receive the largest payoffs will find ways to *combine* the Liberal Arts with the sciences so that each can benefit the other.

The third major criticism of the Liberal Arts, that the disciplines are so utterly politicized on one particular side—the "left"—is for me the most difficult and uncomfortable to address, particularly in the current climate of hyper-partisanism in America that arose in the wake of the 2016 presidential election and only got worse through the pandemic. It seems to me that it is almost impossible to discuss political issues without inflaming people's passions, so I fear that this section of the chapter, in which I try not to take a side, will anger many and please few. But avoiding or dismissing this criticism would undermine the entire purpose of the book. An effective defense of the Liberal Arts requires engaging with the strongest and most emotionally powerful arguments against them.

It would be silly to deny that although America as a whole is fairly evenly divided in political preference,[251] an overwhelming majority of the professors who teach in Liberal Arts in American higher education are on the left side of the political spectrum. Extensive survey data as well as the preferences revealed by political donations show that between 80% and 90% of all faculty have generally leftist politics, and I believe even the higher of those two numbers understates the skew in the core Liberal Arts disciplines. There are about 120 professors on the faculty where I teach; I have been at this institution for twenty-eight years; and I have met exactly *one* openly conservative colleague, and he retired a decade ago. Yes, my institution is located in Massachusetts, the most leftward-leaning state in

[251] For the purposes of this argument, it does not matter if the divide in contemporary America is 50/50 or 30% left, 30% right, 40% who do not really care, or some other basically even distribution.

the nation, but I also did not know any conservative professors or graduate students in the urban, Roman Catholic institution in the midwest where I did my PhD and only one or two conservative students (and no professors) at the large state university (also in the midwest) where I was for an MA. This is not an unusual experience for a scholar in the Liberal Arts, and I think it is likely that the true number of scholars in these disciplines who are on the right side of the political spectrum is closer to 1% than it is to 20%.[252]

Critics from the right would explain this seeming political imbalance as the result of the capture of academic institutions by the left, a subsequent multi-decade purge of right-leaning scholars, and the maintenance of leftist political orthodoxy through a range of behaviors running from intellectual disparagement of student opinions to intimidation of colleagues to conspiracies against hiring conservatives or even allowing them to speak on campus. In this view, left-wing academics discourage students with different political opinions from entering graduate school and then actively discriminate against those who seek employment in academia, maintaining a leftist political orthodoxy through dishonesty and force. People on the right, then, are not under-represented in academia because they lack intellectual ability or desire, but because they are never given a fair chance to enter the profession and rise through its ranks.

It is certainly true that starting in the 1960s, left-leaning academics began to replace their right-leaning predecessors throughout American academia. Up through the post-World War II era, college professors were

[252] Up to the end of the 1990s, some critics argued that academia was really not as left-leaning as it seemed because there were conservative faculty concentrated in law and medical schools and in engineering and science. My undergraduate education was at an engineering-focused university—Carnegie Mellon—and I never met a conservative professor (although there were some conservative students). I assume that the denial of reality was intended to defend academia against charges of bias, but it seems pointless, since there is no external body that has the power to change the political make-up of academia, nor any large pool of conservative faculty who could somehow be inserted into professorships to bring about artificial "balance." More recently, scholars have stopped denying that the political make-up of Liberal Arts faculties is primarily of the left, as the evidence for this is simply overwhelming.

more conservative than the general population; since the 1980s, the opposite has been true. But it is not at all clear that this change was the result of conspiracy or even active effort by leftists. The shift in ideology happened at the same time as massive changes in the demographic makeup of the faculty. Before World War II, American professors were ethnically, socially, culturally, and economically much more homogeneous than they were afterwards. The giant expansion in higher education after the war brought new students, and thus soon afterwards new faculty, to the universities from a much wider range of racial, ethnic, and class backgrounds than had previously been the case. Ideology usually tracks demography (or, put in Marxist terms, ideology arises from class interests), so change in the latter could be enough to explain the change in the former.

However, although I think that the changes in the social, ethnic, and economic backgrounds of faculty were by far the most important factor in the original creation of the political skew in Liberal Arts faculties, I do not think the current ideological monoculture can be attributed entirely to this cause. I have observed enough instances of hostility (both deliberate and unconscious, though almost never face-to-face) to right-leaning positions and people over the past thirty years that I find it easy to believe that American academia, particularly in the Liberal Arts disciplines, can be a very unwelcoming environment for a conservative student or professor. Although I did not witness overt discrimination in graduate school, I did hear both professors and fellow graduate students speak dismissively of two or three openly conservative students when they were not present. Worse was the case of the one openly conservative colleague at Wheaton, who was socially shunned and regularly mocked not only politically but also personally by a substantial minority of other faculty, some of whom were at the time very influential on campus. It would be unwise to base too much on this one example, since it is probably impossible to separate hostility due to ideology from enmity arising out of a long history of personal interactions, but colleagues from other institutions have never been surprised when I tell them this story. They know of similar examples of politically generated hostility, usually occurring between 1995-2000 and directed at older colleagues who had been hired in the late 1960s or early 1970s and were thus holdovers from the previous intellectual culture. Fortunately for these professors, they were protected by tenure and reputation, but the experience must still have been miserable. Thus, even if there is no official political discrimination, informal social pressure must surely discourage people with right-leaning political beliefs from choosing academic careers; so there is likely some truth in the conservative assertion that contemporary academia is a hostile social, cultural, and political environment for certain points of view that in the rest of society are not out of the mainstream. But whether this environment is a primary *cause* of the massive political skew among professors in contemporary academia is much more difficult to determine because there are other possible explanations.

Many of my colleagues believe that the current ideological makeup of the professoriate arises from academia being biased in favor of high intelligence, with people on the left being more intelligent than people on the right. There are many problems with this self-congratulatory explanation, but the simplest refutation is the somewhat different ideological distribution in fields like medicine, law, and engineering, which require cognitive abilities at least equal to those required by Liberal Arts academics. Both groups are made up of equally highly intelligent people, but each has different balances of political opinions, indicating that intelligence alone cannot be the cause of the political leanings of professors.

Another possible explanation is that careers in Liberal Arts academia usually do not provide the same level of financial benefits as those in business, medicine, or law, and right-leaning people are more concerned with personal economic success than those on the left, so each group gravitates towards differently remunerative careers. Such an explanation, however, can only work if we ignore the value of the non-monetary but tangible rewards of working in academia, including summers free of classroom responsibilities, regular sabbaticals, and flexible daily and weekly schedules. Add 25% to a professor's salary for the summer and winter breaks and an additional 10% for only having to come to the office three or four days per week and another 5% for being able to come in late or leave early; add in free or heavily discounted tuition for faculty children, and note that all of these non-monetary benefits are not taxed, and the total compensation is quite similar to that of people in other careers that on paper may be more highly paid, thus undercutting the idea that there are so many left-leaning professors because the right-leaning people have gravitated to careers that compensate them more.[253]

I do not think that Liberal Arts professors are significantly more intelligent than doctors, lawyers, financiers, or engineers, or that we professors are any less materialistic than people in other professions. Nor have I seen evidence that in aggregate people with left-leaning politics are so much smarter or less interested in being compensated for their labor than right-leaning individuals that these differences could explain a nine-to-one ratio of political opinions. But I do think that there are some rather consistent differences in personality types between Liberal Arts professors and other highly educated professionals. Scholars of the Liberal Arts choose to study ill-defined problems that rarely have objective, optimal solutions. It may be that people who are comfortable with that kind ambiguity and incomplete knowledge tend to hold certain political opinions (for good or ill), whereas those who dislike the intellectual messiness of the Liberal Arts disciplines, and so are drawn to other fields, hold a different group of political opinions (also for good or ill). Similarly, the types of personalities drawn to the Liberal Arts may differently value the *kind* of compensation they receive for their labor. For example, Liberal Arts professors may value individual autonomy in their day-to-day work and having long periods of "alone time" much more highly than do the individuals who take up careers in professions like medicine, law, and business, which may require more formal and constant teamwork. Likewise, many professors place a high value on their freedom to pursue a line of inquiry regardless of the time required for the research or its practical utility, trading this freedom for potentially less monetary compensation.

[253] I can testify that Liberal Arts professors ferociously defend these non-monetary perks. In negotiations with administrators over compensation and benefits, the most idealistic and otherworldly professors in the most esoteric fields suddenly transform themselves into flinty-eyed, never-give-an-inch bargainers who can out-patience a Galapagos tortoise and out-stubborn an Army mule.

Professors in general also may be more risk-averse and thus willing to sacrifice upside potential (very few of us will ever become really wealthy from our jobs) in order to be protected against financial downsides, while people in other careers may be more willing to risk losses if there is a chance of large rewards in the future. These kinds of value-judgments may very well be correlated, at any given time and place, with some set of political opinions. The current ideological culture in Liberal Arts academia, therefore, may not have a single cause but may instead be the result of the interplay of various factors: some discrimination, some self-selection, and some shared values. In literary terms, we would say that the political skew is "overdetermined," in that any one factor *might* be sufficient to explain the phenomenon, so it is impossible to determine which one is the actual cause.

Someone who wanted to defend the current dominance of one side of the political spectrum could argue that the opinions currently held by Liberal Arts scholars are closer to the truth, that there is a logical inevitability to these political positions, and therefore that intelligent, thoughtful people will generally share them. We would all like to think that our own political stances are obviously correct, but even the most cursory study of intellectual history shows that every political position is seen by those who hold it as being the inevitable conclusion of logical reasoning. Previous generations of scholars certainly thought that their own positions —sometimes diametrically opposed to today's consensus opinions—were reached through rigorous logic and based upon carefully considered evidence. Supporters of eugenics, for example, did not think of themselves as racist, murderous monsters intent on killing the non-conforming but instead as being strong-minded altruists willing to see uncomfortable truths and take unpopular actions in order to "save" the human race from a crisis (imaginary) of accumulating negative mutations.[254] The conclusion

[254] What proponents of eugenics actually said in support of actions—such as forced sterilization and infanticide—that we now perceive as almost inhumanly cruel is actually more frightening than the way they have been characterized by later commenters who want to portray them as monsters. Instead of hatred and disdain for those they considered inferior, their "more-in-sorrow-than-in-anger" writings, which warned of the looming disaster for the human race that would be caused by the accumulation of genetic defects

that any specific political opinions are the inevitable result of the logical reasoning of intelligent, thoughtful, educated people founders on the brute fact that the specific opinions of the intelligent, thoughtful, educated people of the past are massively different from the specific opinions of the intelligent, thoughtful, educated people of the present.

This argument might be salvaged if there really were a directionality to historical development, if it were certain that each generation was progressing inevitably towards some sort of perfection in its culture (the "arc of progress" trope). The institutions of the Liberal Arts today, then, would necessarily be better than those of the previous generations, and we could be confident that the next generation's would be better still. Undoubtedly some people do believe this, and certainly when it comes to technology and our knowledge of the natural world, for several centuries each generation has progressed beyond its ancestors by standing on the shoulders of giants. But any equivalence between continuous improvements in technology and those in politics or culture is difficult to substantiate. Both the Whigs in the eighteenth and nineteenth centuries, and the original Marxists in the twentieth, believed that history was inevitably progressing towards their preferred forms of social organization. Their imagined perfect societies, however, were distinctly different from each other despite being built upon the same basic material foundations, and, more importantly, the actual path of history turned out to be not at all what their theories predicted. No objective evidence allows us to conclude that either culture or politics progresses steadily and inevitably towards some ultimate perfection. Any teleological interpretation of human progress can only be maintained if it is so abstract as to allow for continuous reinterpretation.

Although I do believe, as I have argued above, that studying the Liberal Arts leads to a better understanding of humanity, and it would seem that such improved understanding would eventually lead to better

(entirely illusory) if the "unfit" were not prevented from reproducing, lamented the harshness of the actions they were advocating. In an eerie premonition of those who in 2021 argued that people refusing to be vaccinated against Covid should have their children taken away from them and be placed in camps, the eugenicists saw themselves as clear-eyed followers of science in a society about to be destroyed by too much compassion.

political ideologies, the evidence is not on my side. The wild variation in the actual political opinions that we find arising after deep study in the Liberal Arts, including the truly weird things that some brilliant scholars of the past have believed and the similarly bizarre obsessions that some present scholars develop, does not support the conclusion that the distribution of political opinions in contemporary academia—as congenial as it may be for many of us—is necessarily better than some other arrangement, and the history of the Liberal Arts suggests that a seemingly stable balance can shift rapidly as the result of a preference cascade. Those of us who are comfortable should also be self-aware, open-minded, and mindful that our disciplines are of their very nature corrosive of orthodoxies.

Furthermore, in practical terms, students and scholars have substantially more intellectual and political freedom than the seemingly overwhelmingly one-sided distribution of political opinions in the contemporary Liberal Arts would suggest. In more than two decades of being a professor I have never personally observed political intolerance filtering down to treatment of individual undergraduates—even in the hyper-political environment that has prevailed since 2016.[255] In fact, my experience at Wheaton has shown me that even the most politically left-wing of my colleagues regularly become devoted to students who occupy a different part of the political spectrum. The "conservative" students at Wheaton are probably still pretty far to the left in absolute terms, but even here they occupy noticeably different places on the political continuum than most faculty. Yet it seems that these are exactly the students who end up being most intensely supported and mentored by the most liberal professors. For example, one of Wheaton's alumnae, a former Republican governor and cabinet official, was supported throughout her studies and her early career by two of my colleagues whose personal politics were (in their own words) "proudly *very* left-liberal." These colleagues, who were both regular campaign volunteers and consultants for Democratic political campaigns, went far beyond even the high expectations students at a small Liberal Arts colleges have for their professors: working individually with

[255] At least not yet.

the student, directing research, arranging internships, preparing for graduate study, writing multiple letters of recommendation, and using every bit of leverage they had to support the student's career. This was not an isolated incident; it was regular practice even in some of the most contentious decades of the twentieth century, and, as best I can tell, it holds true even today.

I think it is more likely than not that we professors end up closely mentoring students whose politics differ from our own because teachers of the Liberal Arts tend to value independence in our students. We love what we teach and want to share our passion with others: disagreement, even vigorous disagreement, is much better than indifference. A student who cares enough to debate with us actually cares about our subject! Teaching such a student, one who has the intellectual strength to argue for a position different from that of the teacher, is such a great intellectual pleasure that we end up supporting that student even if we disagree with everything he or she concludes. Students who have received such intellectual challenge and support in their studies are then much more likely to attend graduate school and eventually become faculty. It may be, therefore, that we faculty are unintentionally laying the groundwork for a new generation of scholars whose opinions differ greatly from our own. Indeed, such a dynamic may be the ultimate source of the regular shifts in faculty opinions that have characterized the history of the Liberal Arts.

Ideological shifts also occur because of the corrosive power of the study of the Liberal Arts with regard to political orthodoxies of every kind. Any political program that can appeal to a large enough coalition to bring about electoral success in a country of hundreds of millions of people must of necessity either contain internal contradictions or be so abstract as to allow multiple interpretations of its stated ideology: there are simply too many conflicting and constantly changing interests in a complex modern nation for any logically coherent political program to remain consistent through time and space.[256] Thus the only way for political orthodoxy to

[256] You can see this if you trace the changes in the platforms of the two major political parties from 1956 to 2024.

persist is by preventing people from knowing the details of history[257] and from being exposed to different points of view; otherwise the orthodoxy will not survive continual challenge by data.[258] The study of the Liberal Arts requires both history and engagement with many ideas and beliefs. The transmission of intellectual history within a discipline works against efforts to erase variations in culture—I have never met a Liberal Arts professor who believes that the monsters of the Khmer Rouge were correct in trying to eliminate previous culture and start from "year zero." Professors and museum curators may currently be almost uniformly leftist, but their work supports neither left nor right because it transcends politics: art and literature and music have the power to move us long after the immediate political contexts in which they were created and the political enthusiasms of their makers has been forgotten by everyone—except scholars of the Liberal Arts.[259]

The intense politicization of the contemporary Liberal Arts can be frustrating, even to those professors who share most of the same opinions as the dominant orthodoxy. The very nature of an orthodoxy is that people under its hegemony never say anything new because they all already agree. Political discussion (by non-specialists) therefore tends to be intellectually shallow, trending rapidly towards the lowest common denominator of "us vs. them," even as it drowns out other topics in a vicious circle of competitive virtue-signaling. As a great deal of what academics published over the past ten years demonstrates, the politicization of everything is a remarkably effective method of making smart, interesting people say

---

[257] Satirized perfectly by George Orwell in *1984* by the EngSoc government's assertion that "Oceania has always been at war with Eurasia" when Oceana had been at war with Eastasia the previous week.

[258] Intense enforcement of orthodoxy is also a sign that the orthodox position is wrong; otherwise it would not need to be enforced through such strong political or social pressure.

[259] It is hard to imagine a more furiously partisan writer than John Milton, but despite filling books with explanatory footnotes and employing our most impassioned tones in lectures, we just cannot get students to care, even a little bit, about the specific politics of seventeenth-century England that so motivated the author of *Paradise Lost*. Of the dozen colleagues I know who love *Paradise Lost* with passionate intensity, not one does so because of Milton's devotion to Parliamentarianism.

boring, repetitive, and predictable things. Politicization also allows people to hide their ordinary academic politics (i.e., personal efforts to obtain resources and status) under a moral cloak: professors can *say* that they are trying to move a department or organization towards a more politically favored stance, when their true desire is merely for increased power for them and their allies. The camouflage provided by intense politicization makes it more difficult to recognize, and thus prevent—or punish—such undesirable (but very common) behavior.

Political orthodoxy is also dangerous in the long run, not so much to the Liberal Arts themselves, but to the particular people and institutions that currently constitute them. The problem is not the particular positions that are currently orthodox in Liberal Arts academia (although that is easy for me to say, since most of them don't particularly bother me), but the acceptance of *any* political orthodoxy in general. The politics of the day are always ephemeral. As human culture evolves to adapt to changing material circumstances, current hot-button issues will eventually fade away and be replaced by others. Orthodoxies, however, by their very nature prevent incremental adaptation to new conditions and so tend to collapse in very dramatic ways. Accepting any single political orthodoxy makes us less able to resist the imposition of some different one that we will likely find less congenial than what is now in place. My sense of the current situation is that although there is no real objection among the vast majority of faculty (or students) to the *content* of the current political orthodoxy, there is a widespread discomfort with how much space politics of all kinds takes up in our institutions. After all, most scholars of the Liberal Arts prefer our own subjects to politics—otherwise we would have studied political science! We may, therefore, be on the edge of the kind of "preference cascade" that occurs when large numbers of people suddenly realize that beliefs they had avoided expressing—either out of fear of contradicting an orthodox position or because they believed them to be idiosyncratic—are actually widely shared. I hope that if a preference cascade does occur, Liberal Arts academia will replace the current political orthodoxy not with a different one, but with no orthodoxy at all, but I fear that such a happy result is not particularly likely.

I have just criticized politicization at length, but I also want to acknowledge that in at least some ways its existence is highly encouraging for a partisan of the Liberal Arts themselves rather than of any one political "side." The very fact that people fight so vehemently about these subjects, trying to harness the powers of the disciplines for their own factions, demonstrates the importance of the Liberal Arts. If the Liberal Arts really were frivolous relics of the past that produce nothing useful and can now be safely ignored, no one would care enough to argue about them so intensely.

The final of the four major critiques of the Liberal Arts comes not from outside the disciplines, but from inside, or at least from one subset of insiders. These critics believe that the institutional Liberal Arts contribute substantially to the maintenance of America's class structure—that they help to preserve the current social hierarchy. Note that this critique implicitly assumes the truth of my thesis that the Liberal Arts are the "tools to rule," but with the difference that the tools are used not for problem-solving or general societal improvement, but for social domination.

Professor John Guillory is one of the most prominent scholars who argue that a Liberal Arts education is primarily valued because for students it produces "cultural capital" that can help students to rise up in the social hierarchy.[260] That interpretation is not entirely opposed to many elements of my argument for the value of the Liberal Arts, although I would call the result Guillory identifies as "increased cultural labor-power" rather than his term, "cultural capital" (if we are going to use quasi-Marxist terminology, it should at least be accurate). But while I have focused on the ways that the study of the Liberal Arts can improve a person's decision-making and leadership skills, Guillory emphasizes how Liberal Arts knowledge can be used to signal class membership and thus to draw boundaries around social classes.

In this view, education in the Liberal Arts is much like the work of what in previous eras were called "finishing schools." These institutions

---

[260] John Guillory, *Cultural Capital: The Problem of Literary Canon Formation* (Chicago: University of Chicago Press, 1993).

prepared women from upper-middle-class backgrounds to enter higher ranks of society by training them in the manners and customs of the higher social class. Finishing schools taught people the subtle signals of dress, speech, posture, and movement that indicated membership in an elite. At finishing schools, people also learned the proper topics for and structures of conversations (i.e., rhetoric, though in a restricted sense) and the correct opinions to express in order to enter into the highest social classes.

The more difficult a social signal is to counterfeit, the more valuable it is, so the great cost of a Liberal Arts education actually supports the "cultural capital" thesis. In biology the "handicap principle," first formulated by Amotz Zahavi, suggests that metabolically expensive but physically unnecessary features of an animal, like peacocks' tails, evolve for the purpose of signaling genetic fitness to potential mates by indicating the possession of superior resources.[261] The social signal of an expensive education similarly demonstrates resource surplus and so indicates to potential allies or mates the high status of the person who possesses them.

The weakness in the "cultural capital" thesis, however, is that any expensive course of behavior could be just as effective a social signal as a Liberal Arts education. The *content* of the education, the discipline studied, is irrelevant if that education is being used purely as a signal; what matters is the cost. The "cultural capital" thesis can explain why people pursue expensive and time-consuming paths of education for their children, but it does not explain why aristocrats have for two thousand years educated their children in the *specific* disciplines of the Liberal Arts. This is not to say that the particular books read, artworks viewed, or music listened to cannot be used as signaling devices—indeed, social signaling through culturally exclusive "taste" is a well-documented phenomenon—only that there are many other more obviously effective ways of sending those particular signals than studying the Liberal Arts.

For these reasons I think that the "cultural capital" hypothesis is not entirely accurate, but like all the major critiques of the Liberal Arts, it does contain elements of truth. Study of the Liberal Arts can and does

---

[261] Amotz Zahavi, *The Handicap Principle: A Missing Piece of Darwin's Puzzle* (Oxford: Oxford University Press, 1997).

signal social class membership in ways that, because they require a great investment of money, time, and effort, are difficult to counterfeit. More importantly, however, education in the Liberal Arts broadcasts information about a person's *individual* abilities and experiences. Mastery of some field within the Liberal Arts demonstrates that a student is intelligent and self-disciplined and so will likely be able to solve complex problems, communicate effectively, and become a leader of an organization.

As I said above, I tell the parents of my students: "Studying medieval literature shows that your kid is *wicked smaht*." Humans value many other qualities in addition to intelligence, but intelligence is both harder to prove and easier to fake than physical strength, health, or attractiveness, so it is very valuable to have a hard-to-counterfeit way to signal your intelligence to potential employers, partners, friends, collaborators, or mates. This is why I do not think "cultural capital" is a particularly good description of what is acquired by education. "Capital" is accumulated value that can be used to generate new income without the owner performing labor. Education in the Liberal Arts does not so much store value that can be used independently of a person (like a machine or a factory), but instead increases the labor-power of the individual student.[262] Mastering a discipline of the Liberal Arts signals the truth that people so educated can be expected to perform valuable work in the future—because they have demonstrated that they know how to learn. Studying the Liberal Arts transforms your brain's work from unskilled to highly skilled labor. Although signaling that you have such skill is valuable, being skilled is far more important.

I am not so naïve as to believe that in this brief space I have fully refuted every aspect of the four major criticisms of the Liberal Arts. There is some truth in all of the critiques because the contemporary institutions that

[262] The ability to signal social status acquired by students of the Liberal Arts is only "capital" in a very sloppy, non-economic and non-Marxist sense (which is ironic in light of the politics and affiliations of the people who most frequently use the word this way). In this case "capital" merely means "something valuable," which is a reasonable colloquial interpretation but is only explanatory in a vague, metaphorical sense.

house the study of the Liberal Arts and the people who pursue that study are imperfect in many different ways. All human institutions are flawed, and the academic Liberal Arts are human institutions. But, as I have tried to show in this chapter and throughout this book, the benefits of the study of the Liberal Arts outweigh even the very high costs of the institutions in which they are currently housed. Study of the Liberal Arts can lead to both material success and societal improvement, and this learning is also a path to personal understanding and fulfillment.

Over the past decade, I have recorded thirteen audio college courses. These are purchased not primarily by college students, but by people who are outside of the university system, usually because they have already completed their formal education in non-Liberal Arts disciplines. I have received emails from doctors, lawyers, accountants, military officers, bankers, heavy-equipment operators, writers, artists, comedians, diplomats, and teachers, all of whom tell me that they have discovered (or re-discovered) a love for the Liberal Arts. They listen to my courses and study these disciplines not because they think doing so will produce immediate material rewards, but because their learning brings them joy.

In T.H. White's novel *The Once and Future King*, Merlin advises a young King Arthur that learning is the cure for sorrow:

> The best thing for being sad...is to learn something. That is the only thing that never fails. You may grow old and trembling in your anatomies, you may lie awake at night listening to the disorder of your veins, you may miss your only love, you may see the world about you devastated by evil lunatics, or know your honor trampled in the sewer of baser minds. There is only one thing for it then-to learn. Learn why the world wags and what wags it. That is the only thing which the mind can never exhaust, never alienate, never be tortured by, never fear or distrust, and never dream of regretting. Learning is the best thing for you. Look at what a lot of things there are to learn—pure science, the only purity there is. You can learn astronomy in a lifetime, natural history in three, literature in six. And then after you have

> exhausted a million lifetimes in biology and medicine and theocriticism and geography and history and economics, why, you can start to make a cartwheel out of appropriate wood, or spend fifty years learning to begin to learn to beat your opponent at fencing. After that you can start again on mathematics until it is time to plough.[263]

The Liberal Arts contributes to happiness and success by teaching people how to think, providing tools to rule and thus giving people power to make the world better and the knowledge of how to do so. These disciplines link individuals to a vast continuum of human knowledge, accomplishment, and experience. Each person is made more valuable, and more human, by learning how to think and by being connected to the great tradition, benefiting from the accumulated wisdom (and error) of the past, struggling with the complex problems of the present, and pushing forward the boundaries of knowledge to create the future. The Liberal Arts are the study of humanity and its works. There is no subject more fascinating or noble.

---

[263] T.H. White, *The Once and Future King* (London: Collins, 1958).

Afterword

It's the Liberal Arts That can Save Us From the Looming AI Slop-tastrophe

The tortuous path of the writing, revision, and publication of this book should have led to disaster. A lot of things happened in the dozen years between the time I recorded the initial audio course in 2013 and the appearance of the current physical volume. A *lot* of things. You might expect—I certainly did—that big sections of the book would have had to be rewritten multiple times in order to still be relevant twelve years after their were first discussed, but except for the cascade of incorrect predictions I made about the evolution of Presidential rhetoric (discussed in Chapter 10), there really was not much material that I had to update or correct in the final proofing. It is hard to imagine a better demonstration of the timeless applicability of the Liberal Arts than this consistency across more than a decade of some of the most rapid and chaotic social and cultural change in recent history. So I am quite confident that the Liberal Arts will weather the systemic shock to our educational institutions and practices by developments in what most people are calling "Artificial Intelligence."[264]

Whether the higher education system in the United States will itself survive, and how different it will be from what it is in 2025, is much harder to predict, and given the track record of my prognostications (see above), you would be wise not to put too much weight on predictions—and I would be wiser not to make any. All I can say with a reasonable amount of certainty is that some practices that are absolutely fundamental to the current system are going to have to change, and rapidly, or the system itself will no longer be able to educate students.

---

[264] Although ChatGPT and similar programs are not "Artificial Intelligence" but are instead just "Large Language Models," it is futile to try to avoid the now-omnipresent generic term "AI."

My gut feeling is that we are currently in yet another speculative technology bubble, this one caused by a somewhat bizarre but very powerful combination of viral marketing, wishful thinking, fear-mongering, and straight-line extrapolation.[265] In almost every article or news story about AI, there seems to be an unstated and naïve assumption that AI will get much better than it currently is at separating truth from falsity and eliminating "hallucinations." But no one knows how to make Large Language Models do these things, or even if it is possible to do so. It is well documented that the inclusion of AI-produced material into an AI's training data rapidly degrades the performance of the software, regardless of whether that AI-generated material is "slop" or carefully vetted and hand-revised writings or images. Unfortunately, there has been an explosion of AI-created material not just on the open internet but in ostensibly curated and evaluated knowledge bases, including scientific journals and supposedly authoritative news sources. Thus almost all sufficiently large collections of training data are becoming more and more contaminated with AI-generated material at the same time that current approaches to improving AI are based on training LLMs on larger and larger datasets. It is not obvious what the technical solution to this problem will be, and in many ways it does not matter, because we already have a set of techniques for determining whether or not writings are true or false: the Liberal Arts themselves.

However, for the purposes of education, it does not matter if AIs improve very much or not at all because students are using them now. The problem is not to find clever methods of catching students using AI to

[265] Tom Renner argues that the current hysteria over AIs is based on our cultural expectations that information that comes out of machines is always reliable despite this no longer being true. Most individuals have not yet adjusted to this new reality, so it is no wonder that our culture has not figured out how to handle AIs. Renner also notes that LLMs are trained using "Reinforced Learning from Human Feedback" and that this training is massively more effective in making AIs interact with their users in pleasing ways than it is in separating true statements from false. The creepy parasocial relationships some people form with AIs have the potential to be very damaging to both individuals and the wider society. See https://tomrenner.com/posts/400-year-confidence-trick/.

cheat but to reform the educational system so that students are motivated to do what is best for their own learning.

Still reeling from the substantial damage that the institutional responses to the pandemic did not just to colleges but to the entire educational pipeline, higher education was blindsided by the advent of ChatGPT and other Large Language Model chatbots that could write papers for college students. Although our colleagues in Computer Science had been telling us about advances in machine learning and hidden-layer neural networks, many professors (myself included) initially believed that most of what we were hearing was typical marketing hyperbole spread by credulous journalists. However, with shocking speed, we went from easily ignored hype about the supposedly unlimited potential of Artificial Intelligence to problems that were far more significant than the development of some new techniques for cheating. Academic journals reported being swamped with computer-generated content; lawyers were sanctioned for submitting documents that included fake citations an LLM had hallucinated; and the tics of AI-created writing began appearing in book reviews, letters of recommendation, and even the *personal* statements of candidates for academic jobs.

It is all a huge mess.

Dealing with the mess is going to be one of the major intellectual projects of the next decade. Somehow we will have to stop AI-slop from overwhelming, through sheer quantity, true human writing. We will have to track down and remove all the LLM hallucinations that have already gotten into our knowledge base, and we will need to block further contamination. Most difficult of all, we will need to discover ways to prevent ourselves from being manipulated through AI. But as serious as all these problems are, in the short term, they are dwarfed by the problem of figuring out how to educate our students now that LLMs can effortlessly generate the essays that have been the primary means of evaluating learning for more than a century.

Education at the college level is going to have to change, and change fast, or the entire rickety edifice is going to collapse. The current system cannot function if students do not do their own writing and professors do not read and give feedback on that writing. Very soon—within a year or two—we will find ourselves in a situation described in wry tones by workers in the former Soviet Union: "We pretend to work, and they pretend to pay us." Professors will be pretending to teach; students will pretending to learn; and money will be exchanged for a credential rather than for actual education. This is not a sustainable business model, to say nothing of its complete lack of morality or social utility. But although it might be better if AI had never been invented, or if students at every level could be denied access to it until their educations were complete, that is certainly not possible now (and probably never was), so we are going to have to adapt. Otherwise, it will not be long before we will be graduating college students whose writing abilities are limited to the composition of AI prompts, and contrary to the cheerleading by AI companies, this will *not* be a good thing.[266]

"The only writing that most people will have to do after college will be composing AI prompts" is an awfully large prediction based on less data than my presidential-rhetoric forecasts, and it is even less likely to be correct. Assuming the predictions of an AI-driven future will come true and concluding that therefore "*We only need to focus on training students to write effective AI prompts*" is educational malpractice.[267] Even if writing in

[266] Preempting the argument that if higher-quality AI becomes ubiquitous, designing effective prompts would be all the writing most people would need to do.

[267] It is more than a little disturbing that the people most strongly advocating for not just encouraging AI use but for spending time and effort *teaching* students to use AI more effectively are exactly the same people who most vehemently asserted that the "asynchronous teaching and learning" that arose during the pandemic was just as good as traditional approaches. It is now undeniable that all pandemic-era education, particularly asynchronous teaching, was massively inferior to traditional methods. Indeed, it was obvious at the time, which is why I completely ignored all such directives, spent my own money to purchase sufficient electronic equipment to livestream my classes, and managed to keep my classes as close to their pre-pandemic forms as was humanly possible. My student evaluations and, more importantly, the performance of my pandemic-era students strongly imply that my approach was superior to the asynchronous approaches that institutions like the Modern Language Association claimed were just as good (in hindsight, these claims seem to have been intended to prevent parents from suing for

the future really does turn out to be merely the generation of prompts, people will still need to learn all the other things in addition to writing that we teach in college, and they will not be able to if we simply add the indiscriminate use of LLMs to contemporary college practices.

It is true that LLMs are just tools and college-level instruction has previously survived the introduction of tools that drastically changed the day-to-day practices of both students and teachers. The paper-and-pencil calculation that used to be a significant part of engineering, physics, and even mathematics itself through the first half of the twentieth century is now accomplished using MATLAB and other software, which itself replaced simpler software, which replaced pocket calculators, which replaced slide-rules. Few people would say that there has been a concomitant collapse in mathematical skills.[268] But the analogy is imperfect. Pure calculation had stopped being central to the college mathematics curriculum even before the development of calculating machines, which is why the people who specialized in accurately performing complex calculations were not called mathematicians but *computers*.[269] Writing, in contrast, pervades every aspect not just of the humanities, but of the arts, sciences, and social sciences: we create, evaluate, transmit, and preserve knowledge through writing. We often do not know what we think until we struggle to write it down. Outsourcing writing to software, therefore, does far more damage than preventing students from developing their writing skills in English classes: it risks crippling their learning and even their thinking.

Unfortunately, to this point almost all the debate over these issues has focused on the problem of how to evaluate students if their writing is being done by AI. But there are straightforward solutions if all we are concerned about is end-of-the-course evaluations (i.e., student final

---

tuition refunds as a response to the inferior instruction their children received).

[268] We don't actually know whether or not there was a loss of intuition that had previously developed from making long and complex calculations and if that intuition would have led to greater progress in mathematics, physics, and engineering. It is a mistake to assume that there are no trade-offs. There are always trade-offs.

[269] What we call computers were originally named electronic computers to distinguish then for the people who worked as computers.

grades). Either we will have students write graded essays in an AI-free environment, or we will adopt other methods of evaluating student performance, probably through the "high-stakes" exams that much of academia has spent the past two decades vilifying and eliminating.

Far more concerning is the potential loss of professors' ability to monitor students' learning and provide feedback by reading and critiquing student essays. If students are using AI to write their papers for them, professors will lose an important tool for determining how well their students are understanding the material—not for the purposes of grading but in order to know how to adjust the class's pace, repetition (or lack of same), and focus. Even worse, students will no longer get accurate feedback on their understanding of the material being covered and their ability to discuss and contextualize it.

I am reasonably confident that higher education will eventually adjust, but the process is going to be chaotic and confusing, uneven in its implementation, and suboptimal for everyone. It is also going to take quite a while to get the whole mess sorted out, and my fear is that, during this interregnum, student learning will suffer greatly, and some students will never get a chance to make up for the lost opportunities.

Fortunately, there is a solution for any individual students who want to maximize the intellectual benefits of their college educations: avoid using Large Language Models and other kinds of AI in your academic work, and study the Liberal Arts.

For years, my go-to metaphor for helping students and their parents work through their college choices has been to compare picking a college to selecting a gym to join.[270] There are many different kinds of gyms because people have many different reasons for joining one. People choose a gym based on the price, the location, the equipment, the amenities, the quality of the personal trainers, the kinds of people who work out there, and various other criteria. You can see how this is a decent metaphor for recognizing that the "right" college for any given student is not necessarily the most famous, most expensive, or most prestigious but the one that has

[270] Okay, a gym membership that costs more than the car you would use to drive to the gym. Metaphors—even extended ones—do not need to match up in every detail.

the particular combination of features that *fits* that student's needs and desires,

Now extend that metaphor to what students do in college. Imagine that you have joined a gym with the goal of becoming stronger. As part of your very expensive membership, you get the services of a personal trainer, who designs a program of exercise that, if followed, will help you meet your goal. To help motivate you, the gym will award you a certificate for completing each stage of your program. But when your trainer tells you to do a certain number of reps at a particular weight, instead of doing it yourself, you pay Bruno, the huge guy who is always hanging out at the gym, to lift the weights for you when the trainer isn't looking. Your trainer doesn't find out, and you get your certificate. But you actually haven't gotten any stronger, so the money you spent on your membership has been wasted.

Yes, Bruno = AI. Students using Large Language Models to write college essays might end up with impressive looking certificates, but they won't actually be able to do the stuff that the certificate implies they can do because they haven't developed the strength and skills that the essays were intended to help build. Students will have paid an enormous amount of money for a credential, not the actual knowledge that the credential is supposed to indicate, and although in the short term, this may allow people get interviews at prestigious employers or have a better chance of getting into a particular professional school, it won't be long before the mismatch between what the credentials imply and what the students can actually do starts to cause problems for them.

That said, I completely understand why students are so strongly tempted to use AI to write their papers. It is difficult to turn down a short-term advantage, even one that you know isn't good for you in the long run, particularly when the inevitable end-of-semester time-crunch comes. Having grades and their associated rewards involved makes the use of AI that much more tempting. Although Large Language Models produce blandly average writing—what my current students disparagingly call "mid"—students who think they are below-average writers see themselves benefiting in the short term if they outsource their writing to AI.

Understandable, but a form of educational self-harm from a more long-term perspective. Students who want to get the greatest possible benefits from their incredibly expensive educations will need to resist the temptation to outsource their writing to Large Language Models just as the people who want to grow stronger need to resist the temptation to get Bruno to lift their weights for them.

Unfortunately, this prescription is insufficient because it does not address the problem of the "arms race" dynamic of continual escalation that can pressure—even coerce—people to adopt technologies that they would rather avoid in order not to fall behind those who have adopted them. This is the same dynamic that occurs with performance enhancing drugs in athletics, and as with drug-use, AI-use comes at a cost that users will still be paying long after the temporary advantage has faded. In these kinds of circumstances, only wide-scale solutions have a chance of working. The ban on performance-enhancing drugs has to be implemented consistently across the entire sports-league, or it will be ineffectual. Likewise, the elimination of AI from graded writing will most likely need to be done across the board to have any chance of working. It may be possible for the educational establishment to accomplish this via some kind of collective action, but it seems more likely that some set of rules will be imposed by governments. Until that time, we are in a chaotic situation in which every institution—if not every teacher—will take an idiosyncratic, ad hoc approach to AI. The inconsistencies alone will make it very difficult for people to navigate the rules and regulations. Thus it will always be safer personally to avoid using AI for writing essays and exams, and students who do so will get the added benefit of learning more, and more thoroughly, than those who rely upon the electronic tools.

Avoiding using Large Language Models is a negative solution to the problem of the use of AI undercutting student learning. Actively studying the Liberal Arts is the positive solution to another set of problems associated with AI that extends well beyond the classroom and the campus.

One of the reasons I personally have little desire to use Large Language Models[271] is that whenever I have experimented with AI, invariably the results have always contained some information that I knew to be wrong. For example, in early 2024, I asked ChatGPT to give me a capsule biography of the science fiction writer Robert A. Heinlein. The LLM did produce clear, grammatically correct sentences, and it is important not to lose sight of how difficult that feat was to achieve. Additionally, many of the facts were correct. But ChatGPT also wrote, "Heinlein's study of engineering at MIT contributed to the technical accuracy of his early short stories..." There is a small, technical problem with this sentence: although Heinlein did study engineering, it was at the Naval Academy, not MIT. Presumably, because in its training data the words "studied engineering" were more frequently followed by "MIT" than by "Naval Academy," the Large Language Model "hallucinated" that Heinlein had gone to that school.

In the middle of 2025, wanting to make sure that I had not missed any relevant essays, I used Grok to see if anyone had made a particular point about *The Lord of the Rings*, asking the AI if anyone else had noted that for a brief moment towards the end of the narrative, the hobbit Frodo and the Dark Lord Sauron both have only nine fingers. "That is an original insight," Grok replied. "Yes! After Shelob's attack has severed Frodo's finger, the hobbit and Sauron both have only nine fingers (Wilson 2016)." As nice as it was to be buttered up by an AI and told I was original, there were problems with this statement in that the giant spider-creature Shelob never bites off Frodo's finger (that is done by Gollum), and worse, there is no author "Wilson" who published a paper in 2016 noting this. Indeed, there is no one named Wilson who published anything on *The Lord of the Rings* in 2016, and worse still, if such an article did exist, Grok's assertion

[271] I have not used them at all for the two books that I have written or revised since ChatGPT became available. The book you are reading and my *The Tower and the Ruin: J.R.R. Tolkien's Creation* are 100% artisanal writing.

that no one had noted the parallel before me would be wrong.[272] What a mess!

I also tried Google's AI, asking for parallels in other works of fantasy or science fiction to the unexplained reference to "the Cats of Queen Beruthiel" in *The Lord of the Rings.* The program returned a sample quotation: "'We must be careful,' said Aragorn. 'The Cats of Queen Beruthiel are spying on us.'" But Aragorn never says any such thing, and in fact, no one has ever said any such thing, as the exact phrase "the Cats of Queen Beruthiel are spying on us" does not appear in any internet-searchable text. Oops.

From these examples, you might think that AI hallucinations are limited to biographical or literary details but that scientific facts should be immune because the internet should not have a lot of examples of incorrect numbers for, say, the atomic weight of aluminum. Sadly, no. My wife was looking up information on various lead/tin solders, and the LLM that Google has made a part of its search-results page gave her a lot of information—including links—on the properties of the element "Snellium," which somehow it hallucinated from Sn, the symbol for tin.[273]

These might seem like trivial mistakes, and in a sense, they may be in that no one's life and health are threatened, but multiply these hallucinations by the millions of times people use LLMs every day, and realize that some of this incorrect information will end up being incorporated into various knowledge bases, which will themselves be used to train future Large Language Models, and the contours of a truly

---

[272] That Grok invented a citation for its hallucinated argument is ironic because the only thing I have found Grok to be useful for doing is finding citations if I cannot fully remember the author or title of an article but can summarize the argument and note some distinctive feature.

[273] To be overly charitable to Google's AI, perhaps it got confused because the Latin word *stannum*, from which the symbol for tin was derived, only came to mean "tin" in the fourth century; before that time, *stannum* meant a silver-lead alloy and tin itself was called *plumbum candidum* ("white lead"). "Snellium," however, was said to have entirely different characteristics. Unfortunately, the details are sketchy because the URLs the AI offered in support did not correspond to actual links, making it impossible to determine if "Snellium" could be used to create less-toxic solders. It is sad that this remarkable element has been so neglected by science.

immense intellectual problem become apparent. In all three of these cases, the hallucination was a pseudo-fact that was obviously wrong to me, a specialist in a particular discipline, but which would seem reasonable to someone outside the field who was using ChatGPT for an essay or a news story. The pseudo-facts could then end up cited in other articles, and from them, other pseudo-facts could be generated.[274] The eventual result will be a knowledge base so contaminated with error that it will be impossible to trust anything in it. The thought of the accumulated knowledge of the human race, brought together and finally made widely accessible only with the development of the world wide web in the 1990s, becoming thoroughly contaminated is too depressing for words.

Perhaps a technical solution to this problem will be developed in time to prevent human knowledge from being completely corrupted by hallucination and error. After all, ten years ago almost everyone would have asserted that it was impossible for get a computer to do things—such as producing paragraphs of grammatically correct sentences on a particular topic—that Large Language Models do so consistently that we are surprised when they fail. But straight-line extrapolation is not a particularly effective method for predicting the future, and the risks of a solution not appearing in time are significant. Additionally, there are some good reasons to doubt that Large Language Models can ever be configured to evaluate truth or falsity, not because of any intrinsic problem with computers or AI, but because of the way language works.

Vervet monkeys have three different alarm calls that they use to warn other vervets of danger. When a vervet spots the approach of a predator, it makes particular noise that depends upon whether the threat is a leopard, an eagle, or a snake. Upon hearing an alarm call, the other monkeys respond with appropriate evasive action, climbing out onto the ends of branches if they hear "Leopard!"; rushing in towards the trunk of the tree if they hear "Eagle!"; and standing up on their hind feet and

[274] Two students, upon learning they could edit Wikipedia pages, had inserted their own nickname for the coatimundi, calling it the "Brazilian aardvark." Before editors removed the invented nickname, various reporters—and even an academic book—had taken the nickname from the Wikipedia page and used it. According to Wikipedia's own rules, those media sources made the nickname authoritative, so it was retained on the page.

craning their necks to look at the ground if they hear "Snake!" Some scientists have argued that this system of alarm calls is the most primitive form of language—there is match between a noise and a thing in the world. And if vervet calls are the simplest system of language, then lies have been a part of language since its very origin.

Because some vervet monkeys lie. If a vervet sees another monkey about to get a tasty bit of fruit, it will make an alarm call, even though no predator is present, and then swoop in to grab the food abandoned when the other monkey retreats. And not only to vervets lie, but they also lie in the way most likely to move their rival away from the food, calling "Eagle!" when the food it out on the tip of a branch or "Leopard!" when the food is on the ground.

The ability of the vervets to lie even with the simplest possible "language" demonstrates both the power of language and its great weakness: language is not tethered to reality; it can describe things that do not exist. Not only can we say anything we can imagine, but the combinatoric and recursive nature of language means that there are uncountably many grammatical sentences. Humans determine the truth of statements drawn from that enormous pool of possibilities by comparing what they say to their knowledge of the world. Large Language Models have no such knowledge—they are machines for producing sentences that are similar to other sentences in the data that has been used to train them. In fact, the very nature of Large Language Models almost guarantees the production of false statements (i.e., hallucinations). ChatGPT builds sentences by adding one word at a time based on the probabilities the program calculates from its enormous set of training data. One of the key breakthroughs in the development of the program was the discovery that the sentence it produced seemed more natural if there was a certain amount of randomness in the choices of each next word rather than always choosing the word with the highest probability. But although that randomness makes ChatGPT's sentences sound like they are produced by humans rather than an algorithm, it also ensures that sentences will be generated that are not true to the physical world—and there is no way for the program to be able to differentiate those sentences from sentences that are true. Hallucinations and errors, therefore, are unavoidable.

And so someone—many someones—will have to check the statements produced by AIs to remove the errors and hallucinations.[275] This will not be the traditional "fact-checking" in which some poor intern uses a search engine, phone calls, or even reference books to confirm dates and numerical values in an article. Indeed, it may be possible to develop other kinds of non-LLM "expert systems" to fix those sorts of errors. Human evaluators will be most valuable when they are able to provide what my wife, an engineer who has spent the last three decades working on extremely complex military hardware, calls a "sanity check," a fast, intuitive once-over on any design, calculation, or process to make sure that what is being proposed is reasonable—or at least possible. To be able to perform sanity checks, people need to have a fairly complete and accurate understanding of not just the particular item being designed or produced, but the processes by which it is made and how the human beings involved in creating it are likely to behave. Being able to sanity check AI-productions is going to be one of the most valuable skills a person can have, since any productivity gained by using AI will be lost if what the programs produce is filled with errors and untruths.

Not only will we have to develop methods—almost certainly human-performed methods—to prevent bad information from being incorporated into our scientific, social, cultural, and historical data, but in the very near future, we are going to need to do a deep clean of our knowledge bases. These are already becoming polluted with unreproducible results, fake or at best trivial papers that exist solely to meet some performance metric for university employment, and mendacious pseudo-research concocted to support various commercial and political agendas, and the adoption of AI is only going to make the problem worse.

[275] This state of affairs is the opposite of what science fiction writers have been predicting for the past 75 years: that machine intelligence would have a complete grasp of facts about the world but would struggle to produce language that sounded fully human. Indeed, the current situation in which fluent human language is produced but the machine cannot evaluate the content of those sentences is such an inversion of expectations that it makes me wonder if the cosmos has a sense of humor.

Although much of the rooting out of falsehood and error will have to be done by specialists in individual subdisciplines, there will be still be an enormous need for intelligent generalists who can orient themselves in unfamiliar disciplines. The people who will be best at doing all this work will be those who know how to think because that is one thing that AI cannot do. Fortunately, it is what the Liberal Arts are best at.

A Final Thought:

I personally do not use Large Language Models because of their hallucinations, which have the potential to do serious damage to the human race's long-term intellectual project of understanding our world and ourselves, and because I like to think I can write better than the overall average of the best writing LLMs can produce. I've argued above that students should similarly avoid using AI in order to maximize their development of writing and thinking skills. Nevertheless, I do think that AI may produce useful knowledge that we do not already possess: LLMs have the potential to help us better understand how our own thinking works—or at least how it goes wrong.

If you train an AI on a lot of real-world data, it can often do an average job of drawing pictures, writing essays, and answering frequently asked questions. But problems arise if you incorporate those AI-generated images or texts back into the data set: when the AI is being trained using AI-created material, you rapidly get more and worse hallucinations. Researchers believe that the data out in the "tails" of the normal distribution of input, the rarer and more unusual images or words or phrases, is essential to the creation of non-hallucinatory output. Even though the influence of the extreme data is not at all evident in the initial, non-hallucinatory output, somehow their presence helps prevent runaway recursive processes. Without the weird stuff, the AI goes crazy, and not in helpful ways.

Might we apply this insight to ourselves? Perhaps in order to be usefully creative, we need exposure to odd, out-of-place material—the things that appear irrelevant are in some strange way essential.

Some circumstantial evidence for this inference may be found in the well known tendency of extremely popular, long-running media series being unable to recapture—or even maintain—the creativity and entertainment quality that led to their initial success. There is widespread agreement that the more recent episodes of *The Simpsons* animated series are not as clever, original, or funny as the first ten years (although we should not lose sight of what a remarkable accomplishment this longevity is). Similarly, despite immense improvements in computer-graphics and special effects, plus seemingly unlimited budgets to hire the very best talent, none of the six Star Wars prequels and sequels match the emotional power and audience engagement of the original three films. There are many other examples.

I hypothesize that the same underlying process is at work in the decay of the quality of AI output when its own products are fed back into its training data and what happened in the minds of the writers and directors of *The Simpsons* and Star Wars. The original writers were exposed to a huge diversity of media—films, television shows, radio dramas, Broadway musicals, pulp fiction, popular music—none of which included *The Simpsons* or Star Wars. The current generation of writers, however, has been trained on hundreds of episodes of *The Simpsons* or on all the Star Wars films and probably the graphic novels, animated series episodes, video-game stories, and novelizations that have been produced over the years. Indeed, according to a few of my former students, to maintain continuity and prevent repetition when new writers are hired in the entertainment industry, part of the "on-boarding" process is to give them access to the complete archives of the franchise for which they are now writing—"content creation" in the entertainment industry. This obviously sensible process, however, may be akin to feeding many AI creations back into the training data: the central, "average" signal now blocks the subtle influence of the rare and unusual inputs that contributed to the success of the original works.

If this hypothesis is correct, there really will not be a single simple fix, since it is hard to imagine how a new writer could contribute to a long-running franchise without actually reading or viewing the earlier versions.

But it may be that increasing writers' exposure to original and high-quality creative works—deliberately including more outliers in the dataset—can mitigate the problem of recursive feedback leading to degradation. If not just depth but also breadth are essential for real creativity, then nothing could be a better foundation than an education in the Liberal Arts, an education that goes far beyond a small, standardized set of texts or tightly focused professional training.

Maybe the antidote to "slop" (both AI and otherwise) is eclectic, exploratory, and deep engagement with culture. If so, then it will be not just tragic but also ironic if colleges turn away from the traditional Liberal Arts on the assumption that AIs will do most of the jobs that humanistically educated people now do. If the only thing that can prevent the impending slop-tastrophe is what is being abandoned, it would not be the first time that the Liberal Arts turned out to be far more relevant and valuable than what was supposed to replace them.

About the Author

Michael D.C. Drout is the Frances A. Shirley Professor of English and Director of the Center for the Study of the Medieval at Wheaton College, Norton, Massachusetts, where, since 1997, he has taught Old and Middle English, science fiction, and the works of J.R R. Tolkien.

Drout is the author of *The Tower and the Ruin: J.R.R. Tolkien's Creation, How Tradition Works, Tradition and Influence in Anglo-Saxon Literature,* and *Drout's Quick and Easy Old English,* and he is co-author of *Beowulf Unlocked: New Evidence from Lexomic Analysis*. He edited J.R.R. Tolkien's *Beowulf and the Critics* and the *J.R.R. Tolkien Encyclopedia* and co-edited *Transitional States: Cultural Change, Tradition and Memory in Medieval England*. One of the founders and a co-editor of the journal *Tolkien Studies*, he has published widely on Tolkien, fantasy and science fiction, and medieval studies.

Supported by three grants from the National Endowment for the Humanities, Drout has co-developed "Lexomic" methods of computer-assisted statistical analysis that have led to discoveries about Anglo-Saxon, Old Norse, Latin, and Modern English texts. The Lexomics software can be accessed at http://lexomics.wheatoncollege.edu.

A consultant for *The Lord of the Rings Online* MMPORG, Drout has appeared in two History Channel miniseries: *Clash of the Gods* and *True Monsters*, in National Geographic's *Beyond the Movie: The Return of the King*, and in *Icons Unearthed: The Lord of the Rings.* He has recorded 13 audio courses, one of which, *A Way with Words Part IV: Understanding Poetry*, was a finalist for the 2010 Audie award for best original work. Among his more recent audio courses are *How to Think: The Enduring Value of the Liberal Arts, The Norsemen: Understanding the Vikings and their Culture,* and *Singers and Tales: Oral Tradition and the Roots of Literature*. His website is http://michaeldrout.com.

Professor Drout lives in Dedham, Massachusetts.

Publications by Michael D.C. Drout

Books

Beowulf and the Critics by J.R.R.Tolkien (editor). *Revised and Extended Edition* (editor).

How Tradition Works: A Meme-Based Cultural Poetics of the Anglo-Saxon Tenth Century.

J.R.R. Tolkien Encyclopedia: Scholarship and Critical Assessment (editor).

Tolkien Studies, volumes 1–21 (co-editor).

Drout's Quick and Easy Old English.

Tradition and Influence in Anglo-Saxon Literature: An Evolutionary, Cognitivist Approach.

Beowulf Unlocked: New Evidence from Lexomic Analysis. New York: Palgrave

Transitional States: Cultural Change, Tradition and Memory in Medieval England (co-editor).

Poems from the Edge of the World: Translations from Old English.

Poems from the Heart of the Land: Translations from Old English.

The Tower and the Ruin: J. R. R. Tolkien's Creation.

How to Learn How to Think: What the Liberal Arts Are Good For, Anyway.

Audio

Bard of the Middle Ages: The Works of Geoffrey Chaucer.

Rings, Swords and Monsters: Exploring Fantasy Literature.

From Here to Infinity: Science Fiction.

A Way With Words: Rhetoric, Writing and the Art of Persuasion.

The History of the English Language.

A Way With Words II: Approaches to Literature.

Beowulf: Masterpiece Library. Old English Edition.

Beowulf Aloud.
A Way With Words III: Grammar for Adults.
A Way With Words IV: Understanding Poetry.
Anglo-Saxon Aloud: Greatest Hits.
The Anglo-Saxon World.
Tolkien and the West: Reclaiming Europe's Lost Literary Tradition.
The Norsemen: Understanding the Vikings and their Culture.
How to Think: The Liberal Arts and their Enduring Value.
Singers and Tales: Oral Tradition and the Roots of Literature.
The Tower and the Ruin: J.R.R. Tolkien's Creation

Audio Lecture Series
Exploring Beowulf available in the Signum Collaboratory at collaboratory.signumuniversity.org

www.ingramcontent.com/pod-product-compliance
Lightning Source LLC
LaVergne TN
LVHW010643110826
845149LV00014B/2934